The Medici
A Great Florentine Family

The Medici
A Great Florentine Family

Marcel Brion
Member of the *Académie Française*

Translated by
Gilles and Heather Cremoncsi

Photographs by Wim Swaan
and others

Crown Publishers, Inc.   New York

© Paul Elek Productions Limited 1969

Library of Congress Catalog Card Number: 72–82317

First published in the U.S.A. by Crown Publishers, Inc.

Designed by Harold Bartram

Printed in Italy

Contents

List of plates

Jacket front: View of the Piazza della Signoria with the equestrian statue of Grand Duke Cosimo I in the foreground; in the background the Neptune Fountain, the Michelangelo *David*, *Hercules and Cacus* by Bandinelli, and the Loggia dei Lanzi; bas-relief in *pietra dura*, crystal and gold, made by Gaspare Mola (about 1580–1640). (18 x 25.5 cms.) *Palazzo Pitti.*

Jacket back: A commemorative terracotta plaque by Luca della Robbia, made on the occasion of a wedding, and showing emblems of the Medici and Bartolini families. *Bargello, Museo Nazionale.*

Front Endpaper: Detail from *Scene at a Tournament* by Domenico Morone (about 1490). (45.5 x 49 cms.) *London, National Gallery.*

Back Endpaper: A pair with the front endpaper.

Unless otherwise stated in the captions, all buildings and museums mentioned are in Florence.

Foreword

The political power of the Medici family, which they wielded at first discreetly, then rather more arrogantly, and finally completely arbitrarily, seems strangely at variance with the Florentines' passionate love of legal rights and liberty. It is, in fact, paradoxical that these touchy, suspicious people should have tolerated the pretensions of the family of the future Grand Dukes of Tuscany long before they had secured their princely status. By so doing the Florentines allowed the Medici a kind of *de facto* monarchy, with precisely those autocratic overtones which they traditionally detested and against which they rose whenever some upstart attempted to rule them. Thus the history of the Medici's acquisition, maintenance and re-acquisition of power, reveals how cleverly, moderately, and diplomatically they dealt with their compatriots. Their history, starting as it does in the fourteenth century and ending only in the eighteenth, is really the story of Florence; tolerated, adored, and hated by turn, the Medici remained inextricably involved with the fortunes of all who lived in the shadow of the rose-tinted lily. Posterity has declared their fates inseparable, their fame identical. And they have received immortality for the works of art which grew from their patronage, or rather which sprang from those men of genius who were their contemporaries and whom they favoured with their extensive, highly intelligent, and generous friendship.

Indeed the history of the Medici clearly illustrates the difference between patron and collector: unable to find or to stimulate new artistic movements, the later generations fell back on knowledge and on science, and at that point also they became collectors rather than patrons. Simultaneously with their preoccupation with economics and industry —in which science itself became interesting through its applications—the sixteenth-century Grand Dukes of Tuscany provided a rather passive encouragement of the arts in the place of the vigorous patronage of the Medici in their heyday in the fifteenth century, of Cosimo *Pater Patriae* and Lorenzo the Magnificent. Of course one can say, as their excuse, that there was no equivalent genius in the sixteenth century to Alberti, Brunelleschi, Michelangelo or Leonardo da Vinci; but this may well have been because the atmosphere of Florence, which in the fifteenth century had so encouraged the growth and output of great artists was destroyed as the republican liberties of the city were suppressed in the sixteenth. The formidable creative impulse of the Italian Renaissance, of which Florence had been so much the centre, gradually gave way to a kind of intellectual and cultural stagnation.

In other parts of Europe patronage was generally aristocratic and came from princes of ancient feudal lineage or from princes of the church, popes, cardinals and bishops who themselves came often enough from noble families. Italian patronage in the Renaissance, however, was not aristocratic in so far as the masters of the little Italian states—so often themselves men of considerable intellectual distinction—sprang from the land. The condottieri who acquired power, fortune and glory, through the business of conducting wars, were originally peasants bored by the plough, workmen or small shop-keepers; they had no noble ancestors and their nobility was acquired by the strength of their fists; nothing was inherited, their position had to be renewed and reaffirmed every day.

The Italy of the Middle Ages had managed to rid itself almost completely of its feudal masters and the *communes*—or small city-states—had shown the citizens, even when they only lasted for a very short time, the superiority of democratic rule over that of the princes. In the Middle Ages the sources of power were outside society or above it, and were to be found in the shape of the Pope or the Holy Roman Emperor; in the Renaissance effective power, one might almost say *natural* power, came from below: the ancestors of the Sforzas of Milan were Lombard peasants; those of the Medici, farmers in the Val d'Arno, who worked with their own hands in the fields of the *podere* which provided their grain and wine. The Medici bank, the alum monopoly, the income from money itself, the speculation in wool and silk, all came later; and when in the mid-fifteenth century the Medici had become the most sophisticated of citizens, masters of the political, intellectual and artistic life of Florence, the preference that they showed for their villas—which were not princely castles but rather enlarged farms—reveals how much they remained attached to their land. In this way the history of the Medici was deeply interwoven with that of Florence, of Tuscany, of Italy itself, as a direct result of their character as statesmen and as businessmen, not as a result of an inherited or feudal position.

For nearly four hundred years they provided a deeply influential example of a certain attitude to the arts, and their name has become associated with the idea of collecting and patronizing art, as much as, in the ancient world, that of Maecenas himself; this example was so important, however, precisely because their patronage underlined the inherently popular character of Tuscan culture and art. It was a culture that was immediately comprehensible to the entire population, quite unlike the official art of the courts, which was aimed at a very limited audience. In contrast to the aristocratic art that flourished at Versailles under Louis XIV and Louis XV, and at Fontainebleau under François I, or in the German courts of the eighteenth century, Florentine art in the Renaissance had the same unpretentious *bourgeois* atmosphere that the Medici had themselves. This situation obviously changed when they mounted the throne of the Grand Dukes of Tuscany, created for them, and supported by, the Emperor; and at that moment also there appeared in the new Medici palace, an official court art of which the most brilliant examples are their portraits by Bronzino. The period of their individuality was over.

The Foundations of the Dynasty

An old popular tradition, which the Medici circulated as evidence of their ancient lineage, told how once upon a time a very cruel giant appeared in Tuscany and laid waste the area called the Mugello near Florence. One fine day a French knight, who was on his way to Rome in Charlemagne's retinue, entered into battle against the giant, whom he vanquished and slew. The knight Averardo's redoubtable adversary was armed with six balls and chains, which he wielded with such ferocity that they left six marks on the doughty Averardo's shield. Charlemagne ordained that Averardo's coat of arms should commemorate the event with six *gules* balls on a field of gold. This champion then settled in the vicinity of his adventure and gained possession of vast domains, where he and his descendants lived the quiet life of landed gentry.

This was the first Medici to be recorded by history—or rather, by legend. It is, of course, most unlikely that the red balls of the Medici owed their origin to feats of warrior heroism, a trait which is scarcely discernible in later members of that family. This can be dismissed as an amusing fable. The Medici's 'Coat of arms' should more realistically be called an 'insignia', as they were not of aristocratic lineage. Since there is no evidence that they were ever anything but professional businessmen, the *palle*, as they are called in Italian, are more likely to be the arms of a pawn-broker's house, six round coins, or, in heraldic terms, six besants. Besants would ordinarily have been *or* on a *gules* field, but then Florence was never over-particular about heraldic refinements, since, after the aristocracy had been routed and the commune had won its independence, the appurtenances of the old aristocracy were regarded either with total indifference or with open hostility.

Some historians have tried to argue that the name Medici might have something to do with the Italian word for doctors, *medici,* and that the red balls were the symbols for pills rather than coins. This also seems unlikely, as, search back as one may, there is no trace of a single Medici who practised medicine or pharmacology, and who would thus have entered his name on the registers of the guild which united both professions. Furthermore the exact status of the medical profession in Florence remains rather vague until the beginning of the fourteenth century, after which we know it was held in poor repute. It was not a profession likely to recruit members of a family whose main preoccupation since its historical beginnings had been business, buying and selling merchandise and, of course, dealing in money. Further-more, the Medici's interest in politics was not professional, nor did it aim at gaining power simply to acquire titles as did the Italian princes and *condottieri.* It was, at first at least, strictly limited to the pursuit of commercial prosperity. As in any democratic system, such political power has no historical origin and no transcendental justification, and must be founded on the consent of the people; but the people only accord this power to men who know how to make themselves popular.

The mass may be persuaded to give support to active violence (as it did to Michele di Lando during the Ciompi uprising), or to discursive violence (as it did later to Savonarola's fiery sermons), but prestige won by such precarious, accidental circumstances cannot last very long. In a society organized to involve public opinion, money has the power to buy out opposition, or to buy out enough of it to guarantee favourable elections and favourable reactions in the assemblies. A rich man is thus better prepared to rally round him the support of friends and partisans than anyone else. This was the practice in ancient Rome, where the clients of a public figure used to crowd into his antechamber every morning to receive their subsidies and present their petitions. In both cases this 'clientele' constituted a considerable block of pledged support in elections and in public debates, and it could also be relied upon to sway and control the people in the streets. An equivalent kind of clientele were the more or less peaceful regiments who were in the pay of a *condottiere* or soldier of fortune. The political power attached to the condottiere by virtue of his command of a regiment had, however, to be wielded with a masterly discretion so as to avoid treading on popular sensibilities.

Florence had rejected the idea of being ruled by an aristocracy of any sort, even an aristocracy of merit, talent, or learning. Uprisings and the street riots had, on the other hand, given Florence a taste of an unstable proletarian government, which lacked political awareness because it was politically uneducated to any but the needs of one class, and incapable of grasping the complex requirements of a large industrial and commercial centre. In the people's eyes the Medici had great advantages: they were not of noble origin; they practised a trade (that it was the most lucrative trade did not worry them because they too profited from it); they always appeared to be simple, modest folk, benevolent but not condescending, and at ease with people from all classes; and they seemed to be the equals of small shopkeepers and artisans.

The din of civil wars between the Guelfs and the Ghibellines, the family feuds and clan hatreds between Whites and Blacks, had died down before the first Medici emerged from obscurity to gain prominence in contemporary chronicles. It was to their credit that they never appear to have changed their minds or their partisanship of the popular cause throughout the fourteenth and fifteenth centuries and even later, no matter what turn Italy's fortune seemed to take. Confirmed democrats (in the Florentine sense of the word), they had always embraced the people's cause and nothing could persuade them to the contrary. Dino Compagni claims they were aligned with the Blacks at the end of the thirteenth century, but partisanship of this sort does not seem to have been a real passion. Their true interests—those which they were to spend their lives upholding—rested with the people. Compagni describes them as 'potenti popolani' at the dawn of their power in the thirteenth century; and Machiavelli gives a wry, paradoxical turn of phrase, 'una nobilissima famiglia popolana' when they were at the height of their power. This 'popular' stock did in the end become 'very noble' indeed, advancing from great secular and ecclesiastical dignities to be made Dukes of Tuscany by Imperial decree, and giving two Popes to the Church and two Queens to France.

The first Medici are distinguished only by their lack of importance in Medieval Florentine chronicles. Quite some time would have to pass before their business 'house' became a royal 'house'. There was an Ugo de' Medici who was mentioned by merit of his banishment in 1280 for his infraction of the peace ordered by the Pope to reduce the death-rate caused by the Guelf-Ghibelline struggles. Two years later one encounters another Medici, Ardingo di Buonagiunta, who was elected a prior of Florence. A certain Francesco is known only because he was caught up in a feud between the Ricci and the Albizzi clans: the latter were 'noblemen', or were regarded as such, and therefore enemies of the Medici. Giovanni di Bernardino, who inherited the bellicose heroism of the Medici, invaded the wool sector of the town and the domains of the Adimari in 1304. He was leading a band of men bearing crossbows, who were participating in an uprising which, though shorter in duration, equalled the destruction perpetrated at a later date by the infamous Ciompi uprising; Dino Compagni records the razing and pillaging of one thousand nine hundred buildings. This Giovanni di Bernardino was also partner to the conspiracy to oust the Duke of Athens, Gautier de Brienne, who had been appointed governor by the Florentine Signoria, but in 1341 his head was lopped off for these efforts. After his death he became the inspiration of a violent reaction which won such universal appeal that it sent the Duke of Athens packing two years later.

These disputes were never the outcome of two opposing concepts of power nor two opposing political ideologies, because all Florentine parties were unanimously upholders of democracy and freedom. Such disputes were rather between powerful rival business groups. The Strozzi, the Albizzi, the Bardi, the Donati were not professional politicians, but businessmen and financiers whose livelihood and prosperity were largely dependent upon political prestige. The peculiarities of Florentine institutions, their whimsical taxation system, their malleable assemblies, their use of banishment and even capital punishment to rid themselves of fallen idols, all contributed to making popularity a key to individual fortune. Machiavelli defined this state of affairs when he put the reproaches of his native city in the mouth of a Florentine notable, judging his city severely but nevertheless with affection: 'There is nothing more soul-destroying than to see the different party chiefs pretending to put liberty before their party interests and, while their actions prove that they are sworn enemies of liberty, their popular and oligarchical governments grow oppressive in the name of preserving liberty. The reward which they hope to reap by defeating their enemies is not the glory of delivering the state from her adversaries, but rather the pleasure of vengeance and the eventual enslavement of their own country. No sooner have they usurped their authority than they indulge in all manner of extreme injustice, cruelties and violence; this gives rise to laws and regulations whose sole objective, heedless of public good, is the furtherance of private gain; these give rise to wars, treaties, and alliances, which are undertaken to satisfy the ends of a few grasping individuals and certainly not to make their state the more glorious. Now, if you say that these disorders also reign elsewhere, I would reply that your Republic is more unlovely than any other because her laws and regulations are never established as they should be in a free state, but only by the whim of those who have ousted their rivals.'

The death of Giovanni di Bernardino in 1341 and the defeat of his 'clientele' gave the Strozzi new prestige and more business. Andrea, head of the 'house', calculated that the confusion following the expulsion of the Duke of Athens (1343) provided a good opportunity to seize control of the government. First he distributed free wheat to the needy. Then he secured a following by means of gold and promises. Four thousand are said to have rallied round him. Finally, he leaped into the saddle and rode off to seize the Signorial Palace. The attempt was unsuccessful, but he renewed his assault with the additional help of the Duke of Milan's troops. The Signoria opposed him with mercenaries recruited from Siena. Florence was again on the brink of civil war. But the day was saved by the formation of a solid coalition of a few eminent notables, the avowed enemies of 'tyranny'. A Medici was at the head of the coalition: Salvestro. The *popolani* clashed with the *ottimati* in the streets for three hours, at the end of which the 'people' were the victors. As so often happens in such circumstances, the people avenged themselves against the threat of oppression by destroying the possessions and families of the vanquished faction. Thus the untimely Strozzi *coup d'état* ended in one of those periodic orgies of brutality, cruelty, murder, and pillage, which, in Florence as elsewhere, followed in the wake of revolutions.

The part played by Salvestro de' Medici (1331–1388) in the restoration of law and order made this wise businessman arbiter of the situation. Since Salvestro's first task was to assure the people that he had in fact become the head of government, he proposed, and obtained, a modification of the constitution. The eight *signori* of the city would be chosen from the three divisions of the population in new pro-portions: three would be appointed by the 'middle classes', three by the 'lesser classes', and only two by the great families. In this way the republican system would function fairly and ensure that the artisans and small shopkeepers held a majority. It was a fickle populace, given to instant enthusiasms and instant disillusionment, prey for anyone who knew how to handle it, a weak people who, despite the power they were guaranteed, continued to follow any attractive leader. Even Andrea Strozzi had managed to move them to action by dangling the carrot of riches for all.

The banishment of the Strozzi in 1343 was a blow to the anti-Medici faction who, under the Albizzi's continued leadership, did not disarm. In 1354 they managed to get a decree passed that reopened the Guelf-Ghibelline wound. This law stated that anyone suspected of being a Ghibelline sympathizer—proof of his sympathies was not necessary—would be duly punished. Arbitrary factionalism reigned again: anyone who supported the *ottimati* was a Guelf and anyone who supported the Medici was, of course, Ghibelline. Over the years Salvestro managed nevertheless to retain his prestige and popular confidence, and ultimately (April 1378) was elected Gonfaloniere, which put into his hands the command of the police force and responsibility for maintaining law and order. To achieve this success Salvestro had to arm the people to intimidate the *ottimati*, and once roused, they were difficult to calm. The prisons had been thrown open and the offenders in them were released to add fuel to the riot.

When the lesser people saw itself master of the streets, it decided that it was time to stop shunting to and fro between Medici and Albizzi. In 1378 the wool carders, the Ciompi, who were one of the lowliest rungs of the proletariat initiated a movement to set up a people's dictatorship. Machiavelli was right when he added to the popular proverb 'he who sows the wind reaps the whirlwind', that to start a revolt does not guarantee that one will afterwards have any control over it. The Gonfaloniere, the eight signori and the forces of order kept to the safety of the Palazzo Vecchio, leaving the people to take over the town. Salvestro came off lightly as a result of his well-known championship of the popular cause; his house remained intact while the houses belonging to the 'enemies of the people' were burned. The people, drunk with new power, bestowed almost royal status and authority on their leaders. They dispensed justice quite arbitrarily, and they even went so far as to promote certain of the proletarian trades, which had never had any political power or representation in the assemblies, to the exalted ranks of the greater guilds. A certain Michele di Lando, a wool carder who hypnotized the mob with his eloquence, dynamism and fanatical revolutionary spirit, was appointed Gonfaloniere by popular acclaim. Michele di Lando had the faults and qualities common to the 'tribunes', those darlings of the masses, but he was also upright, level-headed and modest and when he felt out of his depth he consulted Salvestro de' Medici. Salvestro took advantage of these consultations to temper the excesses of anarchy, to the great displeasure of the Ciompi, who were determined to hold on to their new liberty and to the benefits they derived from the anarchy and from its resulting pleasures and profits.

The people were soon outraged that their own leaders should listen to the counsel of a banker, a representative of order, prudence, circumspection and moderation. They turned against Michele, who was constrained to deal harshly with his own former comrades in arms in order to keep the peace and prevent the destruction of the entire city. The Ciompi had, however, by this time succeeded in alienating those among the lesser population who disliked revolutionary measures, leading to wanton vandalism, and compelled them to close down their workshops and shops. Internal and external business was languishing. This was reason enough for the re-establishment of social peace. Michele di Lando, who now represented the law and the superior interests of the city, decided, with Salvestro's endorsement, to put a stop to the insurrection and to all the democratic nonsense which had raised him

1. View from *Loggia dei Lanzi* showing the *Perseus* by Benvenuto Cellini, *Hercules and Cacus* by B. Bandinelli, and the bridge linking the *Palazzo della Signoria*, or *Palazzo Vecchio*, with the *Uffizi*.

to power. He led out the militia, and accompanied by a standard-bearer unfurling the banner of liberty, went to confront the Ciompi. The Ciompi had also decided to put a similar stop to things by gaining control of the Palazzo Vecchio, but had not gone far before they encountered the regiments of the faithful. Not a blow was exchanged but the outcome of the whole operation was of the most lamentable and grotesque nature.

The lesser and greater *bourgeois* had been quite terrified by the revolution. Once it was over they joined forces to regain control and come down really hard on the poor Ciompi, depriving them of all their newly-won privileges. They did not treat Michele di Lando as harshly as the rest because he had made an effort to preserve a modicum of law and order amid the chaos; he was banished along with Salvestro, because he had collaborated with the revolutionary régime. He lived in Modena for five years until his death in 1388.

At this time several hundred Florentines, including some of the best families, were living in exile in Genoa, Venice, and even as far afield as the Holy Land. These exiled *ottimati* now returned to Florence, where their supporters took advantage of the defeat of the proletariat to regain their power and reduce civic rights to near non-existence. The old names cropped up in the list of leaders who were to be in control for some time: the Albizzi, and the Capponi, who had been alternately friends and foes of the Medici; and later Niccolò da Uzzano (1359–1431), who was one of the most remarkable men of his time with a sensitive political intelligence of the most subtle and powerful kind.

When Donatello modelled a bust after this great Florentine, he seems to have harked back to the Roman republic for inspiration (see plate 57). He gave Uzzano's face the energy, sternness, authority, decisiveness, discernment and febrile strength of a Cicero. It was in 1417 that Niccolò da Uzzano joined in an unacknowledged triumvirate with an Albizzi and a Capponi. After Salvestro died, the Medici had kept away from the political vortex. Salvestro's son, Veri, was invited to play an active rôle as the people's leader, but he did not have it in him to make a success of it and he was too fearful lest involvement in some luckless adventure might jeopardize his life or endanger the Medici house's business interests. His retreat to political obscurity permitted him to stay on in Florence while his brother Alamanno followed the well-trodden path to exile. Veri's business concerns made a safe life of modest well-being preferable to one guided by the political ambitions of his ancestors and his successors. Since exile from Florence was tantamount to courting financial disaster, he stayed. He may have been biding his time until the propitious hour when he could return to public life, but this happy hour never came. When Florence finally decided it was time to call upon another Medici to put an end to the disorders and intrigues that had lacerated her for so long, she beckoned to Giovanni di Bicci (1360-1429), who was not a direct descendant of Salvestro de' Medici.

Giovanni di Bicci was the son of a certain Averardo who had been nicknamed 'Bicci'. This name became the patronym of his children, who, in the Italian manner, were called 'di Bicci' (the sons of Bicci). Unavoidable circumstances had drawn Salvestro into the thick of the political fray and forced him into political prominence while Averardo had managed to keep to the wings where he skilfully pursued his financial and commercial interests. He never took sides and his advisedly incon-spicuous behaviour made it much easier for him to build up his fortune, which had become fairly sizeable by the time his son Giovanni inherited it. This branch of the family were known as the Medici 'da Caffaggiolo', because they lived at Caffaggiolo, in order to distinguish them from the main Florentine branch, the 'Great Medici'. The Caffaggiolo Medici retained a certain rustic mien which Bronzino brought out when he painted Giovanni di Bicci's portrait from old records (see fig. 2): the nose is strong, a trait common to the whole family; the closely-pursed lips seem to

2. Courtyard of the *Palazzo Vecchio*; it was rebuilt by Michelozzo in 1454, the stucco decoration on the columns being added in 1565 on the occasion of the marriage of the Grand Duke Francesco de' Medici with the Archduchess Joanna of Austria. The fountain is by Verrocchio.

hide some secret, or a promise, or an unwise investment; the deep-set eyes recede beneath arched, bushy eyebrows. The expression is bold and frank as well as being sensitive and wholesome and not without a trace of melancholy. This wise and discreet businessman did not think fit to enter the political scene till 1421 when, at the age of sixty-one, he was elected Gonfaloniere. It was only then that his valuable qualities came to light, his modesty, his generosity, his benevolence, his lack of greed and worldly ambition. After his death he was enthusiastically described—surprisingly so in view of the facts—as being 'of a nature more divine than human'.

His lavish expenditures on the city were never regarded as ostentatious. When he (together with seven other families) commissioned Brunelleschi (1377–1446) to re-build San Lorenzo (see plate 39) in which the Medici were to establish their family chapel, this was not merely intended to draw attention to himself or to keep ahead of the other banking families, such as the Pazzi, the Rucellai, the Capponi, the Sassetti; all of these families shared a craze for building and vied for pre-eminence in architecture, as they did in the money, wool and silk markets—the principal sources of wealth for the great families of Florence, the *popolo grasso*. He also initiated reforms that were directly beneficial to the *popolo minuto* or poorer classes, such as the reduction of the salt tax, which had always most gravely afflicted the proletariat and was thus unpopular. During his three tenures of office as a prior, in 1402, 1408 and 1411, he had always voted and pressed others to vote in favour of certain measures which might appear demagogic, but which were necessary in view of the fact that after the failure of the Ciompi movement more was taken away from the artisans and the proletariat than their brief victory had won them. In 1414 he had been unwillingly appointed one of the Ten War Councillors; this position was doubtless forced on him because he was reputed to be peace-loving and cautious. The truth of this reputation was illustrated in 1424 when Florence became involved in a risky war, but later managed to extricate herself by heeding the advice of this 'pacifist'.

Disputes with Milan and Venice usually represented the surviving antipathy between the two Medieval Italian factions, the Guelfs and the Ghibellines. The Ghibellines were partisans of the Emperor who had bestowed titles, domains, offices upon them, thereby elevating them to aristocratic status. Although they did not share a common origin with the French and German nobility, or belong to the same category as the old feudal families, they were nonetheless set on an equal footing with these. This newly-created nobility swore allegiance to the Emperor, to whom they were beholden. Although their active participation in trade would have been almost inconceivable for aristocrats in other countries, they regarded themselves as an incontestable élite at the very summit of the social scale. Much of this aristocratic pride had survived the Guelf-Ghibelline feud, which had had a considerable effect on the thoughts and the passions of these 'aristocrats' of money and of the wool and silk trades, who formed the bulk of the *ottimati*. This attitude goes some way to explain why the *ottimati* and the anti-Medici always sought pretexts for precipitating their city into wars: war was a *noble* enterprise in which there was profit for the leadership. The opposition, the 'democrats', were of the opinion that such adventures were silly, anachronistic Medieval follies which did untold damage to business and prejudiced the interests of the lesser citizens. As these saw it, war was just another excuse for prohibitive taxes to pay for the hiring of mercenaries and their captains: the warmongers had the same interests as the aristocrats, and were indeed usually the same people—Albizzi, Uzzano, Capponi. They were opposed by the champions of moderation, wisdom, unity and a more democratic approach—the Medici.

Florence had no direct interest in the war into which Milan sought to entice her in 1424. The Duke of Milan, Filippo Maria Visconti, pursued a traditional Lombard policy of trying to keep Venetian expansionism under control. He tried to persuade

Fig. 2 Posthumous portrait of Giovanni di Bicci de' Medici by Bronzino. *Museo Mediceo.*

3. Façade of the *Palazzo Vecchio*, with its tower; the main block of the building was put up between 1298 and 1314, possibly from the plans of Arnolfo di Cambio.

Florence that it was in her interest also to arrest the growth of Venetian commerce with the countries which provided the Tuscan workshops with their raw materials. The ever-increasing number of Venetian banks and the proportionate increase of trading privileges accorded them by Eastern Mediterranean countries would soon permit Venice to control, and eventually to monopolize the silk trade routes. Filippo Maria Visconti dazzled the Signoria of Florence with descriptions of untold profits to be won by the suppression of their rival. Florence hesitated for some time before agreeing to military collaboration. The condottieri, who were free to conduct their operations as it suited them, then proceeded with their habitual torpor inspired by totally whimsical or self-interested motives. The uncertain alliances, the sudden reversals, and the carefully masked betrayals which ensued finally convinced Florence of Milan's duplicity. Milan had wanted to engage Florence in an expensive war only to weaken and impoverish her and thus make her easy prey to Visconti's real intentions.

Since Giovanni di Bicci's position was much enhanced by this turn of events, which had the merit of reinforcing his peaceful convictions, he set about unmasking the 'war-mongers'. These were among the richest men in the land; the best way to bring them to heel would be to introduce some badly-needed tax reforms which would wear holes in their pockets. Reforms would have the double advantage of reducing his rivals' fortunes and pleasing the people by giving them the satisfaction of seeing that, for the first time, money was being collected from those who had it. The fiscal system was so arbitrary, biased, and unjust that it really amounted to a weapon which the governing power could levy against the 'opposition'. Giovanni di Bicci's benevolent outlook had not, as we know, restricted his helpful activities to the workers and the destitute; he had always been ready to answer big business-men's and bankers' pleas for financial support. This had also proved an effective means of securing them as friends and controlling them by permitting him to become their creditor. Many of the important men from the greater guilds were greatly indebted to him; by means of this he was able to obtain their political support and backing for the tax reform known as the *catasto*.

The prestige that Giovanni di Bicci had won by opposing the Milanese war and the belligerent policies of the *ottimati* gave him the opportunity to push Rinaldo degli Albizzi, one of their leaders, into carrying out this reform in 1427, not long before he died. The main weakness of the earlier *estimo* system had been that the tax burden was unequally divided, favouring the big landowners at the expense of the smaller. Similarly, all direct and indirect taxation had been formulated and enforced by the governing factions to their own advantage. Giovanni di Bicci, now in a position of considerable indirect power, was generous enough to forego this method of pressurizing his adversaries, or at least to do it in a more subtle way. His attachment to institutions and his friendship for the people led him to show an apparent disinterest in tax matters, which none of his rivals ever dared equal. Since to advocate the *catasto* meant that one was willing to publicize the sources and the growth rate of one's own business, one put one's cards on the table and thus forced one's fellow players to do likewise. These revelations showed, of course, not only the Medici's fortune, but also their strengths and their rivals' weaknesses. From now on any Florentine was allowed to examine official tax declarations and to verify the declared amounts. In this way the system provided a further check on existing official revenue inspection; it created a new popular inquisition, which was doubly efficient by virtue of that individual spontaneity that jealousy, envy and malice quicken.

The *catasto*, for all its originality and novelty value, was obviously not faultless, because both Cosimo de' Medici and Lorenzo the Magnificent later modified and improved it. The reform was, however, revolutionary enough to provoke heated

4. Part of the façade of *Palazzo Strozzi*, begun by Benedetto da Maiano for Filippo Strozzi in 1489, continued by Cronaca until 1504, but not finally completed until 1536.

public controversy, dividing people all the way up and down the social and economic scale into those in favour and those against the new system. The word *catasto* refers to the adding up, or 'piling up' of assets. It was a tax on capital and not on income, which was easier to conceal. Once the rate of taxation had been established it was possible to levy a further tax on revenues from capital. A body of verifiers or inspectors was set up to obtain truthful declarations of wealth that bore some relation to reality. The inspectors were given full powers of inquiry. They worked side by side with a host of voluntary investigators, whose zeal was rewarded with a fat bonus. Dissemblers were hunted down and made to pay half the undeclared sum to the treasury and a quarter of it to the denouncer.

Giovanni di Bicci realized that the fairness and legality of these new methods of taxing wealth were not beyond reproach, but that the system did have the merit of actually sharing out fiscal dues according to each citizen's real wealth. The main effect was in fact that real property was more efficiently taxed than was total wealth, and the tax turned into a method of penalizing ostentation: it did, however, put a stop to the random, arbitrary, bullying methods of tax collection which had characterized the *estimo*. Giovanni di Bicci's modesty made him admit that his *catasto* did not solve the problem as well as it might. But then, a man of measured temperament, such as he was, readily becomes a man of half-measures. Going half-way, he used to say, was infinitely preferable to the risks entailed in going the whole hog when the effect of extreme measures might well be total ruin. He applied this policy to business and politics alike; it proceeded from the tradition of calculating, temperate moderation which had made the Medici rich. *Bourgeois* pragmatism, *bourgeois* prudence and utilitarianism—these were the virtues he held up against the wilder enterprises and schemes advocated for Florence by the Strozzi and the Albizzi, who were not always successfully held in check by the level-headed common-sense of their intelligent partner Niccolò da Uzzano.

It might appear that this cautious merchant abandoned these traditional principles when he actually embarked on a risky enterprise of his own: the defence of 'Pope' John XXIII at the Council of Constance (1414–1418). One wonders what led him to defend and finance a pontiff of such doubtful legitimacy, who was on the verge of losing his tiara. What could have persuaded this man to do something so out of character as to hurl himself into an enterprise that was certain to involve him in loss and to strain the vast resources of the Medici bank to the same extent that the disastrous Wars of the Roses had strained those of other Florentine houses? The loans that the Medici made to John XXIII were probably so considerable that Giovanni di Bicci adopted the gamblers' time-honoured system of not quitting half-way in the hope that by the end of the game a change of luck will recoup their investment. It may be true, of course, that, realistic and hard-headed businessman that he was, he may have wanted to rescue the Pope in distress for purely altruistic reasons. Or perhaps he was persuaded to take this personal interest by his son Cosimo; Giovanni di Bicci had sent Cosimo to the Council of Constance as his observer and the impetuous generosity of the young man's entreaties may have influenced his father.

The Medici appeared at the Council of Constance not because they were fascinated by the conciliar debates and canonical courts that adjudicated the claims of the three Popes and finally repudiated John XXIII and Benedict XIII, but because the councils drew enormous crowds of prominent ecclesiastical and lay dignitaries. They had as much to gain by attending the council as do modern business-men by attending business conventions. The difference between modern conventions and the councils is that today's gatherings are exclusively for specialists, whereas the councils were peopled by nobles, artists, writers, financiers and bankers from Venice, Genoa, Paris, Bruges, Antwerp, or Augsburg, milling around with the discordant legions of churchmen. A Medici from Florence could meet a Fugger from

Augsburg at one of these councils and transact a remunerative deal.

When Cardinal Colonna was finally upheld by the Council of Constance as the true Pope and became known as Pope Martin V, his unfortunate rivals were ignominiously thrown out and denounced as usurpers and impostors. John XXIII lost his tiara and left Constance, but he was ambushed by the Emperor Sigismund's men and promptly thrown into prison. Sigismund, who had organized the Council, fixed the ex-Pope's ransom at 35,000 florins. Cosimo de' Medici, who had managed to escape the 'Pope's' captors, left the prisoner in order to be able to continue working for him. He entreated his father to pay the ransom. All Florentine historians, Capponi in particular, stress the effect of the young man's intervention. It was an enormous sum and one which few could even dream of paying or repaying. John XXIII, who had befriended Cosimo, had intimated that he would make him his heir, but no one could tell what such an inheritance might amount to. In fact, when he died it turned out to be a very modest one: the Medici intervention in fact resulted in a financial loss for them. In spite of all this, Giovanni di Bicci paid up the ransom and asked John XXIII to come and live in Florence where he would be honourably received in accordance with his rank and personal worthiness for, despite the Council's judgement, he still regarded him as the true Pope. In the event, the Medici gained enormous prestige from playing host to a sovereign pontiff, even though his title was contestable. Not only did their popularity grow, but so did the good name of the bank, which was evidently so secure that it could throw away 35,000 florins on a lost cause.

The portrait the contemporary chroniclers and Machiavelli paint of this first great Medici represents him as a citizen who was devoted to the public good, merciful to his enemies, given to a lenient vengeance that was exceptional at a time when the normal treatment of the defeated was bestial cruelty and methodical viciousness in the torture chambers and on the scaffolds. Giovanni dealt with criminals leniently because he regarded them as unhappy souls rather than guilty parties. He elicited people's gratitude by not putting himself forward for election to civic offices; the more he protested, the happier they were to appoint him. Whether this self-effacement came naturally and spontaneously to him or whether it was the result of cunning calculation, it served him well. The testament he left for his children when he died on February 28, 1429 is a touching specimen of paternal counsel, benign and modest. He enjoined his sons to distinguish themselves by the exercise and excellence of their virtues, rather than by the external pomp and the ceremony of public status, for as long as they did so, they would be storing up riches in heaven, while on earth they would win all the success that justly accrues to true worth.

II Cosimo Pater Patriae

Giovanni di Bicci's son Cosimo (1389–1464) carried on his father's traditions. Like his ancestors, he was a moderate, prudent man who increased his family fortune and political prestige. He was moderate, but he did take risks, too—calculated risks. Cosimo was always suspicious of political adventurers whose schemes could involve the whole population in ruinous exploits. The golden mean, so much praised by the ancients, did not preclude risk-taking, but it did restrict risk-taking to very safe bets. Cosimo would not have minded being called cautious to the point of meanness; indeed he would have taken it as a compliment to his acumen. 'You may pursue the infinite,' Cosimo said, 'but I pursue the finite. You may set your ladder against the vaulted heavens, but I set mine firmly on the ground.'

He was convinced that a settlement was wiser than law suits, that a dubious peace was better than a victorious war, and that all problems could be solved by skilful negotiation. When Sacchetti wrote that 'a good businessman cannot be a soldier', he described the Florentine notable. Cosimo claimed that all was possible, if a little wit and goodwill were employed, provided that one's sense of timing was perfect, and provided one could pay the price. Cosimo was an excellent judge of men. His intuitions were instinctual and not intellectual. A few minutes of conversation sufficed to inform him how much he could expect from anyone and how much he should trust him. Vespasiano observed this in his *Vite*. He remarks that 'he was discretion itself, and could judge men by looking them in the face.'

Cosimo was born in 1389, and was nearly forty when his father died, the right age to accede to a glorious succession. Immense financial wealth and political power came into his hands, and no one but the other notables begrudged him these. The people were now used to seeing one Medici succeed another. What was good for the bank was good for the Signoria and for the Councils, too. Cosimo inherited and maintained both Giovanni di Bicci's fortune and his popularity and saw them multiply almost unfalteringly until his own death in 1464. As the Florentine historian Guicciardini was to write, 'He enjoyed these benefits totally unopposed for thirty years' (actually thirty-five years). This view of Cosimo, by a chronicler who was perhaps more faithful to the glory of the Medici than he was to historical fact, might lead one to suppose that Cosimo contentedly sat back and watched his financial and political security accrue unchallenged by adversary, ambition, or risk. This was far from being true. His thirty-five years of public life were turbulent years, riddled with intrigues, threatened by rivals, accusations, plots by the *ottimati*, and by constantly impending reverses of popular favour—thirty-five years by permission of the shifting, jealous, temperamental mob.

Twenty years before he became head of the house of Medici, Cosimo was introduced to the business world by his father, whose example he followed assiduously. And he was well advised to do so, for his father had already proved himself as a businessman who had reconciled love of money and power with a life and public image of generosity and modesty, which had earned him the reputation of a true democrat—as indeed he was in his own fifteenth-century Italian style—characterized by the formulae, 'All in good time' and 'Everything in moderation'. Cosimo is said to have advanced the public good by turning everything to his own profit.

5. Detail of torchholder on the façade of *Palazzo Strozzi*.

This was only partially true. The love for his country—Florence, since no one then thought of Italy as an entity, with the possible exception of Machiavelli—and the keenly-developed sense of community which all Florentines shared, down to the most egotistical, did motivate many of Cosimo's successful enterprises. It was not all done to earn extra popularity and prestige.

The democratic concept shared by all reasonable, intelligent, experienced men in the plutocratically organized Italian republics provided for popular participation in the affairs of state, but this was truer in theory than in practice. The notables, who clutched all the reins of government in their own hands, were probably right to distrust the capacities of the *popolo minuto,* the lower classes, the workmen and labourers, to decide the fate of the entire community. The constitution did require that they be consulted. But as Guicciardini put it, 'the people are quite senseless, they are a monster of misapprehensions and confusions and their vain opinions are as far from the truth as is Spain in the maps of Ptolemy from India'. Matteo Palmieri, the pharmacist, made a similar observation from his shop at 'Swallows' Corner': 'It is lunacy to have a cobbler tell us how civil laws are to be enacted, how the Republic is to be administered, how wars are to be conducted'. And finally, there was Machiavelli, who believed that one should work for the good of the people but without consulting them at all: 'The only thing one owes the people is results'.

The governmental system of Florence was in fact immensely complex and was continually altered either to suit the group in power, or to reverse the effects of earlier changes. The system was based on a series of elected councils and officers chosen in a variety of ways, which aimed to give opportunities of holding office to a representative cross-section of people. There were of course many methods used to make sure that the friends of the most powerful groups got in, and it was precisely their skill at manipulating the institutions which gave families like the Medici their political pre-eminence. At the beginning of the fifteenth century the principal legislative body in Florence was called the *Signoria.* It was composed of nine officers, comprising the *Gonfaloniere di Giustizia,* the senior executive officer, the *Capitano del Popolo* representing the interests of the greater guilds, and seven *Priori.* These were empowered to initiate legislation and to direct policy. Separate from the Signoria was the office of the *Podestà* which was given to someone from outside the city and held for a year. The Podestà was the Chief Judge of the city and leader of the army in war. By the time of Cosimo's return from Venice in 1434 the Podestà had been made subservient to the *Otto di Guardia* (Eight Guards), who controlled a kind of political police force and had the power to arrest political enemies and criminals designated by the Podestà. In times of war a special council, called the *Dieci di Balia* (Ten Baillies), was appointed to handle all aspects of war, including finance.

To these offices and groups were attached advisory committees of experts called *Pratiche* whose function it was to give specialized advice on particular aspects of government. To the Signoria also were attached twelve *Buonuomini* (good men) and sixteen captains of the companies or guilds. The number of additional advisory committees varied from time to time; the aim seems to have been to divide the responsibility for decisions among as large a number of people as possible, although obviously in times of danger those in the senior offices would gain special powers. To provide democratic checks there were also councils representing the people as a whole, such as the *Consiglio del Popolo,* which was elective, and the *Parlamento* which was an assembly of all the citizenry called together by the *Vacca,* the great bell of the Palazzo della Signoria (see plate 3). Election for offices was originally by casting lots; the names of eligible candidates (drawn from a list of 2,000 senior citizens) were placed in a bag, and the number required would then be drawn out. During the course of the fifteenth century the decision on eligibility became increasingly

6. Column of Justice in Via Tornabuoni opposite the church of Santa Trinità; the medieval *Palazzo Spini* is on the right.

important, and the short-lists of names considered increasingly dependent on the party in power. The clerks in charge of elections, the *accopiatori*, gradually became the arbiters of what names would be selected and placed in the bags, and these accopiatori in turn became the agents of groups seeking power; rich and powerful as the Medici were, they were obviously able to have a decisive influence on the choices the clerks made. After the Pazzi conspiracy had been quashed in 1478, elections were stopped for ten years, giving the supporters of Lorenzo the Magnificent a chance to consolidate his position in the city. Sudden reversals such as that faced by Lorenzo's son, Pietro lo Sfortunato, in 1494, however, could never be ruled out.

All in all the system allowed the voice of the poorer classes to be heard, but it also enabled the dominant groups to manoeuvre each other in and out of office and influence. The Medici always posed as friends of the people, and appeared on the side of constitutional correctness, although they were willing enough to alter the system to their own advantage if they could do so with impunity. In the last resort the ability to rouse the rabble and overturn the government was decisive, and was a danger that had to be faced by any Florentine politician and was frequently faced by the Medici. Their long-lasting power rested on their ability to survive these reversals of favour in the streets, and in their clever manipulation of the extremely fluid constitutional arrangements.

While his father was still alive, Cosimo travelled Europe for several years, meeting influential people and setting up branches, at Bruges, Venice, London, Geneva, and Avignon. He made wealthy, respected men his agents. He sent Giovanni Tornabuoni to England, a respected citizen (whose family name was given to one of the main streets of Florence) who was wealthy enough to commission Ghirlandaio to paint him a fresco (recently restored) in the choir of Santa Maria Novella. The characters of the *Life of the Virgin* were given Medici faces and those of their servants, their humanist friends, and of course the Tornabuoni themselves, who were also related to the Medici. When Tornabuoni's son Lorenzo married the beautiful Giovanna degli Albizzi in 1486, he asked Botticelli to decorate the walls of his villa

Above:
Fig. 3 Tomb of the Anti-pope, John XXIII (died 1419), commissioned by Cosimo de' Medici from Donatello and Michelozzo, in the Baptistry.

Left:
Fig. 4 Frescoes taken from the Villa Lemmi, by Botticelli, showing Lorenzo Tornabuoni and Giovanna degli Albizzi (the two figures on the left). *Paris, Musée du Louvre.*

7. Borgo Sant'Apostoli, as it turns into Via Tornabuoni.

at Pian di Mugnone near Florence with symbolic scenes of the young couple's happiness. (These frescoes were later detached from the walls of Villa Lemmi, as it came to be known, and are now in the Louvre—see fig. 4).

Cosimo's relations with the anti-Pope John XXIII (see above, p. 24) were an example not only of his constancy, but also of his understanding of the fact that his support for the prelate after he had lost his papal crown at the Council of Constance, would do him great good in the eyes of the world. Cosimo was as generous with him after his death as he had been during his lifetime: he commissioned a magnificent sculpted tomb in the Baptistry for which he employed the young Donatello (see fig. 3). The anti-Pope's misfortunes put him in Cosimo's debt to the tune of 100,000 gold florins, excluding the ransom of 35,000 florins. Cosimo had also risked another unwise 120,000 gold florins on the King of England, whose circumstances were precarious. But Cosimo could allow himself the luxury of losing money—a luxury only afforded by the immensely rich, who can also afford to be farsighted. It was not an act of folly but of largesse. It reinforced his credit and his reputation as the richest man in Florence. He wanted not merely to be the richest man in the city, but the only really wealthy man. He set out to absorb, and did absorb, rival bank after rival bank, helped by his political ascendancy which naturally favoured his calculated, steady progress towards total hegemony and monopoly.

In Cosimo's mind, glory and gain walked arm in arm, helping each other along the path to success. He aimed to draw some advantage from every event. In 1439, when the Pope decided to convoke a council at Ferrara, Cosimo did not rest until he had persuaded the Fathers of the Council to meet in Florence instead. Local trade would greatly benefit from it and, at the same time, the crowd of foreigners that spent their money in the shops would provide splendid entertainment for the Florentine populace. It would enjoy the exoticism and the incessant to-ing and fro-ing of clergy and laymen up and down the streets of Florence. The most appreciated spectacles were indeed those that took place in the street: the arrivals of sovereigns, religious festivals, civic commemorations, carnivals, holy processions, circus parades with strange animals. The exoticism of the 1439 Council was, in fact, one of its most relished features, for it brought to Italy a host of Eastern European prelates and Byzantine princes, accompanied by Moors and Mongols in their retinues and every sort of curious animal in tow.

Profit and prestige were also present at the union of Cosimo to Contessina de' Bardi, heiress of one of the most famous Florentine families, which brought him the Bardi's palace and the directorship of their bank. Cosimo left the house in which he had been born to live instead in the beautiful Palazzo Bardi. Then his ever-increasing riches dictated that he have a still larger, more beautiful house. In 1444 he had his own palace built by Michelozzo on a broad street, a tall, airy, distinguished building (see fig. 5). There was one problem. Brunelleschi, the family's official architect, who had designed the San Lorenzo church which was to become the bankers' 'palatine (royal) chapel', and who displayed the most extraordinary daring in the execution of the cupola of the Cathedral of Santa Maria del Fiore (see plate 28) had proposed a palace of such splendour and magnificence as to make Cosimo nervous as to the advisability of such ostentation. If the Medici residence were in any way excessively rich, big, opulent, or elaborate, the purpose it was intended to serve, that of publicity, would be self-defeating for it would be used against him. He might even lose his popularity. Anyone who fell from popular favour had only to make one innocent slip, one clumsy imprudent error and he would be made to forfeit his money, power, often his freedom, or even his life. Michelozzo was more modest, more discreet and therefore preferable to Brunelleschi. And even this discretion excited some acid souls to observe that the 'Medici are living like princes now'.

8. Detail of the façade of *Palazzo Rucellai* built between 1446 and 1451 by Bernardo Rossellino after a design by Alberti, himself a member of the Rucellai family.

Fig. 5 Window in the façade of the *Palazzo Medici-Riccardi* in the Via Larga, built by Michelozzo (1444-52).

9. Detail of the fresco of the *Adoration of the Magi*, painted between 1459 and 1463 by Benozzo Gozzoli, showing Piero il Gottoso and Cosimo il Vecchio de' Medici. *Palazzo Medici*.

It was very dangerous to become an object of public jealousy; Cosimo, like his ancestors, went to great pains to ensure that he was beloved by the people and he relied on them to protect him from the nobles. The demagogy that achieved his ends was of a truly refined and subtle nature. It was founded on the appreciation that if one deliberately and rigorously excluded the people from government, one had to distract and even destroy their political awareness by giving them other pastimes. Today these distractions would be material prosperity, sports, leisure-time amusements. In Cosimo's time it was sufficient to furnish the public with frequent festivities to hide the more disturbing questions. The infantilization of the masses as a means to making them more malleable was a highly successful tool in the Medici system of controlling the government.

This system, which was to vary in its applications, owed its origins to an accident—the war declared against Lucca in 1429. It was an ugly, almost pointless war. Florence wanted the tiny republic to feel the weight of her authority. Lucca was not strictly dependent upon Florence for her prosperity and her security, but she lived in her great neighbour's shadow and Florence was to show her that she should never try to steal a ray of the limelight from her. Brunelleschi, whose plan for the house in Via Larga was to be rejected, was a universal man, as were all great artists of his time, and took an interest in military strategy as did Leon Battista Alberti, Michelangelo, and Leonardo da Vinci. Thus Brunelleschi proposed an ingenious method of hastening Lucca's defeat. The river Serchio's course could be redirected so as to inundate the city; the plan failed, however, and the Florentine regiments were the ones who were nearly drowned. The war dragged on for four years, and Cosimo's position suffered, as the expense involved and the protracted victory were unpopular. Cosimo himself had not really been in favour of the war, but had been forced into it because the populace had naively transformed it into a question of national honour. Just as they had loudly acclaimed the onset of the campaign, so they now loudly protested against tax increases and the rising cost of living that the war had caused. The war, in fact, bled 30 million florins from the public treasury.

Cosimo was able to gain the public's confidence by pointing out that he had opposed the whole enterprise with all his might. The negotiated peace for which he pressed was then wholly attributable to him, regardless of its humiliating and profitless nature. In one mighty shift of popular opinion, Cosimo emerged more powerful than before. He heaped the entire responsibility for the disastrous enterprise onto the shoulders of his political adversaries, the nobles. The nobles in return decided that they would be undone if Cosimo obtained popular consent to assume broader, more openly-established powers than he had had hitherto. The extremists of the anti-Medici factions, whose belligerence the prudent Niccolò da Uzzano was no longer there to temper as he had died during the war, aimed to bring Cosimo down by legal and constitutional means. Rinaldo, the most daring and fiery of the Albizzi, who were, after all, hereditary enemies of the Medici, started the ball rolling by demanding that severe punishment be meted out to this man who was trying to 'raise himself above his neighbours and reduce them to slavery'.

Everything that the republic owed to Cosimo and the Medici, its commercial and financial prosperity, its magnificent feasts, its beautiful monuments, the charity to pauper girls, his gifts to the poor, Medici-financed hospitals—all was forgotten. The benefactor suddenly became a public enemy. Rinaldo was sufficiently circumspect to have his friend Bernardo Guadagni, whose debts he had paid, appointed Gonfaloniere. By the powers of his office, Guadagni controlled the police and was of consequence in the assemblies. Instead of barricading his palace doors, which, like all other Florentine palaces, could have withstood a siege, or asking his friends and clients to take up arms in his defence, Cosimo offered no resistance and agreed to appear before the assembly of the Signoria. They responded by throwing him

immediately into prison in 1433, pending the appointment of a special commission to conduct his trial.

The cell in which the great banker was locked was a tiny room at the very top of the Palazzo Vecchio's tower, nicknamed the *alberghetto,* the little hotel. Political prisoners were placed in it. Cosimo adapted himself to its discomforts; knowing that his enemies would stop at nothing to get rid of him and knowing that poison was one of the preferred means of dealing with awkward problems, he fasted for four whole days. He spent these days in lengthy conversations with his gaoler, Federico Malvadri, who finally agreed to assist him to communicate with the outside and to deliver 1,100 florins to the Gonfaloniere Guadagni. This generous gift had the effect of suddenly changing the Albizzi's client's mind; the Gonfaloniere proclaimed his devotion to the Medici and saw to it that Cosimo was escorted to the frontiers of the Florentine republic in 1433, fearing lest he fall foul of some treacherous attempt en route.

His departure, half banishment and half voluntary exile, was used by his supporters to turn the situation round once again. Cosimo they said, had gone off to Venice to set up his bank's new headquarters, taking with him all the countless business concerns in Florence in which he was interested, in addition to his own. Florence would thus be robbed of a source of enormous income which benefited the entire population. The Medici may have made their fortune in Florence, but they had also *made Florence's fortune.* Their departure, considered in this light, was a national disaster. Scarcely a year had elapsed since his escape from the *alberghetto* when the same assembly which banished Cosimo, after they had failed to condemn him to death or have him secretly assassinated, clamoured for his return. He left a public enemy, a virtual tyrant; on his return in 1434 he was acclaimed at the gates with garlands and banners.

The chronicles and historical records of the fifteenth century all celebrate Cosimo. According to them, the title of Pater Patriae, Father of the State, which the humanists in his entourage elected to bestow upon him when he died, instead of the less acceptable titles of 'triumphant' or 'imperator', was thoroughly deserved by him on his victorious return. Paintings and medallions outdid themselves in emphasizing the modesty of style that Cosimo loved to cultivate. They portray him sitting down in an armchair in the calm of evening, reposing after a hard day's work. He sits peacefully, leaning slightly, his head to one side, his hands clasped reverently enough, though not in prayer. The gesture of the hands reminds one more of the shopkeeper, who when he finishes his cramping book-keeping, rubs his hands to get the circulation going again. There is another less conventional portrait of Cosimo, unlike the others he probably sat for, painted posthumously by Pontormo (see plate 14). The artist drew upon reliable documents, pictures, sketches, sculptures, engravings and took from them the features of the Father of the State. In the same way that the historian's greater detachment gives him the freedom the chronicler never knows, so Pontormo's portrait is freer than those executed by Cosimo's contemporaries and can and does portray his *history,* its economic and political importance. He interprets Cosimo's physiognomy in relation to his past life, which posterity could judge as a unified whole.

The long hooked nose, the thick ears, the coarse lip do not reveal a particularly aristocratic nature. It is a popular, robust, primitive face, which shows a rustic or an artisan, with all his virtues and vices, but also it has an incongruous look of a man of destiny, heir-apparent to a vast fortune, which he was bound to increase. He also looks the part of the political personality who uses to his best advantage the privileges he is heir to, and who ensures that none should envy or hate him other than his equals, his political and business rivals. He is the democrat who plays to the gallery, who is friend of the people; he plays the democratic game which convention demands

10. Detail of the fresco of the *Adoration of the Magi* by Benozzo Gozzoli, showing an idealized portrait of Giuliano de' Medici as one of the Magi. *Palazzo Medici.*

but which is always secretly or even overtly overruled by the power of money, which the people can resent, but more often tolerate or pursue.

Wisdom and resignation were characteristic of Cosimo Pater Patriae, of the Medici dynasty as a whole, and of the Florentine notables as a class, whose lofty and noble fatalism came from classical philosophies. Towards the end of his life, Cosimo went about with his eyes closed; when his wife asked him why, he answered, because he wanted to get used to not seeing the things he loved. When Lorenzo the Magnificent

was dying, he turned his face to the wall to avoid the panting onslaughts of Savonarola, who pursued him with wild anger to his very death bed. Florentine politics required that the *haute bourgeoisie* be both ostentatious and simple, modest and munificent. But excessive ostentation, or the merest trace of avarice could well destroy popularity, which had to be refurbished, re-established, and merited every single day. Pope Pius II Piccolomini, a man of great learning and refined tastes, once wrote to Cosimo, 'you are royal in everything but name'. But that name made all the difference, for the Medici domination of Florence depended on the people's goodwill and bore no resemblance to the divine rights of the Emperor or the King of France or the King of Naples.

If the *vox populi* in Florence was more of a *vox dei* than elsewhere, it was because a throne built on the wobbly consent of the masses is fragile and precarious. The aristocratic politicians, who wished to dispense with popular suffrage, made futile attempts to perpetuate their power by force, and were never very popular in Italy. Feudalism was a foreign importation; the indigenous communal system was generally preferred. What actually happened was that those who sought power or needed it had to be subtle and cunning enough to persuade the people of their basic freedom, while influencing them to adopt decisions which were really dictated by the ruler's needs. Propaganda and publicity are the traditional ways of persuading without commanding among democratic peoples; Cosimo's skill in directing and wielding

38

public opinion, indispensable to his position and wealth, proves his rare genius and in itself illustrates the tenacity and prudence which were his life tenets.

Cosimo strove throughout his career not to appear to be 'raising himself above his neighbour', while never allowing that neighbour to forget his financial distinction and therefore his effective superiority. The Florentines may have been hostile to titles of nobility, but they were subject to the strong influences of *bourgeois* prestige; their egalitarian persuasions enabled the paupers to forgive the privileged their wealth, for they reasoned that craft and a little luck could make them as rich. The difference between the *popolo grasso* and the *popolo minuto*, between banker and the lowliest artisan, was a matter of degree, whereas a chasm separated the aristocrat from the commoner. It was a moral chasm, a social barrier, and there was the rub. The Florentines, like all true democrats, preferred an opulent *bourgeoisie* to an indigent aristocracy. Their king would have no divine rights, no holy unctions, no elections. He would be theirs by their kind consent and they would turn a blind eye for as long as he lived up to his name and prestige, a prestige that they accepted and understood because it was theirs to bestow.

Cosimo never broke the Medici tradition of reliance upon popular support against their own class: they were *popolani* as opposed to *ottimati* and remained so. Machiavelli quite rightly remarked in his *Discorso sopra il riformare lo stato di Firenze* that 'The Medici who ruled at that time were reared and fed by their fellow citizens, and they governed these people with a familiarity that made them feel honoured'. Every word of this acute observation rings true. These Florentines, who so jealously guarded the cult of the invulnerability of their liberty, an idea more important to them than the actual practice of liberty, were as restricted and overruled by the Medici as they had been by any other government; and yet they were indebted to the Medici for not stressing the differences between the butcher, the baker, the proletariat and the financial and commercial magnate, and for their singular lack of arrogance. Was the pleasant disposition that characterizes Cosimo's portraits genuine, spontaneous, true or was it a disguise? His professed love of the countryside, his rustic hobbies, his gardening at the exquisite Caffaggiolo and Careggi villas— was all this real or was it a convenient way of excusing himself from Florence when things became uncomfortable?

On his return from exile he had announced that he would not punish or revenge himself upon his enemies, and that he would work for a restoration of unity to the city. This, however, was asking too much. Magnanimity of this sort would be more akin to imprudence. Cosimo's twenty years' experience in public affairs at his father's side, then his own experience at the head of his bank and in the affairs of his city, had taught him the political habits of the Florentines, their fickle and even vindictive temperament. He was not prepared, therefore, to bank on a return of popularity which could easily be swayed against him again. Soon after his return he took action against the nobles, his policies revealing the determined will to power and implacable severity that lay beneath the external geniality, which appears in his portraits and which was so much admired. He claimed that there had been a conspiracy against his life and he accused the greatest names in Florence: the Albizzi, Peruzzi, and the Strozzi. A massive proscription followed, comparable to those of Sulla in Rome, except that, as Machiavelli stressed, there was no bloodshed—at least, officially. Deportation and exile sufficed to satisfy the Medici wrath, for the Medici always respected that time-tested, ever-valid professional precept: today's enemies may be tomorrow's friends; final measures are imprudent.

Cosimo may never have known, therefore, of the more violent and vicious attacks made on his victims, although if he did know of them he may have justified them as fit retribution. Machiavelli later said that a prince should know how to use both beast and man; his justification was that 'this is what the Ancients meant by their

12. *Adoration of the Magi* by Botticelli, showing members of the Medici family: the young man on the left is perhaps Lorenzo de' Medici (later known as il Magnifico, the Magnificent); on the right is a supposed self-portrait of the artist; the central figure has been identified with Piero il Gottoso, Lorenzo's father, and the leading King (in black) with Cosimo il Vecchio, Lorenzo's grandfather. *Uffizi.*

13. Posthumous portrait of Lorenzo the Magnificent by Vasari. *Uffizi.*

fable of Achilles reared by the centaur Chiron'. Guicciardini, also a man of wide learning and experience, offered a similar justification drawn from his reading of Florentine chronicles: 'All states are violent; no ruling power is legitimate; the emperor who takes his from Roman authority is the greatest usurper of all; and princes' violation is twice as great since they subjugate us to their will with temporal and spiritual weapons'. Few epochs made recourse to such deliberate savagery and brutality as did the Renaissance, which could also boast of sublime achievements in the realms of art and every refinement of life. Men were of violent and impulsive temperament, of uncontrolled passions, whose loving, desiring or hating were always pushed to their extreme limits. The horrors which some of Cosimo's supporters perpetrated upon his return merely reflected the fact that vengeance was then in vogue among Italian tyrants and statesmen. The more morally precarious their power, the more it depended upon force and the more necessary that this force be terrifying and produce ghastly and spectacular examples. The punishment of Ramiro dell'Orco, for instance, was meant to be an example of how felonious governors, or governors suspected of treason, were treated; Cesare Borgia had his body hacked in two. The Duke of Milan, Gian Galeazzo Sforza had Petrino da Castello's two hands lopped off, because he had seen him chatting with his mistress; and he buried Pietro del Drago alive because, justly or not, he distrusted him. And Sforza himself, in his turn, was slaughtered in the Church of Sant' Ambrogio in Milan by a band of assassins led by Giacomo Girolamo Oligiati and Gianandrea Lampugnani.

Tyrants who died peacefully of old age in their beds were few and far between. Pope Alexander VI was poisoned; his son Cesare Borgia drifted into obscurity, became a soldier of fortune, was eventually struck down on a battlefield in Spain. Galeotto Manfredi, Lord of Faenza, was stabbed by his wife; Giovanni Frangiani, Lord of Fermo, was stabbed by his nephew; Girolamo Riario, Lord of Forlì, was stabbed by conspirators; Sigismondo Malatesta, who was poisoned by one of his servants, was reputed to have raped his daughter and his son-in-law. Ferrante of Aragon, King of Naples, according to the historian Commines, who knew him well, was a monster of cruelty, viciousness and greed: he would have his enemies' heads cut off and pickled; he embalmed the cadavers of those he had murdered, dressed them up, and propped them up along the walls of a gallery in which he liked strolling; he would visit his prisoners, whom he kept locked in cages, and mock them between fits of wild laughter. One day he avenged himself on the Signoria of Venice, with which he was pursuing a legal war, by poisoning the holy water in every Venetian church. When the gates of his palace swung to behind his dinner guests, no one ever knew if they would emerge alive. Thus Jacob Burckhardt, the great nineteenth-century historian of the Italian Renaissance, had good reason to write, 'A mixture of good and evil is found in the most remarkable combination in the various Italian states of the fifteenth century. The personalities of the princes were so outstanding, so imposing, so perfectly suited to their circumstances and to the rôles they were required to play that moral judgements risk losing their relevance.'

Cosimo was neither more nor less moral than the rest of his contemporaries. He can be praised, however, for having been less blinded by passions than Visconti, or Borgia, Malatesta, or Sforza, and for having been reasonable rather than impulsive. Behind the revolts, public vengeances, settling of scores, and assassinations the private interests of subordinates played themselves out. Cosimo's return was celebrated with very few murders, probably committed behind Cosimo's back; the leaders of the opposing factions were sent packing, but it is to Cosimo's credit that they actually arrived safely in Rome, Venice, and Genoa. The banishments were, however, exceptionally long and none was ever shortened. Compared to other 'tyrants' Cosimo was distinguished by his modesty and his moderation. Commines praises Cosimo for exercising 'a gentle and pleasant authority befitting a free city'.

14. Posthumous portrait of Cosimo il Vecchio, also known as *Pater Patriae*, by Pontormo. *Uffizi*.

He did not oppress his fellow citizens with arms; he crushed them with his wealth, which was a less painful and destructive if equally effective way of controlling their liberties.

Upon his reinstatement, Cosimo instituted a series of economic and political reforms calculated to increase his popularity. He undertook yet another revision of the *catasto*, which had previously concerned his father. He wanted to make the *catasto* progressive—that is to say, to base it on a series of social categories, taxed on a sliding scale ranging from fifty to four per cent according to income, correctly assessed or, if this were not possible, arbitrarily estimated (which also enabled him to favour friends under the guise of impartiality). This fiscal reform seemed fair since the richest citizens would theoretically pay the highest taxes, but in practice there were all sorts of ways and means of getting round the tax inspectors.

Cosimo believed in the balance of political power. He counterbalanced the proletarian infiltration into the government by placing a few relatively unaggressive 'nobles' in the administrative posts. This gesture was quite revolutionary as the aristocracy had been excluded from public office for a century and a half. Cosimo may have justified the move by showing that the aristocracy had learnt its lesson and need no longer be feared as the enemy of 'liberty'; he was also using this group from the upper class to bolster himself against any sudden pressure or possible insurrection by the proletariat, such as the Ciompi uprising.

His talent for weaving between parties and drawing support from all classes was proof of his rare political genius. In the end, Cosimo became a virtual dictator, but one at whom no one ever levelled the charge of abuse of power. He used it instead to promote all sorts of improvements. He originated, for instance, marriage assurance, which later became a common practice throughout Italy; it provided dowries for brides: the parents deposited a certain sum when their child was born and this sum, with the interest compounded was returned upon the daughter's marriage. Since infant mortality rate was very high at the time, the young girls received often as much as five times the amount that their parents had paid in. Cosimo organized these assurance companies into a state body, the *Monte delle Doti*, which he generously subsidized from his own pocket.

In spite of his habitual modesty, his quiet way of dressing, his relaxed manners with all and sundry, Cosimo knew how to be magnificent when the occasion called for it, when receiving distinguished foreigners, when dazzling and delighting his people. Sober diets prevailed at Tuscan tables, even at ceremonial dinners, but plain cooking was more than compensated by the luxury of the table ware. Plates, silverware, crystal and silver gilt centre-pieces and engraved stone lavishly decorated the sideboards, but all in the most perfect and exquisite taste. Popular feasts were much the same. They were intended to entertain the masses who had the endearing quality of enjoying the sight of the wealthier citizens' pleasures, provided they made a spectacular show. All ceremonies took place in the street in Italy. Even the executions were accompanied by macabre and brutal ceremonies which were geared to captivate their beholders. Equally captivating were the religious processions of cowled flagellants and penitents in the trains of purple-robed Cardinals and mitred bishops. The 'Triumphs' composed by the humanists in conformity to Petrarch's book *I Trionfi*—the *Triumphs of Love, of Time, of Death, of Chastity*—often excited real panic in the audience. In the Triumph of Death, Death was usually acted by a hoary emaciated hag or by a scythe-wielding skeleton, which never failed to terrorize the onlookers.

This 'theatre of horror', which was intended to put the fear of death and damnation into its spectators and move them to remorse and repentance, alternated with a different sort of procession, the royal welcome for popes and foreign princes, which with their exotic trains and animals resembled the arrival of a circus. The entire

15. Pope Leo X (Giovanni de' Medici) with Cardinals Giulio de' Medici (the future Clement VII) and Luigi de' Rossi, by Raphael, 1518-1519. *Uffizi*.

Fig. 7 Bust of Giovanni de'
Medici by Mino da Fiesole
(1461). *Bargello, Museo
Nazionale.*

16. View of the Cathedral,
Santa Maria del Fiore, from
'Giotto's' *campanile.* The
church was built according to
designs of Arnolfo di Cambio
from 1294 onwards, but
completed only in 1436. The
marble panelling of the walls
was carried out in the mid-
fourteenth century.

population of Florence profited from these visits which drew crowds of ready spenders, who lavished their money liberally on silks, gold objects, jewelry and works of art. But the spectacles themselves, aside from all their commercial advantages, were enough to strengthen the popularity of the man responsible for them. Giovanni Villani in his *Cronaca* gives an account of the 1283 spring festivities as if they were a quite normal event: some thousand young men and women in white, led by a figure personifying *Love,* spent two months celebrating, dancing, giving tournaments and banqueting in the streets. In 1459 Pope Pius II, the humanist Aeneas Sylvius Piccolomini—a highly talented poet and extremely generous patron—paid Cosimo a visit and was received with exceptional pomp. (Pius II had an entire town, Pienza, built in his and his family's honour and glory by Rossellino). Giovanni Cambi's *Storie* tells of a magnificent ball given for Pius II under the colonnade of the Mercato Vecchio, which was surrounded by a palisade covered with cloth; the benches were draped with tapestries. 'Sixty young Florentine men of the best families were chosen for their skill at dancing, decked out in pearls and gems, and danced all day, as did the young ladies and girls who were also chosen for their abilities. The dancers changed their clothes several times a day, and all the ambassadors and many cardinals also attended.' This occasion also saw the revival of the ancient sport of watching animal fights, which the Romans had taken over from the Etruscans. In one day alone there were fights between ten lions, three wolves, four bulls, two buffaloes, a cow, a wild boar, a calf and a giraffe. The exotic animals came from the private Medici zoo, the giraffe having been a present from the Sultan Bajazet.

Cosimo maintained good relations with the Orient, whence he imported the crude silk that was made into cloth in the Florentine workshops. He took measures to free himself to some extent, at least, from this foreign dependence on silk by encouraging the cultivation of silkworms throughout Tuscany. It was ordered that every peasant in the Florentine territories should plant a certain number of mulberry trees proportionate to the extent of his estate. One of the most surprising imports from Asia and Africa was that of slaves. Slavery was such a common practice in fifteenth-century Italy, which also saw the flowering of humanist thought, that not a single humanist ever uttered a reproach against the usage or even expressed shock or surprise over it, showing once again what a variety of contrasts were able to flourish in Renaissance society. Slaves were brought in from black Africa, from Asia Minor and also from Russia. The Circassians were in particular demand, for their beauty was widely praised.

It was with a Circassian slave that Cosimo had a son, Carlo, who had an important position in the town of Prato; his portrait was painted by Filippo Lippi among the characters watching Salome's dance and among the spectators of the martyrdom of Saint Stephen in the chancel frescoes of Prato Cathedral. Carlo was the only illegitimate son we know of, but Cosimo also had two sons by his wife Contessina de' Bardi. The younger of the two, Giovanni, was very gifted; Cosimo had hoped he would be his heir, but he died in 1463, too young to succeed him. Mino da Fiesole's beautiful bust of the young man is at the Museo Nazionale in Florence (see fig. 7). The other son, the sickly Piero, nicknamed *il Gottoso,* the gouty one, was Lorenzo the Magnificent's father (see plate 9). That a pious man of dignified habits such as Cosimo should have had a mistress did not shock the Florentines. Italy has always been indulgent to carnal weaknesses. An excellent example of this indulgence was Cosimo's continued kindness to Filippo Lippi (*c.* 1406–1469) after the scandal he caused. Florence was amused, rather than outraged. The story goes that Lippi was very partial to beautiful women. He had to be kept under lock and key in his studio, else he would spend his days running after them. When a convent asked him to do a painting of the Virgin, the artist requested that the youngest and most beautiful nun should pose for him. He was so taken by her that he carried her

off and had a son by her, who also became a painter, Filippino Lippi (*c.* 1459–1504). He finally married her, when Cosimo intervened on his behalf and prevailed upon the Pope to release her from her religious vows.

This worldly broad-mindedness in no way diminished his orthodox observation of customs and faith. Cosimo had the Badia at Fiesole enlarged at his own expense, as well as the Convent of San Marco at Florence, where he had his private cell to which he would occasionally retire to meditate or recuperate from his secular occupations. His concern with spiritual matters is attested by his unstinting support of the group that liked to call themselves the Platonic Academy, which met either in the gardens at Careggi or Caffaggiolo, or in the palace in the Via Larga. The hospitality he extended to humanists, scholars and artists made him a model for what in the eighteenth century was called an 'enlightened monarch'. His generosity was so great that in less than 30 years he spent some 600,000 gold florins on works of art and charity. This sum was twice the annual budget of the city of Florence, and therefore gives some indication of his liberality. He also spent a good deal of time, trouble and money on sending agents to every European city to collect classical works of ancient authors in order to furnish his library. One admirable example of the contemporary devotion to manuscripts is often cited: political difficulties with Naples were settled and a full-scale war was averted when Cosimo finally agreed to part with one of his manuscripts, a precious copy of Livy which King Ferrante of Aragon had coveted for some time.

Cosimo's intelligence, his prudent politics, his diplomatic genius, his skill at ruling kindly but firmly are all traits worthy of a Father of the State. He is sometimes called the first 'apostle of the Renaissance'. He was also a great statesman, who was against war, but who was prepared to hire the best condottiere available to intimidate his enemies, and if intimidation was not enough, to wage war and conquer his adversaries.

Nicknames, like funeral orations, have an eloquence of their own. Public opinion largely endorsed the title of Pater Patriae bestowed on Cosimo by the humanists. By contrast, the Florentines manifested the lack of affection and sympathy they had for Cosimo's heir by emphasizing his physical defects and his bad health. Piero de' Medici is inseparably linked to the name which heralds his entry into history: the gouty one, *il Gottoso*. His portraits accentuate his heavy, dull features, his massive neck which suggests thyroid trouble, and the drooping eyelids that make him look dazed and sleepy. Only his deficiencies were acknowledged. His qualities passed unnoticed. He was resented mostly for having taken the place of his more attractive brother Giovanni, whom Cosimo would have preferred as his heir. Cosimo was apprehensive of the onerous inheritance he was leaving Piero. Nonetheless, despite his unlovely appearance, Piero was neither stupid nor without gifts. He was a mature man of 46, of wide business experience, and considerable cultivation, perhaps a result of his frequent contact with the humanists. His acute and perceptive sensibilities are particularly evident in his account of his father's death: 'He began to tell us about his life from his earliest business experiences; he explained how and why he had acted as he had in such and such circumstances, explaining the state of his domestic affairs and warning me to be prudent. He regretted two things, he said: not having done all he could have done and leaving me such a heavy burden to carry when I was in such bad health.' After laying down the details of a modest, quiet funeral with few churchmen and few candles, Cosimo expired. His son had been comforted by these words (Fabroni reports them word for word), and they overwhelmed him with a great tenderness: 'This turned my hopes to God and despite my deep sorrow, I knew a great joy in seeing how great was my father's soul and how kindly disposed he was to me.'

Unfortunately Piero did not inherit his father's acute judgement; he distinguished

17. The choir-screen and one of the pulpits, about 1200, *San Miniato al Monte.*

51

ill between the counsel of the trustworthy and the suspect. He was indiscreet enough to have as his confidant Diotisalvi Neroni, an intelligent man, but also a cunning and experienced intriguer. Neroni was one of those sharp-nosed Tuscans with pursed, protruding lips, an ironical mouth and eyes that sparked with malice, as Mino da Fiesole's bust of him reveals (see fig. 8). He was highly cultivated, a brilliant businessman, eager to gain the political prominence which Cosimo had denied him. Neroni shuttled between the two parties who vied for power, the Highland party and the Lowland party. The Lowlanders were the partisans of the Medici. They were so called because the Medici palace in Via Larga was situated in the low-lying districts of Florence. One of their rivals, Luca Pitti, built his magnificent house on a hillside which commanded a view of the city; his friends banded together and called themselves *Poggio,* meaning mountain, hill, elevation. The Pitti bank feared the competition of the Medici bank and the Pitti were not against using suspect sources of wealth to increase their prestige and their power. During Cosimo's lifetime, the Pitti conducted their affairs discreetly and in the dark. Their Poggio Party contained some eminent and respected men like Niccolò Soderini and Agnolo Acciaiuoli, whose civic patriotism was irreproachable and whose hostility to Piero came from their fear that he could not possibly rule as adroitly as had his father. The Pitti also managed to come to an arrangement with Neroni, even though, as Machiavelli says, Cosimo charged him from his deathbed to look after Piero and to guide him.

Neroni's first great error, in collusion with Pitti and Soderini (who was Gonfaloniere for a month in 1465) was to persuade Piero to increase his holdings in real estate. Land, he said, is a safer and more stable bet than money. The bank should recall all loans and convert the profits into houses and land. This clumsy measure enraged all the Medici's debtors who had not expected to repay then. Some of the larger debtors risked bankruptcy if they had to realize their assets immediately. Even the most respected families whose standing and credit were generally recognized, might be brought to the brink of disaster. While Neroni was treacherously running the Medici bank onto the rocks, the Poggio party tried to get its men into key positions. Soderini proposed that there should be a new form of scrutiny of votes and called for a new election to replace councils dominated by the Medici's men. For a while it appeared that he and Luca Pitti had a good deal of support, and the Medici, shut out of government, deprived of the support of their clients who spread abroad the rumour that the bank was about to fold, were faced with all the dangers that menaced important men in the Florentine democracy: unpopularity, proscription, confiscation of property, banishment, and even death.

Piero il Gottoso averted catastrophe at the last minute. He cancelled the recall of loans and with the help of his son Lorenzo, collected allies amongst those families who were still sitting on the fence. The Pitti and their supporters in return tried to lure the Medici into battle with other states. The Florentine Republic was always closely involved with the problems and intrigues of Venice, Genoa, Siena and Naples; with Milan, the Medici had managed to keep good relations by paying the Duke, Francesco Sforza, a handsome fee for maintaining troops at the disposal of Florence. But Francesco had just died. Should she renew the contract with his son Galeazzo? The Medici were in favour of renewal and the Pitti against it. It then began to look as if Venice was going to use this opportunity to attack Florence; the advice of the Poggio party appeared in the eyes of the public as inept. When they realized that their tactics were not working to their advantage the Pitti and their friends decided to settle the matter by resorting to force. They sent armed bands into the city and on one occasion when Piero was returning from a visit to Careggi tried to assassinate him. At this point, with the city on the brink of civil war, Piero suddenly revealed hidden resources of energy and political acumen which had never before come to

Fig. 8 Bust of Diotisalvi Neroni by Mino da Fiesole. *Paris, Musée du Louvre.*

18. Façade of *San Miniato al Monte,* dating from the early thirteenth century.

light. By dint of numerous gifts, promises, threats and persuasions, he enticed a large section of the Poggio party to join his own and the trading *bourgeoisie* threw their full weight behind him. There was a celebration to commemorate the Father of the State and to remind all Florentines how much they owed the Medici. Chance had it that Roberto Leoni, an honest man with allegiances to no party, was chosen Gonfaloniere. Leoni realized that the Pitti and their cohorts were striving for hegemony of the city by force and so took a few precautionary measures. He filled the Palazzo della Signoria with soldiers, and rang the great bell to summon the people's assembly in the square. He thus obtained emergency decisions from a packed assembly, whom he had frightened but won over to his side. They decreed that there should be no elections for ten years and that the instigators of the situation should be punished. Although some of the enemy had already left, Piero il Gottoso had the gates of the city closed to prevent suspects leaving and fraudulent accomplices from entering. The keys to the city gates were given to him and he placed them on his table. In a single day, the people had restored to him all of the affection which they had always given the Medici, and which Piero's fears for the bank's money had caused to wander. When the populace learned that Cosimo's son had nearly been the victim of a murder plot they demanded the execution of the conspirators.

Piero had no such wishes. The experience of his ancestors had taught him that excessive cruelty never paid. If the Poggio Party were exiled, they might still conspire but they would be out of touch with the people and thus incapable of winning them over. Diotisalvi Neroni was banished to Sicily, Niccolò Soderini to Provence and Agnolo Acciaiuoli to Apulia—each for twenty years. The conspiracy had cost them dear. Pitti, who had started the whole thing, made amends, and avowed his contrition; he was pardoned, in return for which he swore fidelity to the new master of the city.

Piero il Gottoso died on 4 November 1469, leaving two sons, Lorenzo, who was then twenty and who was to be called the Magnificent, and Giuliano. Five months before his death, Piero took the precaution of marrying his older son off to a Roman princess, Clarissa Orsini, despite his tender years. The Florentines always looked askance at 'foreign marriages'. Furthermore, an alliance with an aristocratic family such as the ancient Roman dynasty of the Orsini was tantamount to wanting to 'raise oneself above one's neighbour', which was intolerable to Tuscan egalitarianism. They were not too harsh with Piero, however, because his reign had been a gentle one. He had restored peace to Italy after a year of war when all of the enemies of the Republic had banded together in an attempt to bring it to its knees. They had been roused by the plots of the banished conspirators, who after the miscarriage of the Pitti conspiracy were eager to return to dominate the city which had expelled them. Venice, her commercial and political rival, then Pesaro, Forlì, Ferrara and Faenza united their regiments under the illustrious Condottiere, Colleone, in whose honour the Serene Republic was to erect a commemorative monument by the Florentine Verrocchio, one of the finest equestrian statues of ancient or modern times (see fig. 9). Contemporaries said that there had never been so many troops led by so bold a captain.

Florence answered this vast coalition with the support of Milan and Naples, which Piero had cleverly managed to obtain. It was a difficult war, which came to a final conclusion on the battlefield near Montefeltro on 23 July 1467, despite this last engagement's inconclusive outcome: the two armies fell asleep in their tracks on the battlefield itself. The chroniclers credited Colleone with having initiated the use of a new and light piece of artillery called the *spingarda*, which scandalized the old-guard condottieri who regarded fire-arms as ungentlemanly and dishonourable. This new weapon does not seem, however, to have been excessively lethal, since, according to Machiavelli, it slew not a single man. Even if the battle cry was

19. Interior of *Santa Croce*, showing the crossing, and frescoes in the choir by Agnolo Gaddi (about 1380). The *Capella Bardi*, containing frescoes by Giotto, can be glimpsed to the right of the choir.

55

'Massacre, Massacre' it was but a figure of speech, a traditional practice that in no way corresponded to any realistic intentions of eliminating the adversary. This was borne out by the comical visits that the captains paid to each other's camps once the battle was over and by the immediate mingling and fraternization of both sides after the heat of battle had scarcely subsided.

Those who really lost from these wars were the conspirators, who had their periods of banishment extended by ten years, whose property was confiscated and who were prohibited from ever holding public office again even upon their return from exile. Peace restored to the city, prosperity assured, the dynasty firmly entrenched by the marriage of the 'prince heir', Piero could boast that in spite of all his ill-health he had in fact acted in the public good and was the worthy son of the Father of the State. He could therefore die peacefully and leave to his son, mature for his age, the family's vast patrimony and that magnificent but overwhelming political inheritance, which, since Cosimo, had become the Medici's burden.

Fig. 9   Detail of the equestrian statue of Colleone by Verrocchio in Venice (1481-93).

Humanism in Fifteenth-Century Florence

III

The Renaissance was a time when men of genius and talent or simply men of good taste and wit tremendously enjoyed being alive. The German Ulrich von Hutten's 'how pleasurable is life' was echoed by a full-throated choir of Italian humanists, poets and artists. The *tedium vitae* of classical antiquity and the *mal de vivre* that was to scourge the Romantics were inconceivable to fifteenth-century man. The magnificent, happy child of the Italian Quattrocento thrived on curiosity and daring exploits; he yearned to discover new continents in the domains of science, art, philosophy and culture. Matteo Palmieri (1406–1475), a Florentine pharmacist, declared that 'Every intelligent man alive should give thanks to God for having been born to this age that has been the flowering of excellent genius such as has not been known for the past thousand years'. Palmieri's social position was indicative of the changes which had taken place in Florence at the time of the Medici. He was by profession a *speziale,* that is literally, a spice merchant; but the *speziale* also sold all manner of pharmaceutical products which brought him into contact with doctors, botanists, chemists, and even alchemists. In his shop at Canto delle Rondine, or 'Swallows' Corner', at the junction of two busy thoroughfares, one was sure to find all kinds of learned men and artists, who bought their painting equipment from him. Matteo Palmieri of the open happy countenance was on friendly terms with all the intellectuals and a welcome member of the ruling Florentines' entourage. The Via Larga's portals were open to all intellectuals including a shopkeeper, such as Palmieri; anyone who knew his Latin and could discourse on literary subjects was as welcome at the Medici table, as were young artists, who were accommodated by the great patrons in anticipation of their future fame.

The illustrious Filelfo (1398–1481), quarrelled over by princes from Naples to Milan, also praised Florence as the supreme capital of the arts. In his Latin epistles he writes glowingly of the magnificence and erudition of the Florentines: 'Florence has infinite charms for me. It is a town which wants of nothing, for its buildings are magnificent, its citizens glorious and rich. I am beloved, honoured, and praised to high heaven by all and sundry. My name is on everyone's lips. When I walk abroad, not only do all leading citizens step aside to let me pass, but so, too, do the noblest ladies of the land. I am shown such deference as puts me out of countenance. I give quite some one hundred audiences a day, sometimes even more, to men of means and import.' Filelfo had nonetheless taken sides against the Medici in the factional disputes and had left the city when Cosimo returned in triumph. Ever arrogant and provocative, he trotted from court to court and fawned upon the Signori of Milan. 'Cosimo', he used to say, 'needs must avail himself of both dagger and poison to protect himself against my genius and pen'. Cosimo, however, did not quake at Filelfo's diatribes, nor even take them very much amiss. There was no other city in Italy, nor in Europe for that matter, that was so tolerant in according its intellectuals the right to express freely whatever came into their heads. To criticize the leading family was not a crime of treason; Cosimo and his grandson Lorenzo were broadminded and forebearing with satirists who mocked at them. Mockery was a puny weapon against the bulwark of power and beauty which Renaissance Florence represented.

57

Those humanists who devoted their entire lives to turning antique pages, scrutinizing and interpreting Greek and Latin texts, were pure intellectuals; their main concern was to secure a rich patron who would provide the shelter, money, and wherewithal they needed to do this work. Little else interested them. Filelfo typified their outlook when he wrote to Palla Strozzi, 'I have devoted myself entirely to writing, so much so that I think I was born to live not only in my own age but also in future ages'. These humanists shunned as much as they could all knowledge of public squabbles, of inter-state disputes, and of political tensions abroad. 'All our zeal is offered up to the muses and dedicated to the arts and to the pursuit of those disciplines which, far from the din of wars, work for a good and happy life.'

The reverse of the coin, however, was the risk these intellectuals ran in isolating themselves completely from all mundane activities, joys, sorrows, difficulties, and successes: the humanist could eventually dehumanize himself; he could grow indifferent to the emotions and sentiments which lesser mortals share; he could think himself above passion, steeled against any stresses or strains that might trouble the mind and the heart. The life led by most Medieval intellectuals was not spent exclusively in the bookish delights of reading and writing, and Dante in particular is evidence of this. Medieval thinkers were capable of living life dangerously. The Renaissance humanist was perhaps more coddled by the solicitude of patrons like the Medici, who guaranteed them their livelihoods and asked no more than that they instruct and distract the connoisseurs. A goodly number sound uncannily like Vergerio's (1370–1444) portrait of them in *De Ingenuis Moribus*: 'A man who spends his life absorbed in literary delights may be dear to himself, but, be he prince or commoner, he will be of little value to the city.' Vergerio reproves him the more because, 'He knows nothing of domestic economics. He lives with his head in the clouds indifferent to paternal honour and responsibility towards his children. He knows nothing of what kind of government is best, whether it should be composed of one man or of several, of few or of many. He shuns public service with the excuse that he who serves the community serves no one, does not rise in defence of his republic in the councils, nor does he take up arms to defend it on the battlefield.'

The exaggerated shading may distort this portrait, but only in places. Not all humanists, of course, were ignorant of public affairs, but many did live in ivory towers. Among these in Florence were the Via Larga palace and the Medici's Tuscan villas at Poggio a Caiano (see plate 70) and Careggi. One cannot help feeling there was something rather noble in that gesture of 'entering into erudition' as one 'enters a religious order'. Once the humanists had settled securely and

Above:
Fig. 10   Courtyard of the Villa at *Careggi* (after 1483).

Below:
Fig. 11   Façade of the Villa at *Poggio a Caiano* (about 1480).

20. The nave, *Santa Maria Novella*, dating from the end of the thirteenth century.

comfortably on the other side of material want they could afford to deny themselves all vulgar ambitions. A genuine aristocracy of intellect was forged in contrast with that aristocracy of money that comprised the rich Florentine families, the big landowners, bankers, businessmen, and industrialists, who offered themselves as the rightful successors to that other aristocracy of blood which in Italy had been superseded by the republican or democratic states, or even the states tyrannized by the princes of the sword, the condottieri and adventurers. All humanists from the humblest teacher to the greatest geniuses, such as Ficino (1433–1499, see fig. 12) and Pico della Mirandola (1463–1494), gave thanks to God for having made them *men of the Renaissance*. The word 'Renaissance', *rinascimento*, was not in common usage until the sixteenth century, when it was used to describe the grandeur and excellence of that century and the preceding one. The voices of praise rise in unison to celebrate the Florentine Quattrocento, the golden age of the Medici, and it was in and around the circle of Cosimo and then of Lorenzo that the eulogies were first sung. 'This century is a golden age that radiates its brilliance over the liberal disciplines so long obscured—over grammar, poetry, eloquence, painting, architecture, sculpture, music, the song of the ancient Orphic lyre, all of which excel in Florence'. So wrote the great philosopher, the archetypal humanist, Marsilio Ficino. And Giovanni Rucellai (1475–1525), a rich and cultivated Florentine merchant, uses the same language as Ficino and the spice merchant Palmieri, to thank God for 'letting him live in this age which all intelligent men agree is the greatest our city has ever known'. Thus it was that a commercial market was transformed into a capital of the intellect by the coincidence of a century fraught with brilliant opportunities and a town of time-honoured cultivation, of a large number of remarkable men in every field of creative and intellectual excellence, and of a family of exceptionally gifted leaders.

The Medici could have been mere patrons like so many rulers who choose to shed lustre on their reigns by patronizing the arts and scholarship. But they were not satisfied merely to subsidize architects, philosophers, and painters. They sought to be their protégés' equals as much as the informed *amateur* can, given the enormous distance that separates the artist from the man who admires and enjoys his work. Cosimo and Lorenzo in particular were the two heads of their house who took most trouble to acquire knowledge and culture to justify their equality; this was true, at least, of the relationship to poets, philosophers, scholars, even if not to the creative artists, musicians, sculptors and painters, whose specialized art made full equality difficult. They were well versed enough as humanists to hold their own in the learned conversations held at their generous dining table in the Via Larga palace. There, or in the cool shade of palm, pine, and cypress at Careggi, would gather some of the most learned and lively minds of their time to try to define the *humanism* which during the fifteenth century became the great preoccupation of Europe's cultivated minds.

The mainspring of spiritual and intellectual concern, which in the Middle Ages had been God, was now shifted to *man* and all his appurtenances. His physical and moral existence, the universe about him, his problems of being and becoming were all brought before the temples of his thought. Man was conceived of as an individual. It was his individuality that mattered, the peculiarities and qualities which made him unique, which made him irreplaceable and *singular*, in the etymological sense of the word, 'without equal'. Whereas Medieval man endorsed collective uniformity in the Christian community that defined his ideals, the principal aim of humanism, especially as conceived in the Florence of the Medici, was to enhance individual development as far as was possible, to mould the individual into a work of art, to emphasize, exalt, intensify his uniqueness, and to distinguish him from all other individuals.

This approach to life was exemplified, almost to perfection, by an artist, but a

Above:
Fig. 12   Bust of Marsilio Ficino by Ferrucci (1499), in the *Cathedral*.

Below:
Fig. 13   Bronze medal with a self-portrait by Alberti. *Paris, Musée du Louvre.*

21. The nave, *Santo Spirito*, begun in 1436 by Brunelleschi; perhaps the most perfect example of an early Renaissance basilica in Florence.

fully-developed artist, who was also a philosopher, a writer and accomplished athlete. It was Leon Battista Alberti (1404–1492, see fig. 13), magnificent architect, a lover of antiquity, a man of astonishing intellectual and physical daring, who laid down the rule by which the artist of his century was to be measured: 'The man who cultivates his personal gifts does his duty by his country'. In other words, the humanist who aspires to complete and total humanism renders the best service possible to humanity; no one should ask more of him. The great Neo-Platonist, one of the most brilliant Florentines and a close friend of the Medici, Marsilio Ficino, traces the extraordinary silhouette of the humanist in his *Theologia Platonica* (the title alone says so much). His perfect or essential man 'spans the heavens and the earth; he plumbs the depths of Tartarus; nor are the heavens too high for him, nor is the centre of the earth too deep. He has mapped the heavens and knows the powers that move them; he knows their destinies and their effects; he has measured their span. Who can deny, therefore, that he is of almost equal genius to the author of these heavenly bodies and that, after a fashion, he himself might also be able to create them? Man wants of no superior, wants of no equal. He will not tolerate the existence of an empire above him which excludes him. He seeks to dominate all things everywhere and demands praise for his works. His predominance is everywhere as is God's. He demands immortality as does God.' There is no intention of sacrilege or blasphemy in this affirmation of man's equality with God, or rather this demonstration of man's divine essence. Good Christians the humanists may have been, but they were clearly not far from believing that it was theoretically and logically possible to be the equals of their God.

The advent of the Renaissance saw the waning of the venerated and time-honoured virtues which men in the Middle Ages had tried to attain. The humanists exalted the virtue of the spirit, '*la virtù dell'animo*' said Landino (1424–1498), above all others. This was the vehicle by which the individual's personal merits attained perfection. The Latinists did not fail to underscore the analogy between this Renaissance *virtù* and the Roman *virtus*. To translate this as *virtue* in the Christian sense of the word would be a mistake. *Virtù* in the Quattrocento resides in the individual's complete and ultimate development of himself beyond all measurable limits, and in his ability to shape his life into a work of art. In this sense the condottiere, the strategist, or the scientist each manifests in his own field as much *virtù*, if not the same *virtù* as the scholar, philosopher, and artist in theirs.

The practitioners of humanism were intellectually and spiritually superior to all other men, given that, according to Ficino, humanism could raise man to divine stature. On the practical level of social and professional advancement, the practice of humanism was the vehicle by which one entered that supreme aristocracy of men who worked in the service of the intellect and worshipped the deity of their own genius. They were the guests of honour at the Medici table (as at those of other Italian princes and leaders of the time), where they received stipends, pensions and subsidies. Should they ever happen to fall out with their patrons, they were always sure of finding board and lodging at some other prince's court. The whole of Europe was the home of the humanist. If there was an international society during the Renaissance, it consisted of these *international humanists*, who included the most brilliant Italian, German, French, English, Spanish and Flemish intellects, and whose learning made them superior to all other men. They were further distinguished from their fellow mortals by the common languages they spoke, the so-called *dead* languages, Latin and Greek.

The Latin craze was so widespread and intense as to inspire translations of Medieval Italian works into the language of Virgil and Horace. Medieval writers, such as Dante, Boccaccio and Petrarch wrote in the *volgare*, in Italian. Some scholars, such as Bruni (1374–1444) and Vespasiano (1421–1498) disdainfully averred that

22. Dome of the *Pazzi Chapel* in the cloister of *Santa Croce*. The chapel was begun by Brunelleschi in 1430 for the Pazzi family (later to be associated with the famous plot of that name against the Medici) and has terracotta decorations by Donatello, Desiderio da Settignano and Luca della Robbia. Two of Luca's roundels of the Evangelists can be seen in this picture.

certain philosophical matters just could not be expressed, in the *volgare idioma*: the humanists even tended to overlook the fact that the most complex metaphysics and the sublimest poetry of the *Divina Commedia* were more than adequately written in Italian. The French historian Monnier has summed up this type of Florentine humanist, who is also representative of similar Italian and European writers generally, when he says that 'Humanism was not simply a taste for antiquity, but a cult of antiquity, so much so that it graduated from mere adoration to attempts at reiteration. The humanist did not simply study his classics to draw inspiration from them; he was so fascinated by their importance that he copied, imitated and repeated them, adopted their models and usages, their examples and gods, their way of thinking and their language.' This language was Latin, as we all know; but so, to a greater extent even, was it Greek.

The extraordinary prestige of Greek in fifteenth-century Florence is due to two contemporary events. First there was the revived interest in Plato by humanist and pre-humanist circles, even before the Quattrocento. Platonism, or neo-Platonism, which was preached by the philosophers was to impregnate all thought in that epoch and in the whole of the Renaissance.

Ficino, the son of a doctor, who had been persuaded by Cosimo de' Medici to devote himself to the study of philosophy in Florence instead of pursuing his medical training in Bologna, pledged himself to the task of reconciling paganism, and Platonic thought in particular, with Christianity. A slight, hunchbacked man, lame and weak, he harboured a sublime and fiery soul, which he threw into his work. His Christian-pagan syncretism was followed by some of the best minds of the century in their efforts to rationalize their devotion to antiquity and reconcile it with their desire to remain orthodox Christians. This approach aimed to show that neo-Platonic and Christian ideas were complementary and that a sort of Platonic Christianity or Christian Platonism would be achieved by emphasizing this harmony. Marsilio Ficino's work was aimed at obtaining irrefutable proof of this—a determination he shared with another great Platonist thinker and universally-acclaimed intellect of his time, Pico della Mirandola, who also worked in Florence.

Every artist was to be affected by these metaphysics. The scheme of a religious masterpiece such as Michelangelo's frescoes in the Sistine Chapel was constructed according to philosophical concepts mixing Christian and Platonic ideas, and contained both Christian and Platonic symbols. The second event which favoured the diffusion of Greek in Italy was the fall of Constantinople (1453). Many scholars and intellectuals who had fled from the East were granted asylum by Italian courts to which they brought their books, their learning, and their teachings. Their entry was made all the easier by the famous council of 1439 which had tried to unite the two churches and which Cosimo Pater Patriae had had the foresight to bring to Florence.

Humanists distinguished themselves by their written or spoken Latin and by their veneration for Greek. The craze for Greek became so fashionable that the smallest children, even little girls, were given instruction in it. The ability to discourse in Greek was regarded as the height of elegance, to be attained even by non-professional scholars. The famous Venetian printer, Aldo Manuzio, adhered to this creed so fervently that he forbade anyone to use any other tongue at his table, under penalty of fine. The appeal of Aristotelian and Platonic thought also served to increase the Byzantine refugees' renown as the latter-day apostles of Greek philosophy. Gemistho Pleto (1355–1450), Giovanni Argyropoulos (1410–1490), were the most prominent of the Hellenists in the crowd of Greeks who came to Italy either for the 1439 Council in Emperor John Paleologue's retinue or after the Turks overran Byzantium or from the Muslim persecutions. Manual Chrysoloras, another Greek, had already been invited to Florence in 1396. According to Ugolino Verino, who witnessed this influx,

23. Detail of the magnificently carved vault of the sacristy vestibule, *Santo Spirito,* by Andrea Sansovino.

the full scholarly corps of shipwrecked Greece drifted into Florence and found there a veritable haven amid the tempestuous seas. Poliziano, a delightful poet much admired by Lorenzo de' Medici, exclaims, a trifle exaggeratedly perhaps, that one would never believe that Athens had been destroyed and occupied by the Barbarian but that she had rather emigrated and resettled in Florence with all her goods and chattels.

The Platonic Academy was an open assembly or group of men who shared the same enthusiasm for culture, the same insatiable hunger for knowledge. It came into being without flurry, formalities or institutions, receiving its name from Ficino. They welcomed among them anyone who endorsed their ideals and their tastes. The group was naturally associated with Cosimo and later with Lorenzo the Magnificent because both were enthusiastic promoters and protectors of all cultural movements. In their homes they never demanded a stultifying adherence to rules of etiquette; everyone was free to speak his mind. Furthermore they awarded a liberal and unceremonious hospitality to anyone who sought it. These early generations of the Medici, like the rest of Florence, were people of simple tastes who felt, nonetheless, that no price was too great to pay for a work of art, an ancient manuscript, or any precious artefact or for the entertainment of literary men assembled in a 'partnership of the liberal disciplines', as Marsilio Ficino put it.

The Medici, with their enormous fortune, their political power, and the prestige culled from their title of 'patrons of the arts and literature' conducted a lively rivalry with the other merchants and bankers in the arts and in learning as well. Their rich friends and enemies soon realized that they might risk being put to shame by the brilliant establishment in the Via Larga, if they too did not make a serious effort as patrons and scholars. They also entered the lists because the Florentines, as Oscar Wilde said of the Athenians, 'were a race of amateurs and art critics', who really did love beauty in all its forms, and whose natural instincts inclined them towards the creation and the acquisition of masterpieces.

Members of all the great families studied Greek furiously. The Signoria declared that its greatest treasures were the four Greek gospels, which they placed on permanent display in the Council Chamber, and the Amalfi *Pandects* stolen from Pisa after its defeat by Florence in 1405. Leading citizens strove to emulate the Medici patronage or vice versa. Niccolò da Uzzano set up a college called the 'Casa di Sapienza' (in 1430), the House of Learning. He was a highly cultivated man, thoroughly devoted to the public good and therefore reluctant to endorse the Medici's meteoric political ascent, which he did his best to arrest. His college gave free instruction and lodging to poor youths who would not otherwise have been able to finance their studies. Similarly, one of the great Strozzi bankers, the handsome Palla Strozzi, collected ancient and modern texts for the library of one of his palaces in the Santa Trinità quarter, which he generously threw open to the public, but which he left to San Agostino in Padua as a result of his exile.

The Florentines may always have had an innate appetite for culture, but the erudite blows dealt in this new battle that followed on the heels of the Guelf-Ghibelline and Black-White conflicts, were to some extent provoked by the example the Medici set for their fellow citizens. Some of these citizens were so absorbed in the craze for antiquity that they pretended to live like ancient Romans and Greeks. One such was Niccolò Niccoli, who was not a professional intellectual, but a merchant, a numismatist, and a collector of ancient manuscripts (he owned 800 at his death). He went about dressed up in togas and drank from Greek goblets, but also ran up enormous debts, which Cosimo paid after he died by buying his prodigious library and installing it in the Convent of San Marco for public use. Vespasiano, it is said, once called on Niccoli to find him amid a group of ten or twelve young noblemen all engrossed in books. Every now and then Niccoli inter-

24. *A Wedding of the Adimari*, showing the Baptistry in the background; painting on a *cassone*, or wedding-chest, by the Master of the Adimari Cassone (early fifteenth century). *Accadèmia*.

25. *A Horse-Race in the Streets of Florence*; painting on a *cassone* of about 1417-18. *Cleveland Museum of Art, The Holden Collection*.

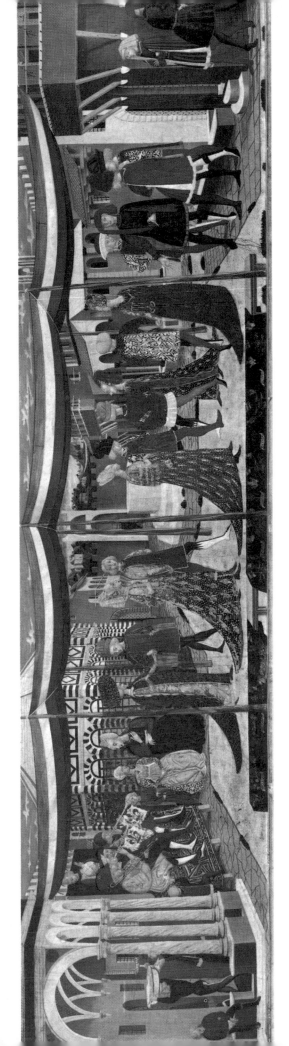

Fig. 14 *Allegory of Spring* or
The Triumph of Flora by
Botticelli. *Uffizi.*

26. Detail showing countryside
with a distant town, from *The
Nativity*, fresco by A.
Baldovinetti (1460), in the
vestibule of *Santissima
Annunziata.*

rupted to ask them what passage they were reading and what were their thoughts
on it. Vespasiano remarks that the self-discipline was so perfect that no one wasted
a minute, contrary to the usual gatherings of noblemen, which more often than not
ended in games.

Ficino's definition of beauty carried conviction with all the cultivated society of
that time, painters, sculptors and poets, although some of them may not actually
have studied the works of Plato first-hand or the works of his disciples in the
Alexandrian school. Ficino taught that beauty resided 'Not in the shadows of matter,
but in light and form; not in the darkling stuff of the body, but in its lucid proportion;
not in the sluggardly sullied weight of flesh, but in number and measure.' One can
almost hear a resurrected Plotinus repeating the old credo of the ancient Neo-
Platonists brought up to date to suit Christian sensibility and thought, when Ficino
says: 'As the ear full of air hears the air, as the eye full of light sees light, so it is
God in the soul that perceives God.' The precepts enunciated by Ficino and
repeated by his disciples in the circle of the Medici explain the aims, aspirations,
and the creations of Renaissance Florence. His immortality owes less to his intellectual daring and the originality of his metaphysics than to the direction he gave
Italian art in his century. This makes his works indispensable for an understanding
of the particular genius of that time, regardless of the form in which it manifested
itself, whether it be Botticelli's *Allegory of Spring* (painted in about 1475 for the
Medici Villa di Castello, see fig. 14), or Michelangelo's ceiling in the Sistine
Chapel or Leonardo da Vinci's *Virgin of the Rocks* (1483, see fig. 15). It was not his
formulae which made him influential but the inspiration he gave artists to discover
for themselves the eternal essential laws of spiritual as well as formal aesthetics.
We know from his own letters that this same Ficino used to accompany the elderly
Cosimo to the villa at Careggi and there play upon the lyre while Cosimo pruned
his vines. The cult of beauty bred another cult, that of friendship, which took root
in this society so firmly and with such intensity as to make it akin to love, founded as
it was, upon an admiration of the two aspects of beauty; the beauty of the body and
that of the soul.

If Ficino was physically handicapped, Pico della Mirandola, who shared Ficino's well-deserved renown as a humanist of great stature, was a splendidly handsome man. He died young, at the age of thirty-one, in 1494. He was a child prodigy, and a dazzlingly brilliant student at the Universities of Padua, Ferrara and Paris. When he was twenty he joined the circle at Careggi. He had studied all the sciences, all philosophical systems, and all religions. He propounded theses on every subject imaginable, but all this without giving himself airs. His intellectual virtuosity was such that he offered seven different interpretations of the Creation as told in the Book of Genesis in his *Heptaplus*. Besides knowing Latin and Greek, he also knew Hebrew, and he was familiar with oriental religions and philosophies, which were hardly known within Platonic circles of Florence. When Michelangelo worked out the iconographic programme for the Sistine Chapel ceiling, he remembered his *Heptaplus*, which he knew well. Pico, who left his universities a confirmed Aristotelian, was converted to Plato by Ficino. It became his ambition to reconcile these two great masters of antiquity, as well as to syncretize a Christian-pagan doctrine, that ambiguous synthesis that permitted the love of Greek gods without alienating the Church. The radiant Pico, the perfect example of the sublime marriage of physical beauty with the beauty of the intellect and the soul, died piously; he requested that his body be 'shrouded in a monk's habit'. He was known to have appreciated Savonarola's fiery arguments, even though he always opposed intransigence in spiritual matters; he respected the Dominican for his steadfast adherence to his ideal of purity, although he carried it to such an extreme and although it was to have such disastrous results on the art of his time.

In the same way that Ficino proposed that every priest should add a Platonic text to the traditional liturgical formulae in the celebration of the mass because Plato's dialogues were as worthy as the Gospels of leading the faithful to the good, the true, and the beautiful, Pico della Mirandola was the apostle of universal reconciliation.

Fig. 15   *The Virgin of the Rocks* by Leonardo da Vinci. (190 × 120 cms.) *London, National Gallery.*

27. *Death of Savonarola* in the Piazza della Signoria; painting dating from the sixteenth century. *Museo di San Marco.*

28. Detail from a later copy of a view of Florence in 1490, called the *Carta della Catena. Museo di Firenze Com'Era.*

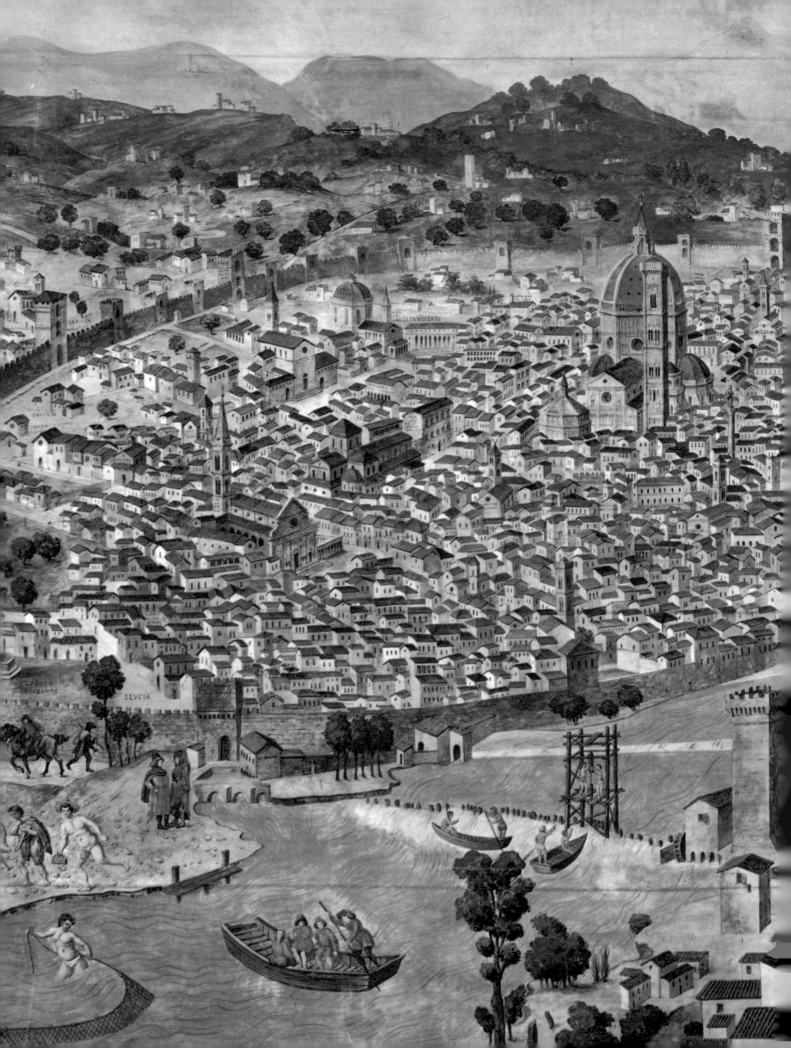

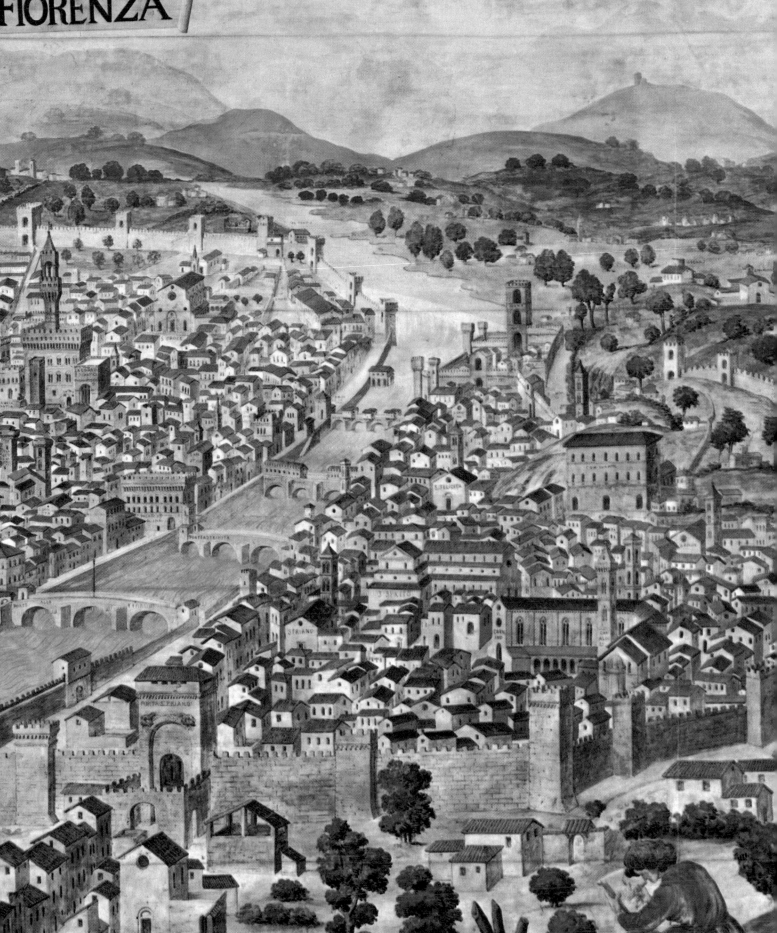

DOMITII CALDERI
NI VERONENSIS SE
CRETARII APOSTO
LICI COMMENTARII
IN SATYRAS IVVENA
LIS AD CLARISSIMVM
VIRVM IVLIANVM ME
DICEM PETRI COSMI
FILIVM FLORENTINVM,

SATY
RA
RVM
GE
NE
RA DVO AGNO
SCIMVS; ALTE
RVM ANTIQVI
VS TAM Á GRÆ

All religions sprang from an original divine revelation which they each interpreted in their own way, but they all possessed a common denominator. This view reappears throughout his nine hundred theses. He undertook to defend these theses when he was twenty-four; five hundred of them were his own personal opinions on theology and metaphysics. In his search for universal harmony, Pico found the conclusive proof of the mystery of the Holy Trinity in the Cabal. His perusal of oriental religious texts provided him with an inexhaustible treasury of symbols which seemed more mysterious and profound than Latin and Greek mythology, the more concrete vocabulary of which had become common usage. Yet this cornucopia of learning in no way dominated the men who possessed it; intellectuals wore their knowledge lightly and gracefully, however erudite they might be. They never renounced the pleasures of beauty and form, of physical enjoyment and entertainment, not even the simple pleasures of the carnival.

The Medici's humanist circle participated in popular pastimes and delighted in the broad humour which peppered popular Tuscan speech. The coarse jokes at the expense of priests, for example, who were often portrayed as simple-minded buffoons, made audiences at Careggi or Via Larga laugh loudly. The Florentine aspirants to humanism did not keep apart from everyday life; this contact gave their philosophy a new significance and broadened its scope. Thus one witnesses the proliferation of occasional verses celebrating particular events. They did not celebrate heroic events but were commemorative poems written on the occasion of a marriage, a festivity, an evening party in the country or a tournament. These poems were not necessarily banal, especially not the *Giostra* of Pulci (1432–1484) or Poliziano (1454–1494). Their exquisite proportions and forms were masterpieces of sheer inventiveness. One might well fear that great poetry had little to gain from humanism, which never failed to bring classical models into prominence, and indeed humanist poetry was both natural and artificial. There are passages and poems which contribute something very much of their own to the body of European lyricism, such as Poliziano's Latin poem on violets which recalls the lines dedicated by the Emperor Hadrian to his soul, *Animula vagula blandula . . .* It has the same rhythm, stresses, music, and the perfect precision of a sculpted cameo, while in the background there are echoes of romantic melancholia. It was the poetry of Lorenzo the Magnificent and Poliziano that persuaded Carducci, the great Italian Romantic to claim them as the precursors of 'modern poetry'.

Angelo degli Ambrogini, native of Montepulciano, hence his Latin name Politianus, or Poliziano in Italian, the poet of the violets, incarnates the most perfect example of lyrical humanism. He is the equal in poetry of Marsilio Ficino and Pico della Mirandola in philosophy. Had Planudus never published his collection of Greek epigrams, the 'Palatine Anthology', Poliziano might not have been as heavily influenced by the past, from which he never seems to have wanted to depart. Grammarian, Latinist, Hellenist, like all his contemporaries, he participated actively in the cult of antiquity. He composed short Latin essays for Lorenzo's children and celebrated nature in the manner of Virgil and Theocritus. Rescued from student poverty by Lorenzo, Poliziano revived the *dolce stil'novo* of Dante, Guinicelli and Cavalcanti, and his Italian compositions matched these models in their elegance and subtlety. It is a shame that his Latin descriptions of Tuscan peasant life are mere stylistic exercises, of little modern appeal, but the Italian *Orfeo*, on the other hand, is of lasting beauty and can move and delight any modern reader. The mythology he revives has the same immediacy, the same vividness and brilliance, and the same modern and eternal appeal, despite its classical source, as Botticelli's *Birth of Venus* or *Allegory of Spring*. He writes as Botticelli paints, but beyond that clarity of line and colour one can already detect the nostalgic tone which, though generally absent in Renaissance art, was to pervade the Baroque.

29. Page decorated with *saturnalia* from a commentary on Juvenal, presented to Giuliano de' Medici by Domitis Calderimus in 1474. *Biblioteca Medicea Laurenziana.* Ms. Laur. Plut. 53-2.

30. Page from *La Vita di
Lorenzo il Magnifico* by Niccolò
Valori (early 16th century),
showing the author presenting
his book to Pope Leo X,
with a view of Florence
through a window, a portrait
of Lorenzo de' Medici, and the
Medici arms below. *Biblioteca
Medicea Laurenziana.* Ms. Laur.
Plut. 61-3 fo 2r. (14.5 × 22 cms.)

Although Poliziano was never a disciple of the astrologers, who practised their trade
even in rational Florence, he did inherit a few Medieval superstitions. He was
seriously convinced that one of the Pazzi involved in the Pazzi conspiracy had sold
his soul to the devil before he was executed so as to avenge himself on his enemies
after his death. When torrential rains threatened to destroy the harvest fields, the
peasants sensed the malevolent hand of the devil and his accomplice. The Pazzi's
corpse was exhumed, whereupon the heavens withheld their downpour. Poliziano
concludes 'that this is proof that the heavens are in accord with the people'. The
body was thrown into the Arno to prevent a recurrence of the deluge.

The Renaissance, this enlightened, learned era which was so modern in its thought
and creative process, was only just emerging from the dark ages that immediately
preceded it. Humanists still believed in celestial omens, and in statues that shed tears.
The humanism of the Quattrocento does not constitute an absolute break with the
past; it links Medieval theology and theocentricity with the High Renaissance of
the sixteenth century which fostered scientific inventions, explorations and discoveries. The scholars and grammarians of the fifteenth century were too fascinated
by antiquity to embark upon a resolutely modern culture. The highest attainment,
so far as they were concerned, was to imitate and equal their Latin and Greek
masters. This explains why Italian literature lagged so far behind the visual arts of
the time, painting, architecture, and sculpture, in developing a truly new, bold and
daring spirit; this spirit was not a genuine Renaissance in the literal sense of a
'rebirth' of classical antiquity, but it was the *birth* of something entirely new.

IN NOBI-
LISSIMA
MEDICVM
FAMILIA
MVLTI PRE
CLARI MA-
GNIQ3. VI-
RI FVERE
IN QVIBVS

IOANNES MEDICES: QVI
MAGNO ET INVICTO ⊘
ANIMO VICECOMITIBVS

Sese opponens sæpius patriæ Nostræ
libertatem & communem omnium sa-
lutem tutatus est. Verius quoq, in
Equestri dignitatę: quæ prima apud
florentinos habetur: sine controuersia
princeps: Nostræ quoad uixit. Rei. pu
extitit rector et gubernator. Quid Cos
mus Ille Magnus: qui in magnis ol

The Florentine Renaissance

IV

While the humanists were busily immersing themselves in the cult and the cultivation of Greek and Latin antiquity, devoting their energies to textual scholarship and philosophical refinements, the artists of the Italian Renaissance were blazing out a new vision of the emotional and intellectual world. They were engaged in the quest for an ideal beauty, for beauty freed from the variance of fickle taste, whose perfection resided in the essence of the ideally beautiful object in which the perfect harmony of matter and spirit would be achieved. This ideal and formal perfection was to rise from a congruence between its earthly representation and the ideal prototype that existed in the Platonic realm of Ideas. Ancient aestheticians had laid down the fundamental laws of structure which were eternally, immutably valid for all future ages, for theoretician and creative spirit alike. It was the task of the moderns to seek out these basic aesthetic principles and inject them with new life for the modern man. The word 'Renaissance', which we use today to describe the principal components and the universally recognized features of this time, was not really used until the sixteenth century, when the era could be observed retrospectively as past history. The word was first used to define the recent past which still inspired the present; for Vasari, who coined the word 'Renaissance', did not belong to the Renaissance, but was a 'mannerist' artist and architect (1511–1574). Perhaps no great artistic eras can be isolated, nor their major features be defined, until their productivity has waned and they have become part and parcel of the past.

Artists and humanists alike believed that before the 'Dark Ages' had shrouded Europe, a Golden Age had lit up the world, and that its art and culture had contained the monopoly of all possible truths. It was the moderns' sacred duty to banish this darkness and bring these truths to light again; whether they be dragged up from the past or taken from later ages was immaterial. The conviction that the ancients had said everything significant and known everything worth knowing inspired architects to study and measure every inch of every Roman building or ruin in the hope that this would give them the key to ideal proportions—or to 'divine proportions': *De Divina Proportione* was the title of a book by Fra Luca Pacioli. They shared the scholars' enthusiasm for assembling libraries of all ancient philosophical and historical texts that they could find, as they were convinced that these pages would reveal solutions to all problems of knowledge and meditation.

The artists believed with the philosophers that the universe was established and could be comprehended through transcendental revelation of divine laws that repeated themselves in all material objects, in the very processes of human thought, and, above all, were most clearly and unshakeably established in mathematical numbers and geometrical figures, which were a hermetic distillation of man's most profound knowledge. Architecture, of all the arts, was the most directly and most clearly marked by these laws. Architectural styles were at a turning point. Gothic architecture, which had exhausted every possible metamorphosis, had reached that exasperated stage of the late flamboyant style, which, less popular in Italy than in the north, had caught on in the Low Countries, Germany and France. Italian sensibilities, when they are not being contrived, tend to lean naturally and spontaneously towards classicism, the model for which had been left by the Romans.

31. A jasper vessel mounted in silver, one of a series inscribed LAUR. MED. that belonged to Lorenzo the Magnificent (the vessel itself is probably from the tenth to twelfth centuries; the silverwork dates from the 1460's). (*Height* 27 cms.) *Palazzo Pitti, Galleria degli Argenti.*

Italian Gothic was by and large fairly sober with strong classical elements, a style adopted by the great religious orders, the Dominicans and the Franciscans. The change from this Gothic style to an architecture of classical shape and proportion—classical here meaning 'ancient'—involved, however, a complete break with the immediate past. The study of classical authors had continued throughout the Middle Ages in monastic libraries and scriptoria, although many manuscripts were lost, which the Medici and other princely patrons and patrician humanists then tried to recover by sending their agents to browse the Orient. During this period, however, the visual arts were inspired by an aesthetic attitude which owed very little to classical antiquity.

Classical art and Medieval thought were incompatible and even antipathetic in many ways: for instance, in the Middle Ages, physical beauty was subordinate to religious devotion, spiritual fulfilment was prized over physical pleasure; the Renaissance, on the other hand, learned from Plato that external beauty could coexist harmoniously with internal beauty, that it need never be an obstacle or a source of conflict. When Medieval thinkers wondered what beauty was, philosophers answered. The Renaissance let the philosophers decide upon aesthetic concepts while the artists themselves created their own images of beauty, free of all the countless erudite theories which sought to formulate in impeccable numbers the indisputable reasons why beauty was or was not as the artist had conceived it. Perhaps no epoch in history persevered so obstinately and so ingeniously to define what was beautiful and why it was so; and no other time responded so immediately to intellectual and sensuous beauty; nor was any other era so totally convinced that it really existed and that they could discover it and did possess it. Never was there an age whose creative impulses were so urgent and so spontaneous and so exuberant or whose instinct for new forms that could satisfy the mind, heart and senses was so felicitously sure and confident.

Renaissance art, despite the apparent clutter of dogmatic treatises on the idea, the nature, and the conceivable realizations of beauty, in practice continually pursued the real experience of the sensual world. This was the artists' infallible guide. They adapted the visual and tangible qualities of this universe, whose essential reality was only accessible through the medium of the intellect, to their own requirements. This system brought it in line with those two Florentine traits: the tendency to think systematically and to regard reality empirically. Although the people of all Italian states accepted the governing principles that made up the Renaissance, each state received and dealt with the Renaissance in a different way. The differences and variations between Lombardy and Venice, or Sicily, do not, however, alter the evidence of their basic unity. The influences which emanated from Italy were then subjected in turn to other national temperaments. Flanders and Germany, for example, used the artistic ideas of the Renaissance as a transitional stage between their High Flamboyant Gothic and their pre-Baroque mannerism. One reason for this shift of emphasis was that the art in these countries was not as deeply rooted in the classical tradition as it was in Italy. There, and above all, in central Italy, it was an integral part of the Latin heritage which hampered and stifled the Italians but also enriched their art.

The word 'Renaissance', however, can be deceptive if the implication of a 'resurrection' or a 'rebirth' of antiquity is exaggerated. In many ways, few eras have been as *modern* as the Quattrocento. It paid lip-service to antiquity to justify and make legitimate its break with tradition. But it saw the development of a real *avant-garde* led by artists like Donatello (1386–1466), Masaccio (1401–1428), Paolo Uccello (1397–1475) or Piero della Francesca (c. 1420–1492).

A significant rôle in the development of this spectacular movement in Florence was, of course, played by the Medici. They were 'modern men' in their own particular

32. One of the bronze doors by Donatello (1430's) in the Old Sacristy (*Sagrestia Vecchia*) of *San Lorenzo*. In the background a fine marble lavabo of the same period.

Caffamn two no ghe purfi agiacere non nene una ni ne inliero
p ch so morti e coloro opani e fermo

and brilliant way. When, therefore, Cosimo Pater Patriae and Lorenzo the Magnificent devoted their intellectual energy and their generosity to their own ardent and learned pursuit of anything that could be exhumed from the past, they also took under their wing those artists in particular who displayed inventive imagination and novel styles. While the Platonists were mustering the raw materials of a coherent philosophical doctrine from a body of contrasting ideas, the Medici were subsidizing and approving aesthetic innovations of a totally unacademic and resolutely individualistic nature.

The Medici had only just acquired their power and money, whereas the old principalities and great royal dynasties of Europe were rooted in a long aristocratic and feudal tradition. It would be correct, and not derogatory, to call the Medici *parvenus*, people who had recently 'arrived'. They really were scions of what was originally a plebeian line, peasants from Mugello, humble artisans and shopkeepers. An important change in the fourteenth and fifteenth centuries was the rise to power and position of a class of rich townspeople who had hitherto been ignored and relegated to the wings of public life. It might be reasonably argued that Renaissance art could have taken the same course without the patronage of the moneyed patricians of the cities, but it would have happened more slowly and would have had to contend with its social environment. Without this change the environment would have been similar to the French and German societies which clung so rigidly for so long to their immediate past and to the conservation of their old ideas and forms. The coincidence of a great aesthetic explosion which reversed the Gothic tradition and the rise of a new social class which positively wanted to relinquish nearly all vestiges of things traditional, is the key to the development of Renaissance art. It really made no difference that the young Medici acted the part of *grands seigneurs* by jousting in tournaments modelled on the festivities and pageantry depicted in Medieval romances of chivalry. Florence knew that the Medici participated in these to offer the proletariat a brilliant, well-loved spectacle. Neither spectators nor participants took the shows seriously; the players regarded them largely as 'theatricals' or 'literature'. The dramatic significance of single combat was banished together with the fading of its mythical and symbolical background. The old 'vows' sworn by the Peacock or the Heron simply lost their liturgical and sacred character and were here enacted with no regard whatever to the religious and ritualistic meanings inherent in the original chivalric codes.

The tournament was therefore not an anomaly in the Medici's otherwise modern outlook, nor a contradiction of their faith in the future. The authentic Florentine sport was, however, *calcio*, a form of football, which also had its share of rules and regulations and rituals associated with the religious and national festivals on which the game was played. It was team sport similar to present-day European football, and had a distinctively democratic flavour such as its modern counterpart has today. One community challenged another, instead of one man another in the lists. This predominance of the community spirit over the individual, of the individual's submission to the group, was a reflection of the principle of majority rule as upheld in the community's assemblies which contained all the legislative, executive, and judicial powers of Florence.

The Medici were always clever enough not to go against the grain of popular and social opinion: they always swam with the current. The Renaissance embodied a way of feeling, thinking, and creating which was shared both by the people and the privileged class, or élite. No one was surprised by the openly revolutionary features of an architecture which returned to Roman models, which built the façades of its churches from tiers of ancient triumphal arches, which preferred the cupola to the pointed arch, and adapted pagan religious symbols to the requirements of quite genuine Christian sentiments: the angel became an 'amorino', a

33. Pen and ink study of a double tomb, linked to the Medici tombs in the New Sacristy, *San Lorenzo*, by Michelangelo (1520's). (21 × 16.2 cms.) *London, British Museum.*

34. Pen and ink study for a door or window, linked to the design of the New Sacristy or the library of *San Lorenzo*, by Michelangelo (1526). (28.4 × 20.9 cms.) *London, British Museum.*

35. Red chalk study of a boy by Andrea del Sarto; the Florentine masters continued their tradition of brilliant draughtsmanship well into the sixteenth century. (37.8 × 26 cms.) *London, British Museum.*

cupid; the fires of Etruscan psychopompic genii flickered at the feet of funeral statues; ornamental themes were borrowed from the ruins of the temples in the Forum; and the rules of 'Vitruvius', in so far as they were known, prevailed unquestioned and unchallenged in all problems of structure and proportion.

Florence turned artistic pleasures into intellectual gratifications. Although Alberti's and Brunelleschi's new buildings delighted the mind, they left the heart cold; but they did convey a curiously sensual feeling of well being, a sort of kinaesthesis which accompanied those intellectual pleasures. This art that was geared to an intellectual rather than an emotional audience—for such were Florentine preferences—was immediately accepted and acclaimed without dispute. Popular support for the artistic revolution stimulated by the Medici was genuinely spontaneous, sincere and unanimous; this is borne out by the fact that the Medici's sculptors and painters and architects were also favoured by the Strozzi, the Albizzi, the Pitti, the Tornabuoni, the Sassetti, and others whose tastes seemed to coincide with those of the dominant family. These families were all patrons of the arts and with the Medici their patronage left a strikingly uniform stamp on Quattrocento art. Even if one does not ascribe to the Medici the original features of this patronage or the current artistic atmosphere, one can safely state that the Medici were involved in every activity that stirred Florence throughout this period although they obviously did not commission and finance every single creative product. Their influence on the Italian Renaissance, and thus on that section of the European Renaissance which was at least partially inspired by Italy, is incontestable. Their influence far exceeds any list that might be drawn up of the churches, palaces, frescoes, statues, gold and silver work, let alone the countless decorative works they commissioned and encouraged. The Medici had a sure instinct for beauty and excellence and their daily exposure to artistic masterpieces made their aesthetic judgements ever more refined and sophisticated. This cultivated instinct of theirs led them to discover the little Buonarroti, whom they first allowed to chip away in the cloisters of San Marco; this boy was to become the genius who sculpted the San Lorenzo tombs and statues; he was to design the new Campidoglio and the Biblioteca Laurenziana and to paint the Sistine Chapel. This art of discovery, this sure instinct for aesthetic evaluation was matched by their equally rewarding gift for perceiving which business and which representative should or should not be sustained or sponsored by their banking concerns.

The differences which are often observed between Cosimo's patronage and Lorenzo's merely reveal that the first was an *ancestor*, a founder and originator, and Lorenzo was the *heir*, whose main rôle was the reception of his grandfather's power and fortune. Their artistic tastes were equally exacting and refined but the emphasis of their selection was different. Cosimo was fascinated by great architectural enterprises, while his grandson was more of a collector whose interests ranged from precious glassware and cut stone—his vases of jasper, agate, chalcedony and quartz decorated with gold are widely celebrated—to gems and antique intaglios. His passion for manuscripts was more inspired by their decorative miniatures than by the rarity of their texts. He also seems to have had a greater predilection for poetry than for philosophy and pure scholarship.

These distinctions arise from the differences in character between grandfather and grandson. Cosimo made an enormous political and financial effort to initiate the embellishment of Florence and extend her public works while Lorenzo only had to continue, or receive the finished products of his grandfather's work. The available inventories of the Medici collections, the silver collection at the Pitti, and the remains of Lorenzo's collections scattered about the various Florentine museums and elsewhere yield a fairly precise and realistic impression of their aesthetic preferences which also correspond to the change of taste between the first

Fig. 18   Page from *La Giostra di Giuliano de' Medici* by Poliziano, 1500. *Biblioteca Medici-Riccardiana.*

36. Study of a boat, wolf and eagle, possibly an allegory of papal ambition; drawn between 1510 and 1516, when Giovanni de' Medici was reigning as Pope Leo X. Pen and ink drawing by Leonardo da Vinci (17 × 28 cms.) *Windsor Castle, Royal Collection.*

37. Pope Clement VII and Emperor Charles V, pencil drawing by Sebastiano del Piombo (soon after their meeting, 1529-30). (31 × 46.2 cms.) *London, British Museum.*

and the second half of the fifteenth century. Giovanni di Bicci's rôle at the beginning of the century should also not be overlooked. He organized the competition for the construction of the dome of Santa Maria del Fiore and had the ingenious idea of asking all the foreign representatives of the Medici bank to advertise the competition abroad and contact architects in Germany, France, the Low Countries. Donatello, who owed so much to the encouragement and the generosity of Cosimo, expressed his gratitude by asking to be buried at his benefactor's feet. And Michelozzo, who refused to be separated from Cosimo when he was exiled to Venice, benefited from this loyalty by building the San Giorgio library with his patron's money and advice.

The name 'magnificent', accorded Lorenzo by his contemporaries and ratified by posterity, might lead one wrongly to suppose that he was more responsible for stimulating and fostering the rise of the Renaissance than his grandfather. The title itself, Lorenzo 'the Magnificent', has such a seductive ring that it alone might persuade the uninitiated to believe that it was the Age of Lorenzo the Magnificent and certainly not that of the Pater Patriae. If, however, their individual energy output were measured in terms of the art and culture they fostered, Cosimo would probably emerge as the mastermind. The Father of the State did more for architecture in the thirty years after his return to Florence from 1434 to 1464, than all his Medici successors put together. Michelozzo's Palazzo Medici begun in 1444, Alberti's façade for Santa Maria Novella begun in 1456 and finished six years after Cosimo's death, Brunelleschi's Santo Spirito begun in 1436, are some of the great works undertaken while he was in power. One can safely say that everything he inspired, encouraged or admired shared a certain simplicity and grandeur, a certain majesty and gravity which were characterized in his aesthetics and his ethics. These were the *commoditas* and the *voluptas,* as Leon Battista Alberti called them, which can be detected in all Cosimo's public and private activities. He sought to realize the simple and dignified life which is supposed to characterize the Florentine and pursued a serious pleasure in architecture, which provided him with a complementary aesthetic satisfaction. As Alberti said in his *De re aedificatoria:* 'Just as deep notes on the zither or the lyre accompany the high and middle notes to produce a harmony which is joyful to the ears; so, too, there is a rhythm in other things, especially in buildings; for when they are ordered and placed in a proper way and in just proportions, they capture and ravish the eyes of those who study them.'

The primary principles of spatial analysis were first propounded in the Quattrocento by Masaccio, Paolo Uccello and Piero della Francesca, among several others, as were the problems of the representation of light and atmosphere that surround material objects. Among the many Florentine sculptors of this earlier period of the Renaissance, whose technical and artistic innovations were also widely admired, were Ghiberti (1381–1455), Donatello (1386–1466), Desiderio da Settignano (1428–1464), Verrocchio (1436–1488) and Benedetto da Maiano (1442–1497). In the field of terracotta bas-relief, a new technique was discovered by Luca della Robbia (1400–1482) which would allow him to cover baked clay (terracotta) with a protective layer of enamel paint containing *terragheta,* a compound of enamel and tin to 'protect it against the calumnies of time', as Vasari put it. These brilliant and colourful decorations (made by Luca, his nephew Andrea and other members of his family) are still to be found in many of the churches of Florence and most picturesquely perhaps on the walls of the Foundling hospital (Spedale degli Innocenti) where small terracotta roundels of babies were placed between the arches (see fig. 19). The hospital itself was designed by Brunelleschi and built with the support of Cosimo de' Medici.

The dominant theories of 'divine proportion' and the 'golden section' or the metaphysics of numbers, which were so important in Renaissance aesthetics were

38. Detail of bronze relief of Christ's Passion, one of the pulpits by Donatello in *San Lorenzo.* The two pulpits, which were carried out towards the end of his life by Donatello and two of his pupils, were assembled in their present position in the sixteenth century; the detail given here shows the *Harrowing of Hell.*

Above:
Fig. 19 **Terracotta roundels** showing babies, in the façade of the Spedale degli Innocenti, by Andrea della Robbia (mid-15th century).

Right:
Fig. 20 *The Trinity* by Masaccio, fresco in *Santa Maria Novella.*

all familiar to the Medieval man, who also used them in his Gothic style; but the Renaissance man decided to codify them, to found an exacting science upon them by which he could define and describe the universe. Abstract geometrical constructions which sought to impose an ideal and universally-valid scheme on all visible forms were developed alongside the growing investigation and appreciation of tangible reality; in other words there were two complementary processes—one of examination of the physical and visible and technical procedures, and the other one of establishing a systematic view of these discoveries—which together contributed to

Above:
Fig. 21   *The Virgin of the Pomegranate* by Botticelli. *Uffizi.*

Above right:
Fig. 22   *The Virgin of the Magnificat* by Botticelli. *Uffizi.*

Right:
Fig. 23   *Calumny* by Botticelli. *Uffizi.*

the entirely new picture of man and his environment that the Renaissance artists and thinkers produced.

The artists inherited from antiquity a very acute and characteristic feeling for physical beauty, which the theocentric Middle Ages distrusted and deliberately played down, for physical pleasure might be a delusion of the devil and so was disguised or at least made subordinate to spiritual beauty. The worship of the nude, which was objectively represented but which was at the same time an ideal, a symbol of inspiration, is celebrated throughout the Italian Renaissance in sculpture and in

Fig. 24 *The Birth of Venus* by Botticelli. *Uffizi.*

painting. This Renaissance ideal is a result of a union of sense and intellect. On the other hand, Cosimo de' Medici's fondness of the work of Fra Angelico (1387–1455) is of course evidence of the survival of certain Medieval traits in the Florentine Renaissance. The symbolical colours and the gentle, tender piety which pervades the work of this remarkable religious painter, belong in many ways to the Gothic tradition. Nevertheless new techniques which had nothing to do with Gothic religious art had influenced him, and in his work he shows the influence of Masaccio whose disciple he became. The extent of this influence is borne out by the spatial arrangement of his figures, by the organization of the fields that surround them, and by his application of Pythagorean principles to proportion, all of which owe nothing to Medieval art, but follow in a modified form the frescoes in Santa Maria del Carmine (see plate 43). Fra Angelico's sweet piety in the middle of this century which was consumed with the passionate pursuit of realism and the depiction of realistic bodies, realistic landscapes, realistic atmospheres and light, transported his fellow monks, whose cells he decorated, out of the real world and into paradise (see plate 44).

The transition from Gothic painting to Fra Angelico followed the same pattern that Cosimo de' Medici's humanist friends pursued in their philosophical development. Forms evolved more quickly than did intellectual awareness so that despite the modernity of his construction, Fra Angelico's spirituality belongs to the fourteenth century. By the time of Lorenzo the Magnificent, the pagan dream lived firmly side by side with the Christian belief, although the former tended to cast back the latter into the shadows of a past that seemed increasingly remote. Thus the authenticity, at one stage at least, of Botticelli's pagan sentiments is unimpeachable. Botticelli (1444–1510) did, however, undergo a crisis of conscience after hearing Savonarola's sermons, became a supporter of the *piagnoni*, and ultimately returned to absolute Christian faith. One can detect a certain pagan-Christian ambiguity in his *Virgin of the Pomegranate* or in his *Virgin of the Magnificat* (see figs. 21, 22). His *Deposition* shows Christ as a smooth-cheeked Adonis, a depiction that completely reverses the traditional evangelical representation. Such ambiguity might imply

39. Nave of *San Lorenzo*, looking towards the west door. The church was rebuilt from 1421 onwards, at the expense of the Medici and seven other families, to the design of Brunelleschi.

Fig. 25 *Pallas and the Centaur* by Botticelli. *Uffizi*.

40. Staircase of the Laurenziana Library by Michelangelo, in the cloister of *San Lorenzo*. The hall, which was designed by Michelangelo in 1524-26, originally housed a wooden staircase; the present marble steps were built by Vasari in 1571 on the basis of a Michelangelo drawing of 1559.

an alternation of, or confusion between, contrary inclinations. *Calumny* (see fig. 23), the *Triumph of Flora* (see fig. 14), the *Birth of Venus* (see fig. 24), *Venus and Mars* (see plate 75) and *Pallas and the Centaur* (an allegory of the Medici's victories over their enemies, see fig. 25) belong to Botticelli's 'pagan period', if one can call it that in the face of his contemporaneous expression of religious faith. He did undoubtedly experience and express an enthusiasm for pagan deities which he communicates through that unique admixture of joyful elation and melancholia

93

which permeates these paintings and the Villa Lemmi frescoes (see fig. 4). It was quite in character that Botticelli went to Lorenzo's and Poliziano's poetry for inspiration for his allegories.

Whereas the pagan and Christian themes and ideals remained antipathetical and mutually exclusive in Botticelli's work, Michelangelo laboured painfully to harmonize them in a unison which was inevitably somewhat contrived. The art and thought of the sculptor of the Medici tombs at San Lorenzo (see plates 41, 42) drew equally upon the Old Testament, on the Gospels and on the syncretists of Cosimo's circle, on the works of Ficino and Pico della Mirandola who aspired to a *reconciliation* between antagonistic worlds. We have already seen how they yearned for such a union, how they arduously tried to pave the way for this reconciliation, and how they never realized the inevitable failure of their great dreams.

The Medici's humanist circle gave Michelangelo (1474–1564) a philosophy of life and a metaphysical faith which permeated his work, and his outlook was as much influenced by the lives of the saints as by Plato. Michelangelo translated Ficino's yearnings and the circle's scholarly ideals and concepts into lasting visual terms. The ideas discussed at Poggio a Caiano and at Careggi and formulated before Michelangelo was even born, took shape years later in the theological composition of the ceiling of the Sistine Chapel and of the *Last Judgement*. Where Botticelli seemed to split his life into shuttling between his two philosophical inclinations, Michelangelo devoted himself to the pursuit of both extremes, grafting voluptuous paganism to Christian asceticism. Living right on into the second half of the sixteenth century, he was never rid of one nor the other and this makes him in a sense the best example to illustrate the kind of Platonism that flowered in the Florence of Cosimo a hundred years earlier.

Patronage as practised in Florence by the Medici and by rival families in the city had a unifying effect on Florentine art. This artistic homogeneity was due to the fact that no Florentine patron demanded exclusive rights to any one artist's work. Ghirlandaio or Lippi saw nothing odd in being employed first by the Tornabuoni and then by the Strozzi or the Sassetti or the Pazzi. That a competing patron should commission an architect or painter, whom another had discovered and 'launched', merely flattered the original patron's self-esteem and furthered his popularity. Every sector of the Florentine community had always taken a lively interest in the arts. The Florentine Chronicles record the waves of public fervour, of collective enthusiasm, which certain works of art excited. Tradition has it that the *Borgo Allegro*, the 'happy quarter', acquired its name when local parishioners bore a magnificent painting of the Virgin to their parochial church at the head of an unusually cheerful procession. This social tradition of acclaiming and encouraging local artists had been sown in the Middle Ages. It prepared the ground for the growth and flowering of its great artistic period. The painters of the thirteenth and fourteenth centuries who worked for the bishops and abbots of Florence also did work for wealthy families there and elsewhere. The Bardi, Baroncelli, and Peruzzi felt very honoured to have their family chapels in the churches painted by Giotto and then by the Gaddi who at the time were more famous than Giotto. There was no break in the Renaissance in the continuity of this wide-ranging and generous collaboration between artist and society; the artist's audience unfailingly supported him regardless of how 'modern' his work might be, regardless of its surprising content or of the shocking effect it might have had on ordinary tastes. Novelty of style was generally acclaimed for it seems that there was no distinction between the artist's aesthetics and those of his general public—unlike the differences that have separated the artist from his public from the end of the nineteenth century to the present day.

The architects who abandoned the Gothic style borrowed structural combinations, principles of proportion, techniques and ornamental devices from ancient

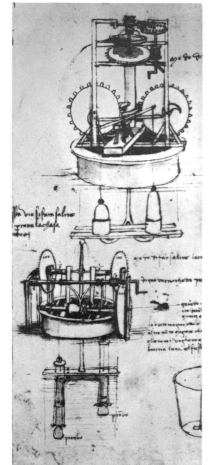

Fig. 26   Detail of a double page of drawings of various machines by Leonardo da Vinci. *Milan, Biblioteca Ambrosiana.*

41. Detail of *Night*, from the tomb of Giuliano de' Medici, Duke of Nemours, by Michelangelo, in the New Sacristy of *San Lorenzo.*

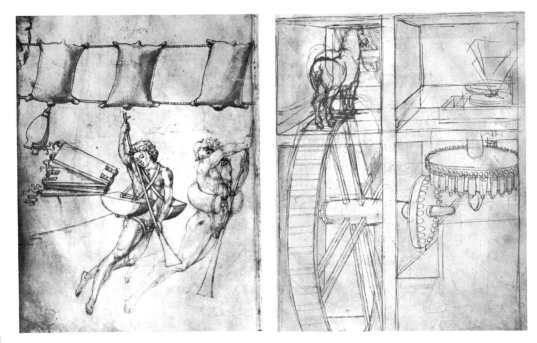

monuments. They did not, however, just copy Roman temples; they invented entirely new structural orders and hit upon new and revolutionary solutions. Artists like Brunelleschi and Alberti were immensely cultivated men, who clearly illustrated the truth of the dictum that the greater an artist's cultivation the greater artist he will be—that is, all artists should have a thorough knowledge of the art that has gone before. Petrarch before them had said 'once the darkness has been banished, our grandchildren may well be able to veer round and return to the pristine brilliance of our past'. The most daring innovators knew that no one was creating anything *ex nihilo*. They listened eagerly to the lessons of their elders and predecessors, particularly of their classical predecessors. Guicciardini's portrait of Lorenzo the Magnificent in the *Storia Fiorentina* tells us how and why he became so important an influence on his time and how his collection of the 'most beautiful objects from every corner of the world' was the envy of every prince in Christendom. His wide interests and his knowledge of music, architecture, painting, sculpture, all arts and skills, was a boon to his city and to artists who wished to learn from the work of others.

These intellectual and aesthetic tendencies of the Florentine Renaissance seem to contradict each other if one does not bear in mind that they all aimed at reconciliation, that perfect *wholeness*, which was the aspiration of all the artists involved. These contrasting tendencies can perhaps be defined as faithful adherence to the doctrines of the ancient world coupled with a forthright and modern inventiveness, the cult of ideal beauty coupled to objective realism, an acute and lively sensibility wed to an extreme clarity of visual perception. Donatello who venerated what he knew of classical art, was also a passionate naturalist, which in a way makes him all the more 'Hellenistic'. When Donatello had completed his statue of the bald-headed Zuccone on the Campanile of the Duomo in Florence, after he had given it every possible corporeal likeness and endowed it with all possible life, he stood back and demanded still more in his famous cry, 'Favella! Favella!—Speak! Speak!'

The absolute liberty accorded every artist to express his personality in all its uniqueness removed the possibility of a dull, academic style. There were studios in which pupils developed their talents and their skills from their tenderest years, under masters who taught them the basic techniques of sculpture or painting (usually both simultaneously because the Renaissance man was by definition a totally accomplished man who would and could easily leave his painting or sculpture aside and paint a shield or facet a jewel, or sketch a triumphal arch or design costumes for a ballet or a masquerade). Leonardo da Vinci (1452–1519) was undoubtedly the most learned and the most erudite man of his century, and yet, whatever leisure time he had from planning his ballistic missiles, his tanks equipped with firing cannons, his submarine vessels, locks for canals, flying machines, diving apparatus, and from his meditations on the secret laws of nature, the mysteries of human physiology and of human, plant, and stellar life, he spent embroidering costumes for theatrical shows and constructing ingenious automatons (see figs. 15, 26, 52 and 53).

Tuscany and ancient Greece both built up a systematic idea of beauty and of its pursuit in accordance with the Ideal, and in accordance with the character and talent of the individual; the Tuscan artists, however, observed nature with new eyes. This fresh appraisal and perception of nature led to a new concept of landscape. In the works of the Pollaiuolo brothers (Antonio 1429–1498, Piero 1443–c. 1495, see fig. 30), or those of Piero della Francesca, for instance, the beginnings of this idea can be found. Their fresh approach to nature anticipated the advent of Leonardo who banished the rather stylized, synthetic and rarely recognizable bits of countryside which had filled in the backgrounds of pictures before he began to work. His landscapes instead were composed of mixtures of fantasy and visionary brilliance, on the one hand, combined with a meticulous attention to the details of plants, pebbles, grass and the minutiae of nature on the other, a combination that was to have a profound influence on the landscape painting of both Florence and Venice in his lifetime and later (see fig. 15). Altogether the Renaissance artists' intuitive and spontaneous translation of the physical world, landscape or human shape, into live, visual forms put them, as we have already said, years ahead of their contemporary humanist philosophers, who were to some extent still groping in the penumbra of Medieval scholastic schemata, and who were later to graduate from these schemata by means of enormous effort, anxiety, initiative and by a quite different process.

This was the artistic and intellectual atmosphere surrounding the artists of the Medici, of Cosimo Pater Patriae and of Lorenzo, *Figlio del Sole,* who imposed their powerful personalities upon their time. When they had gone and when Savonarola's iconoclastic reign was over, artistic patronage was again taken up by the Medici but in a different way, coloured by new interests and ambitions. This second period of the 'Triumph of the Medici' takes in the rule of the Grand Duke Cosimo I and of his successors; and it includes the papacies of Leo X and Clement VII, in whose times the axis of action shifted from Tuscany to Rome.

Above:
Fig. 29   *Hercules and the Antaeus* by Antonio Pollaiuolo. *Bargello, Museo Nazionale.*

Below right:
Fig. 30   Detail from *The Martyrdom of Saint Sebastian* by Antonio and Piero Pollaiuolo. (290 × 210 cms.) *London, National Gallery.*

43. Detail of fresco by Masaccio in the Brancacci Chapel, *Santa Maria del Carmine* (about 1425), showing St Peter enthroned.

TEMPLA DOMVM EXPOSITIS·VICOS·FORA·MOENIA·PONTES·
VIRGINEAM·TRIVII·QVOD·REPARARIS·AQVAM·
PRISCA·LICET·NAVTIS·STATVAS·DARE·COMMODA·PORTVS·
ET·VATICANVM·CINGERE·SIXTE·IVGVM·
PLVS·TAMEN·VRBS·DEBET·NAM·QVAE·SQVALORE·LATEBAT·
CERNITVR·IN·CELEBRI·BIBLIOTHECA·LOCO·

V Lorenzo, *Figlio del Sole*

Lorenzo's contemporaries called him *Il Magnifico* (the Magnificent, 1449–1492) and he is traditionally known as such. This name was used fairly frequently to honour celebrated personalities, and the usage is still current in Italy where university rectors are called 'Rectors Magnificent'. The title posterity should more appropriately have bestowed on Lorenzo is, however, Marsilio Ficino's inspired 'Figlio del Sole' (Son of the Sun). His brilliance, his lucid intelligence, his dazzling energy and youthful vigour shone through his rather ugly features and gave an impression of splendour which few painters have been able to reproduce. Benozzo Gozzoli gives a totally idealized portrait of Lorenzo in his fresco of the *Adoration of the Magi* in the chapel of the Medici Palace (see fig. 31). Verrocchio's bust and Vasari's posthumous painting seem closer to the reality recorded by his death mask which was moulded on his corpse (see plate 13). Its grave and almost terrible grandeur seems to proclaim that the Son of Suns had fallen back into the Earth whence he had risen.

His poetic talents and his exquisite understanding of the art of living which he, the most famous of the Medici, brought to perfection, gave him (and still give him) a sort of golden aura. His cult of Divine Beauty, to which he referred in a letter to Niccolò Michelozzo, was a widely upheld ideal in the Renaissance. It embraced all phases of life and constituted a psychological, as well as an aesthetic, canon. It also had the special peculiarity of endorsing excellence for the sake of excellence (in evil

44. *Burial of Saints Cosimo and Damiano (and other martyrs)* by Fra Angelico. Cosimo and Damiano were the patron saints of the Medici, and their many miracles are recorded in a series of pictures by Fra Angelico at San Marco. *Museo di San Marco.*

45. Pope Sixtus IV and Platina, fresco by Melozzo da Forlì, 1477. Standing in the centre is Cardinal Raffaello Riario, and on the left two other nephews of the Pope, one of whom is Girolamo Riario; some of these were involved in the Pazzi conspiracy to murder Lorenzo the Magnificent and his brother in 1478. *Pinacoteca Vaticana.*

accomplishments as in good), of valuing the intrinsic perfection of all things, including practical action. When Cesare Borgia summoned his suspect condottieri to an isolated castle and slew them, Machiavelli described the stratagem as 'beautiful' ('bellissimo'); and this morally neutral assessment was accepted by many of his contemporaries. The Renaissance made a clear distinction between material and moral beauty, which in the Middle Ages were theoretically one and the same. This new conception of beauty as an attribute, a perfect and integral property of any object, a being or an action, gave this era its aura of aesthetic hedonism. Such an attitude was without precedent in the history of Christian civilization; its antecedents and its roots were to be found in pagan Rome and Greece. The Florentine Quattrocento was marked by a profound Platonic veneration of Beauty for Beauty's sake, and it is present in Ficino's philosophy and in Poliziano's poetry as in Lorenzo's. A similar feeling but carried to absurd lengths was revealed by the 'tyrant' of Rimini, Sigismondo Pandolfo Malatesta, in his crimes. It also lay behind the concept of that 'inimitable existence' whose classical models the Quattrocento yearned to imitate, and which Lorenzo sought to realize in every phase of his own life, attaining such magnificence that he became the envy of the richest and most cultivated courts of his day.

Lorenzo the Magnificent was well equipped for the task of reviving the golden age of antiquity, for he possessed the three qualities that Poliziano declared the indispensable attributes of the perfect man: a splendid mind, cheerful determination, and the green freshness of youth and fortune (Cesare Borgia also vaunted his *green fortune* and knew his end was near when he saw it fade). Lorenzo's native intelligence was helped by the education he received from the best of scholars of his time. Through them he was well qualified to become a complete humanist and, what is more, to embody that human masterpiece, which the great Renaissance teachers, Vittorino da Feltre, Guarino da Verona, strove to produce in their schools. Their ideal was the cultivated and beautiful man, in whom physical and spiritual excellence were perfectly balanced. Lorenzo himself was taught by Gentile da Urbino, by Argyropoulos, by Christoforo Landino, and, of course, chiefly by the family friend, Ficino. He was given a broad and eclectic education, including religious instruction by his mother Lucrezia Tornabuoni. The duality which was the

Left:
Fig. 32   Reverse of the portrait of Federigo, Duke of Urbino (fig. 35), showing a *Triumph*, by Piero della Francesca, 1465. (47 × 33 cms.) *Uffizi.*

Right:
Fig. 33   Reverse of the portrait of Battista Sforza, also showing a *Triumph*, by Piero della Francesca, 1465. (47 × 33 cms.) *Uffizi.*

incessant worry of his contemporaries, attained a harmonious unity in Lorenzo, where pagan aesthetics were truly married with rigorously Christian ethics and metaphysics. The immense patience with which Lorenzo endured all of Savonarola's threats and insults is testimony of his genuine respect and admiration for the monk from Ferrara, that prophetic orator who wished to restore the Church to its original purity and virtue. He was as disposed to understand and appreciate this scourge from God as he was to discuss Plato with the scholars. He detected the ring of true greatness in the Dominican's voice, and it moved him to sympathy despite the orator's contempt for those who venerated beauty.

Lorenzo had no difficulty in coupling his habitual modesty with ostentation and expensive tastes. He used regularly to entertain some fifty people to dinner at the Via Larga palace; all his guests sat together at the same table heedless of rank or class, for the passport to his favours was talent. It is said that at one of these meals, Lorenzo seated an obscure boy of humble origin to his right treating him with fatherly concern; Lorenzo had discerned a certain talent and potential in the young Michelangelo despite his awkwardness. Another anecdote indicates the care he showed for his humblest subjects. A peasant came one day to show him a specimen of iron ore. Lorenzo talked with him for a long time, then accompanied him outside and strolled across the city with him, so completely engrossed in the conversation that he forgot his guests. His fare was simple and his manner always convivial and open. He would often take his guests off to his country villas at Caffaggiolo and Poggio a Caiano, where formalities were discarded and everyone was free to do as he pleased. When the occasion demanded, however, Lorenzo could entertain with a splendour and lavishness that dazzled his most opulent guests and which also satisfied his aesthetic predilection for princely pomp. (The fact that he was always accompanied in public by an armed bodyguard was probably a realistic precaution taken against the murderous plots of the Pazzi or the Frescobaldi and not, as some have suggested, a proof of his tyranny.) Luigi Pulci describes an immensely lavish jousting tournament held in 1468 in which Lorenzo and his brother Giuliano took part. And three years later, an equally splendid festivity was held in honour of the Duke of Milan, Galeazzo Maria Sforza, which cost two hundred thousand gold florins.

The psychological impulse which generated this splendour was derived from his typically Renaissance ambition for glory and immortality. By far the most important of all the Triumphs described by Petrarch in his *I Trionfi* and subsequently represented so often by artists, engravers, painters, and decorators of *cassoni*, was the Chariot of Fame (see figs. 32 and 33). An almost organic need for a glorious immortality was fundamental to the Renaissance cult of eminent personalities who managed by hook or by crook to stand out above ordinary men, to distinguish themselves from the amorphous and anonymous masses around them. Patrons' thirst for posthumous fame was assuaged by the works which the humanists wrote about them and which in succeeding centuries it became the special duty of the court poets to produce. Sculpted and painted portraits fulfilled the same need. Artists even incorporated their patrons in religious subjects, which almost became pretexts for portraits, as is witnessed by the Medici family's appearance in Botticelli's *Adoration of the Magi* (see plate 12). The Renaissance portrait served not only as an historical record but was something akin to deification; for instance, the equestrian monument of Colleone by Verrocchio (see fig. 9) or that of Gattamelata by Donatello (see fig. 34), can be regarded as echoes of the apotheoses of the emperors represented by Roman equestrian statues; the horse here acquires the same rôle as he did in classical mythology, of the glorifying animal who bears the soul aloft to the paradise of divine heroes.

Equestrian statues would not have suited a scholarly patrician such as Lorenzo,

Fig. 34   Equestrian statue of Gattamelata by Donatello, in Padua.

despite his equestrian talents and his distinction in the tournaments. Florence's leading citizens all participated in these jousts, which were, as we have seen, the only relic of aristocratic custom that the city preserved; by the fifteenth century they rather resembled open-air pantomimes, or carnival processions, with the added intention of making a strong impression of the magnificence of the young princes of the city who took part in them on their descendants who would hear tell of the occasion years later. Indeed to make sure that the memory of these displays would endure, poets were commissioned to describe every last detail of the events that took place. The annual Carnival, which was the occasion for elaborate and often brilliantly original processions, belonged to an even more ancient tradition, celebrating the victory of spring-time over winter, resurrection over death. All European civilizations have at all times combined agrarian feasts devoted to obtaining fertile crops with religious rituals that render homage to benevolent deities, particularly to those who govern the fertility of the soil. The feasts and rituals had become popular holidays, on which the people, ignorant or heedless of the real mythological significance of these celebrations, simply delighted in the return of the festivities themselves. The artists of the day helped to design and deck out floats, and make costumes and 'props' to be used by the participants. Poets and musicians also contributed, by composing lyrics and songs for dramas; mythological themes gained prevalence with the growing interest in classical antiquity. Lorenzo would choose a subject and write poems for musicians, such as his favourite lutanist Squarcialupi, to set to music. As already mentioned, another important source for these displays was found in Petrarch's *Triumphs*; the Triumph of Death in particular was never lacking. It seems that the macabre sight of Death drawn by a team of black oxen never failed to dampen the spirits of the heartiest carouser.

In the Middle Ages this dramatic representation of men's inevitable demise was deliberately aimed at inspiring its spectators to take stock of themselves and repent; the Renaissance gave the theme a grandiloquent treatment; later the anxious, restless age of the Baroque amplified the original solemnity and baleful gloom, as if to indulge in the agony of being, rather than to alleviate it. The High Renaissance of the Medici's Florence also witnessed the occasional resurgence of chilling Medieval terror: in 1511 a painter with a genius for weird fantasies, Piero di Cosimo (1462–1521), designed a Death Float that was so unusually horrifying that Vasari has left a description of it. It echoed the blood-curdling sermons with which Savonarola held his audiences rapt in terror some years before, and was perhaps reminiscent also of the wood-cuts accompanying his treatise *On the Art of Dying Well*. This strange exaltation of death, at a time when poets, artists and musicians proclaimed their joy at being alive, is a striking example of the internal contrasts that characterized the Renaissance; the fascination with death is all the more remarkable when set beside the more obvious hedonistic, pagan, or sensual products of the age. Piero di Cosimo worked secretly on his float in the privacy of an annexe to the Church of Santa Maria Novella, where no one was permitted to enter; the impact therefore, when it finally rolled out was immediate, astonishing and horrifying. The monumental catafalque advanced through the streets with a rattling of bones and swaying of white crosses, drawn by the black oxen of the Petrarchan tradition, which assigned unicorns to the *Triumph of Chastity*, elephants to that of *Fame*, stags to that of *Time*, and the four symbolic animals of the Evangelists to that of *Divinity*. A gigantic effigy of Death, scythe in hand, was enthroned in the middle of the float surrounded by closed coffins. At each halt of the procession, the coffins were thrown open and skeletons emerged chanting the sad and soul-searing plaint so familiar to their audience, 'Dolor, pianto, e penitenza' ('Pain, tears and repentance'). A procession of men dressed as skeletons followed on the emaciated backs of the most decrepit nags obtainable, bearing torches and streaming black banners and chanting

46. Detail from the fresco *Egypt's Tribute to Caesar* by Andrea del Sarto (1521) in the Medici Villa at *Poggio a Caiano*. (See plate 70 and fig. 11.)

47. *The Repulse of Attila by Pope Leo I,* fresco by Raphael, 1514. The figure of the Pope is a portrait of Leo X (Giovanni de' Medici) for whom the picture was completed, although it was originally commissioned by his predecessor Pope Julius II (died 1513). *Vatican, Stanze di Raffaello.*

incessantly the lines of the *Miserere*. Contemporaries said that this terrifying invention much enhanced Piero di Cosimo's fame.

Lorenzo's famous float portraying Bacchus and Ariadne furnished a refreshing contrast to the theme of Death. He wrote a hymn for it the initial quatrain of which epitomizes another aspect of the Renaissance philosophy of life: 'How sweet is youth and how quickly spent; make much of today's joys for the morrow is ever unsure.' This invitation to seize the hour and enjoy earthly pleasures is of course a recurring theme in European poetry, and can be found for instance in Ronsard or Marvell. The original idea and its mood came from classical Greece. It is contained in the 'Palatine Anthology' of Planudus, with which Lorenzo seems to have been familiar, and in which a poem by Palladas of Alexandria says: 'This is life and no more than this; life is pleasure; banish all discontent; human existence is so very short; so bring me my wine and make haste and bring on the dancers and bear me crowns of flowers; make haste and bring me women; come let us make merry today for who knows what the morrow may bring.' Such was the motto of the revellers who wanted no more than to enjoy sensual delights. For them, death meant what it did in Horace's *Carpe Diem* and in Lorenzo's *Chi vuol esser lieto sia*, an inducement to enjoy the present all the more intensely. Pico della Mirandola, however, with his nobler vision, attributed a loftier, more serious purpose to life, which possesses a grandeur worthy of Faust. 'Where there is life there is soul; where there is soul there is spirit.' This philosophy of life aims at securing the victory of the spirit over matter, to secure a harmonious unity of these two human components. And Lorenzo's other poems apart from his carnival songs—his rustic eclogues of *la Nencia da Barberino*; his occasional poem on falconry; the *Ambra*, his mythological allegory about a river in love with one of its tributaries; the philosophical debate the *Altercation*; and the *Prayers to the Virgin*, which are so moving and touchingly sincere—are also very different in atmosphere from the plaintive sensuality of Ariadne's chant.

Lorenzo was not, however, the great poet his contemporaries claimed him to be. He did not create any new forms or original themes. Poliziano's Italian and especially his Latin poetry is far superior, subtler and more powerful, and it possesses a more clearly defined individuality. Lorenzo's more inspired moments, as witnessed by his *Bacchus and Ariadne*, do contain a quality of feeling and a graceful lyricism, rare in fifteenth-century Italian poetry. The bulk of his work, however, is rather stereotyped, as for instance the comico-serious eulogies to country-life, which keep to the well-worn track of Virgil's eclogues and the same classical models whom Sannazzaro (1458–1530) and Pontano (c. 1422–1503) also imitated. His pastorals seem more genuine, for he often forsook the urbanity of Via Larga for long spells in the country. Careggi, Poggio a Caiano and Caffaggiolo (see plate 70, figs. 10 and 11) are not castles but agricultural estates, large farms, whose villas were constructed and decorated in a very simple, sober style, quite different in character from the showy châteaux of the French Renaissance. This banker and moneylender knew the soil; he liked to handle it himself; at Careggi he supervised the rearing of Calabrian pigs, and at Poggio a Caiano he raised golden pheasants from Sicily. He ordered a special variety of rabbit from Spain, which he adapted and introduced to Tuscany. Once, when his fortune was in danger of failing, he was able to rely on the yield from his estates to cover any possible deficits in his bank. He might have recited Leon Battista Alberti's eulogy to the country: 'The country villa is a good and faithful friend. If you are in the spring of life and in love, she will not only satisfy your every desire but will add recompense to recompense. In spring she offers verdant trees and birdsong. In autumn she rewards gentle labour with a cornucopia of fruit; all year long she will keep melancholy away.' The Italians did not share that rhapsodic awe of nature in which the German artists of the period revelled. They preferred (and prefer) orderly, man-made countryside to the wild landscapes

48. Cardinal Ippolito de' Medici in Hungarian dress, by Titian, painted after he had taken part in a campaign against the Turks in 1532. *Palazzo Pitti.*

beloved of Dürer, Grünewald, Altdorfer and the Danube school, or the Swiss land-scapists. Their Tuscan landscape lacked the wilder extremes of the North: it was ordered, intellectual, and harmoniously balanced, with clear, simple outlines. Thus Lorenzo's careful poem on the *Nencia* achieves a faithful poetic representation of peasant life as well as an accurate reproduction of classical prototypes.

As we have observed, one of the most curious features of this century was that while there were revolutionary inventions in the visual arts, humanist literature dragged behind in a desire to imitate classical models. Lorenzo's fable of the Ambra's love for the Ombrone, the two rivers that ran by Poggio a Caiano, was borrowed from Ovid; it became a mythological commonplace, one which the Spaniard Pedro Espinosa took up in his *Fabula del Genil,* and which the Portuguese poet Sa Miranda adapted to his native Mondego. What then were Lorenzo's real gifts? What made him 'Magnificent'? It was above all his talent for harmonizing art with life, so that his whole life became a pursuit of beauty. Lorenzo was more than a poet; he was a poem, a masterpiece, a work of art as perfect in himself as a Donatello statue or a painting by Botticelli. He was a master of the art of living, a master who valued every exquisite manifestation of perfection. His collection of mag-nificently worked goblets and flasks studded with semi-precious stones, with jade, lapis lazuli, amethyst, topaz and pink quartz was of the same excellence and catered to the same taste for the exquisite as the volumes he had copied and equally magnificently illuminated with the Medici coat of arms (see title page). When Poliziano once caught sight of Pico and Lorenzo walking down a lane at Careggi, Pico leaning on Lorenzo's shoulder, he commented wryly, 'There goes a phoenix in a laurel tree.' Despite his ugly features, his heavy jaw, his bulbous forehead, his sunken eyes, Lorenzo possessed the natural beauty of a tree: its integrity, its lack of artificiality, its harmonious accord of all its faculties, which was the humanists' supreme ideal. He combined statesmanship and business sense with a love of the arts: he possessed princely grace in public ceremonies, but was given to unpretentious economy and dressed quietly in the same way as other citizens; he ate simple fare at a table laden with rare goblets and vessels tooled by the greatest artists of the day; many of the books in his collection contained masterly miniatures, brilliantly designed and illuminated. Even his servants were masters of their art, or the jesters who distracted him from his many concerns. Florence, in his lifetime, became the supreme example of a society devoted to culture and aesthetic beauty and to all the daily refinements that make for the 'inimitable life'.

The complexity of Lorenzo the Magnificent's character was further enhanced by his political career. He was a highly gifted and flexible politician whose dominant characteristic was perhaps his completely pragmatic approach to the problems of the day. As in his business ventures, he had only one principle—to achieve success. However refined and sophisticated the Medici might have been, they never missed an opportunity of eliminating their competitors or manoeuvring rival banks up to the brink of bankruptcy and then buying them up at ridiculous prices; once taken over these rival banks would be refloated and restored to prosperity. An age which witnessed the moneyed classes' rise to power was naturally geared to a monetary morality, that is, to a struggle for success devoid of ethical considerations. The maxims of Guicciardini or Machiavelli were a reflection of what was at the back of everyone's mind. This outlook guided the brilliant statesmen who liked to enjoy managing their affairs successfully without worrying about the morality of ends and means.

They did not discard all morality, as the moralists of Savonarola's type believed; they simply followed a different approach, with roots and laws which were not Christian in conception. Savonarola was a Medieval man, almost an anachronism. His ultimate downfall was inevitable because his values were out of joint with his age and he only managed to fascinate the Florentines for a brief spell. The Medici, however, were modern men, men of their time. They harked back to antiquity only for aesthetic or intellectual inspiration. For the rest, they repudiated the ethic and aesthetic of the Middle Ages, and lived fully and exclusively in the present and for the future. Moralists have condemned Lorenzo the Magnificent precisely because they have judged him by moral standards with which he had dispensed. They deplore the brutality, and even the savagery, in his action against the inhabitants of Prato and Volterra, but they overlook the context, the complicated network of business, administration and politics which left no leeway for hesitation or indulgence. It was often better to strike a crushing initial blow than to go on scuffling indefinitely. This attitude was of course an essential effect of the will to power so characteristic of the age, which provided so many examples of the 'superman', later embodied in philosophies like those of Nietzsche or Gobineau.

The Prato revolt of 1470 was engineered very shortly after Lorenzo succeeded his father by Diotisalvi Neroni, by the Pitti faction and by the agents of Borso Duke of Este, all enemies of the Medici. Lorenzo suppressed the revolt with notable rapidity and severity. The Volterra case of 1471 was complicated by the dominance of commercial interests over political considerations. Some of the ancient Etruscan town's inhabitants had discovered deposits of alum and were conceded rights to them by the town authorities. The Medici bank furnished the capital to exploit the mines. The strike proved a success and the mines were soon flourishing. The authorities, who began to regret having given this concession to private individuals, tried to nullify the original contract. This would have prejudiced the bankers' interests, as they virtually monopolized the Italian alum trade. Volterra was theoretically an independent city, but Florence had provided her with her Podestà and with her alum proprietor, an 'influential citizen' called Inghirami. The dispute might have been confined to commercial bickering if Inghirami had not been assassinated and if the Podestà had not been packed off to Florence. As in the case of the Prato conspiracy, Lorenzo was still very young and nervous about his responsibilities when this

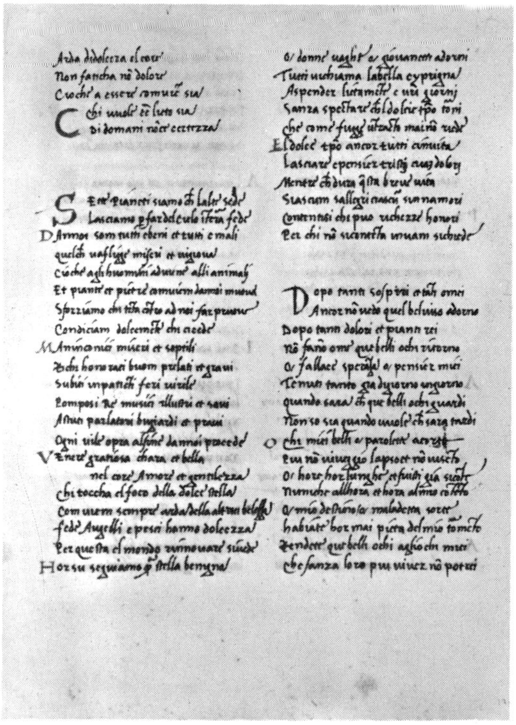

Above:
Fig. 35   Portrait of Federigo da Montefeltro, Duke of Urbino, by Piero della Francesca, 1465. *Uffizi.* (See fig. 32 for reverse)

Left:
Fig. 36   Frontispiece to *Canzone per andare in maschera per Carnesciale* by Lorenzo de' Medici and others, about 1493-7, with a portrait of Lorenzo in the foreground. *Biblioteca Medicea Laurenziana.*

Right:
Fig. 37   Page from Lorenzo the Magnificent's *Selve d'Amore*. *Biblioteca Medicea Laurenziana.*

occurred. His insistence that Volterra's insubordination be punished was opposed by some of his advisers like Tomaso Soderini, who argued that a bad settlement was preferable to a successful lawsuit and that a poor agreement was preferable to a crushing victory. Lorenzo plunged ahead, however, while others of his friends and clients silenced Soderini and the peace party, and engaged the services of Federigo da Montefeltro, Duke of Urbino, who was a very famous soldier, as condottiere (see fig. 35). When Volterra saw herself confronted by such a threat, she soon capitulated. Although Lorenzo tried to prevent the troops from entering the town, they did so and the inevitable sacking and pillaging was not averted, in spite of his efforts. Lorenzo's remedy was radical, more so in the event than he intended, but it achieved its ends: vassal towns would never again cause trouble.

Florence had one enemy, however, that would never be subdued by any measures, ordinary or extraordinary. This was Pope Sixtus IV, who came to the papal throne the same year as the sack of Volterra (1471). This pontiff seems at first to have liked and even to have helped Lorenzo, but the two men were unable to see eye to eye on the political arrangement of Italy. Sixtus IV's ambition was to subjugate Italy under the domination of the Papal States. Lorenzo, on the other hand, was convinced that the only way that Italy could repulse the threatened advances from foreign powers was by putting an end to her internal rivalries and parochial squabbles, and by achieving some sort of balance between the various states. Unification was out of the question at this time. This divergence of opinion and objectives, which led the Pope and Lorenzo to become mortal enemies, coupled with the Pope's stubborn, ambitious and warlike nature, augured ill for Florence. To the rest of the world it may, for a while, have appeared that these two antagonists had a harmonious relationship; Louis XI of France even asked the Medici to intervene with the Pope on his behalf. This misapprehension endured until Sixtus rejected Lorenzo's request, which also carried the support of Milan and Naples, that his brother, Giuliano, receive a cardinalate. The rejection could have been made on the grounds that Giuliano was still young and that to make him a cardinal would have been outrageous; nonetheless, there had been precedents, especially among the Pope's own family. The Pope's refusal and the terms used were tantamount to a declaration of war. Would papal domination prevail, or would the Papal States become part of a more balanced system?

The two rivals engaged in a 'trial by force'. Sixtus IV had won the first round by humiliating the Medici in refusing the cardinalate, but this was only the beginning. His plan was to throw Florence into diplomatic isolation by allying himself with other Italian states and foreign powers and then to weaken her by seducing away her vassal and satellite cities. The Medici were themselves the principal enemies; once their fall was contrived, Sixtus IV hoped Florence would return to her democratic origins and to eternal factional strife, which would eventually diminish her importance. Among the Florentine families opposed to the Medici but whose importance even at this time was considerable (and who were even allied by marriage to the Medici), were the Pazzi; in this family there were some prepared to work for the elimination of Lorenzo and his brother, their aim being in this way to reinforce their own position. Without them in fact Florence would be an easy prey to the ambitions of other families. Thus the views of Sixtus IV and of Francesco Pazzi, in particular, coincided, and they decided to act.

At the time of this plot, which is usually called the Pazzi conspiracy, the papal armies were under the command of a nephew of Sixtus IV, Girolamo Riario, who can be seen together with his cousin Cardinal Raffaello Riario at the Pope's side in the famous fresco of Sixtus IV by Melozzo da Forlì in the Vatican (see plate 45). Girolamo became one of the main instigators of the plot. Another Florentine, Francesco Salviati, Archbishop of Pisa, joined them, as he was angry at being unable

49. Courtyard of the *Bargello*. The building was begun in the mid-thirteenth century, completed in the fourteenth century, and in the time of the republic was the palace of the chief judicial officer, the Podestà. Coats of arms of various holders of the office can be seen on the walls.

to take up his bishopric in that city on account of the Florentine government's opposition to his appointment. The main conspirators, with the exception of Girolamo Riario, then visited Florence in April 1478, where they were joined by Montesicco, a soldier of fortune in the Pope's pay. Francesco Pazzi, who lived at Rome and was closely involved with Sixtus IV's financial affairs, came to Florence at this point also, ostensibly to visit his family; he persuaded his father and other members of the family to be prepared for the assassination of Lorenzo de' Medici and his brother Giuliano, and to stir up the people in the streets at the right moment. Two condottieri were retained at Todì and Imola with their troops to come to the support of the conspirators should need arise.

The murder was supposed to take place on April 25, 1478; a festive dinner was to be the fatal hour. The assassins were to place themselves near the two Medici chairs and strike when the signal was given by the organizers, who had agreed that the two brothers should be killed at exactly the same time, for if one managed to escape he would be the harder to destroy and a double murder's terrifying impact on the Florentine people would be lost. Giuliano, however, was unwell on April 25 and did not come down to eat, so the crime was postponed to the following day. As this happened to be a Sunday, it was decided that it would be easier to kill the brothers in church during mass. (This was how Galeazzo Maria, Duke of Milan, had recently been killed in Milan). There was a slight hitch, however, for Montesicco had sudden misgivings. The unscrupulous adventurer objected to sacrilege: murder, yes, but not in a church. Two priests were found to replace him, Antonio Maffei of Volterra and Stefano da Bagnone, who were apparently unruffled at the prospect of desecrating Santa Maria del Fiore; they were reinforced by Francesco Pazzi himself and another accomplice, Bernardo Bandini. En route to the church, Francesco Pazzi put his arm round his old friend Giuliano's waist in a friendly gesture, but this was to check that his victim was not wearing a cuirass or a coat of mail. In any case, it had been agreed beforehand that the assassins would strike at the heads of their victims at the moment of the consecration of the Host.

And so it was done. Bandini and Pazzi sliced open Giuliano's skull with their swords and Giuliano dropped to the ground. The two priests met with less success; their rapiers only got as far as Lorenzo's shoulder. Wielding his sword and wrapping his cloak about his arm in lieu of a shield, he managed to break through the group of murderers and to run to the sacristy, as did his friends Poliziano, Ridolfi, and Nori, who threw himself on Bandini's sword to parry a thrust intended for Lorenzo, and so died. While the conspirators were trying to ram the heavy sacristy doors, Cardinal Riario, unsure of the outcome of the affair, rushed to the altar and clasped the crucifix to his bosom. Meanwhile, Archbishop Salviati proceeded to carry on with his part of the plan; he marched to the Palazzo Vecchio with a group of men to inform the Signoria of the death of the Medici and advise them to surrender themselves into his hands. In the meantime also the Pazzi supporters appeared in the Piazza della Signoria to arouse the people—which merely had the effect of sounding the alarm. The people rose in a frenzied rage and took up arms to avenge the attack on the beautiful Giuliano and the beloved Lorenzo, whom none that day considered a tyrant. The Gonfaloniere Petrucci, hearing the noise and cries outside in the streets, asked Archbishop Salviati and his men to wait until the Signoria had finished their discussion of what to do, and closed the gates of the Palazzo Vecchio behind them. When he learned of the attempted assassinations, he killed the Archbishop himself and delivered his thugs to the mob, which gleefully vented its wrath upon them and other supporters of the Pazzi, in what was known as the massacre of the *pazzeschi*, whose corpses they dangled from the windows of their homes.

Popular reaction was immediate and quite unrelenting. Francesco Pazzi, who had taken to the surrounding hills, was hunted down and captured by the peasants,

50. Via de' Bardi, fifteenth- and sixteenth-century palaces.

taken into the city, and throttled before the Palazzo Vecchio. Nor was Montesicco spared, despite his refusal to commit the crime. The two priests were tortured and strangled. Cardinal Riario and Bernardo Bandini were the only survivors of the vengeance of the *palleschi* (the supporters of the *palle,* or insignia of the Medici). Bandini managed to get to Venice and from there to Constantinople where he thought he would be safe. When the Sultan heard the tragic news, however, he bound the offender hand and foot and shipped him back to Florence, where he was tried in the court of the Palace of the Podestà, the Bargello, and hanged. Cardinal Riario was taken into public custody and imprisoned until June. Thus ended a methodically organized plot which might have caused Lorenzo's death as well as Giuliano's but which, in the end, greatly benefited Lorenzo's political position.

Sixtus IV, frustrated by the failure of his conspiracy, responded to the massacre of the Pazzi with the Church's most devastating weapon; he excommunicated the whole city, depriving the people of the sacraments, as punishment for the execution of Archbishop Salviati. Fortunately, the Medici power in the city was more solid than ever. Lorenzo knew how best to protect his city from external reprisal, whether on the battlefield or in the corridors of diplomacy. Even the dangerous war prepared in the following year by the Pope, in alliance with Ferrante of Aragon, King of Naples, was not too much for his abilities or his power. At the end of 1479 it seemed indeed that Florence would be invaded and pillaged by the soldiers of the Duke of Calabria, Ferrante's son, and humiliated for ever. There seemed little hope for mercy from Ferrante, whose cunning and brutality were notorious. In this crisis Lorenzo decided to see what personal diplomacy could do; he did not surrender himself unconditionally; he asked instead to be taken to Naples, in order personally to discuss the war with his adversary. He put himself at the mercy of the King and then attempted to persuade him to reconsider his alliance with Sixtus IV. Lorenzo's logic and patience—he stayed in Naples from December to April—his almost chivalrous gesture of appearing to trust in Ferrante's respect, in spite of his reputation, finally led the King to change his mind, and stop the war. The King, disconcerted by Lorenzo's direct appeal, in his own court, to his honour, his intelligence, generosity, and above all to his good sense (for Lorenzo could give convincing reasons for Naples to leave the side of the Pope and to join that of Florence), accepted Lorenzo's proposals. Lorenzo then returned home in triumph to be paid homage and respect by those very citizens who had feared his plan when he set out. This victory set the seal on his position in Florence and Italy as a whole.

In the following years in Florence, Lorenzo introduced several beneficial reforms into the constitution and the city administration, while the situation at the Vatican improved considerably when Innocent VIII, a friend of the Medici, succeeded Sixtus IV on his death in 1484. In local administration, he contrived to exclude the important families from all councils and primary offices and replaced them with men of humbler origins. In this way he won the gratitude of the clerks who owed him their positions, and he deprived the representatives of 'merchant feudalism' access to the spheres of influence, these families being in the main opposed to his power—the Albizzi, the Pitti, the Pazzi, the Nicolini, the Guicciardini, the Ridolfi, the Neroni and so on.

Lorenzo was clever enough to cement and reinforce his position gradually and discreetly. He felt he had to have absolute control in order to govern well, but he also knew that he must move cautiously to avoid rousing the egalitarian and touchy Florentines. He adroitly devised measures which appeared not to hinder the course of true democracy but which in fact hamstrung the figureheads of the democratic constitution; the Podestà and the Captain of the People, who was comparable to the people's tribune in Ancient Rome, and who defended the interests of the poorer classes, were rendered ineffectual. The lesser guilds were reduced from fourteen

Fig. 38 Both sides of a medal showing (above) Giuliano de' Medici with a representation of the fighting during the Pazzi conspiracy and (below) Lorenzo with the same, by Bertoldo di Giovanni (1420-91). (Actual size.) *London, Victoria and Albert Museum.*

51. Entrance to the *Belvedere* fortress, with the Medici coat of arms, built for the Grand-Duke Ferdinando I by Buontalenti in 1590.

52. The main cloister, *Santa Maria Novella.*

118

to five, which made them easier to handle. The councils were modified in 1480, and new ones formed whose effect was to limit the people's prerogatives. The nomination of the ten accopiatori, who were administrative officers, and whose position enabled them to select candidates for the Signoria, also came into the control of the Medici. This arrangement aimed to ensure a stable political structure based on permanent institutions, which would no longer be subject to the precariousness of the two-month sessions to which tradition had always bound political councils and organizations. The 1480 constitution, which had been autocratically conceived by Lorenzo, effectively gave all political power to a council of thirty members. When this council proved to be rather too exclusive, forty assessors were added to it. The Medici empowered the resulting Commission of Seventy to adopt the undemocratic practice of replacing defunct members by co-option rather than by a series of public elections. This was a way of gradually replacing independent members with Medici clients and supporters.

However undemocratic Lorenzo the Magnificent's new institutions might have appeared, they did not alter the atmosphere of confidence, the implicit or explicit solidarity which bound Lorenzo to his fellow citizens, and to which the spontaneous, violent, popular reaction to the Pazzi plot had attested. This confidence was not to be shaken until the day a man spoke out against the Medici, not with the tongue of political reason, nor with popular wisdom, but armed with the slings and arrows of the Old and New Testaments. Thus Savonarola (1452–1498) achieved what the Popes, the Kings of France, the German Emperor, Italian coalitions of princes and all the conspiracies of the Florentine patricians had failed to achieve.

The extent and heights of beauty and power attained during Lorenzo's reign are best demonstrated by the appearance of this 'foil'. The eulogy of pristine Christian virtues was thumped out from the pulpit by a monk of hideous appearance, whose eloquence rang unrivalled and unprecedented through the awed churches of Florence. Savonarola came to Florence in 1482 from Ferrara and installed himself in the Dominican convent of San Marco, which had traditionally been favoured and patronized by the Medici. (They used occasionally to retreat to the cells decorated with the exquisite frescoes of Fra Angelico, where Cosimo often used to stay.) In the last twenty years of that Golden Age called the Quattrocento, Europe stood at the brink of a religious revolution, marked throughout Christendom by outbursts of reforming zeal, in Florence as at Wittenberg, in the Dominican order as in the Augustinian. It was of this revolution that Savonarola was, in a sense, the Florentine representative.

In 1483 Savonarola preached his first Lenten Sermons at San Lorenzo, which was regarded as the Medici church in which members of their family had been buried. Lorenzo died nine years later (on 9 April 1492), and during the whole of this period the Medici never once attempted an act of violence or even of intimidation against this preacher, who unflaggingly criticized and insulted them and menaced them with divine retribution, and even with French invasion, which would in this instance have served apparently as celestial punishment. Except for the heckling to which the more enthusiastic Medici partisans, the palleschi, exposed him, Savonarola was allowed to preach with complete freedom, to insult whomever he liked, to incite the masses to insurrection, to arouse the whole of Florence to repentance and ultimately to achieve a real conversion of the city. At any time during these nine years Lorenzo could have rid himself of this nuisance, in whom he recognized his most serious opponent to date. Savonarola was the only man capable of shaking the confidence on which his harmonious relations with the people were based.

Lorenzo followed traditional protocol by inviting Savonarola to visit him, when he was nominated prior of San Marco. The monk made no reply. He refused to

53. Detail of the *Ponte Vecchio*. The upper storey of the buildings consists of a continuous corridor running from the Uffizi to the Palazzo Pitti, built by Vasari for the Grand Duke Cosimo I in 1564.

receive Lorenzo, when Lorenzo called at the convent to see him. Their only recorded meeting was a dramatic exchange that occurred at Lorenzo's deathbed in 1492. The monk was intransigent, arrogant, and fanatical in the expression of his hatred and caused the ailing Lorenzo enormous suffering. He obstinately commanded Lorenzo to confess and expiate his sins, his indecencies, his pride, his cupidity, and to make a last sovereign gesture: to give the people back their liberty. The Chronicle of Florence reports that the Magnificent did not reply to Savonarola's demands and invective. He merely turned his back on the fanatic in disdainful silence.

This moving scene, which has inspired several painters, emphasizes the impossibility of any dialogue between the two men, because, morally speaking, *they spoke two different languages.* Lorenzo's language was that of the Florentine Renaissance, of lucid and lofty wisdom; the monk spoke the tongue of a fanatical prophet, illuminated and uplifted by a supernatural eloquence culled from the Bible. Savonarola's favourite book was the Old Testament; Lorenzo's was the *Symposium* of Plato solemnly read on every November seventh, the day chosen to honour the Divine Plato who was celebrated with a spirit akin to holy communion. These two books were mutually exclusive and nullifying. However spiritually and intellectually unequal and incompatible the two men may have been, Lorenzo's superiority consisted in his capacity to understand and in some degree to endorse his adversary's religious convictions. Savonarola, in return, blindly accused him of heresy and tyranny, although in fact he possessed the most cultivated sensibility and pursued the most prudent policies of his day. The part played by the natural animosity between ugliness and beauty, between puritanical virtue and sensual delight, and by the more innocent antagonism between an uncompromising Christian asceticism and the pagan-Christian syncretism that Ficino, Pico della Mirandola, and their disciples had tried to devise, only served to aggravate the inevitable conflict between the two aspirants to power. The salvation of Florence could only be won at the expense of the Medici, and Savonarola was to achieve this after Lorenzo's death, during the reign of his son. While Lorenzo breathed, however, the confidence and sympathy the Medici had inspired in their people did not wane, although it might occasionally have wavered among the *piagnoni*, the 'tear-jerkers', as the followers of Savonarola were nicknamed by their detractors.

When Lorenzo died, the opposition to the Medici changed character. Through Savonarola it became a popular, rather than a political opposition, based on moral and not on political issues, on spiritual claims and not on those of prestige and self-interest. Savonarola declared himself to be the envoy of God, selected to chastise paganism and 'restore liberty' to the Florentines; the religious *coup d'état*, which had been long brewing, he claimed would have to take place at the propitious time. This finally proved to be the occasion offered by the weakness and faults of Lorenzo's son, Pietro. It would come as an authentic, popular uprising leading to the replacement of the *palle* on the city's banners by the cross and the peaceable, tolerant government of the Medici by the sovereignty of Christ the King.

Fig. 39   Portrait of Savonarola by Fra Bartolomeo. *Museo di San Marco.*

54. The Viottolone avenue in the *Bóboli Gardens*, laid out on the Bóboli hill behind the Palazzo Pitti for the Grand-Duke Cosimo I, from 1550 onwards, by Tribolo, Buontalenti and Giovanni Bologna.

VI   'The Dictatorship of God'

The advent of the Ferrarese monk Girolamo Savonarola in Florence was one of the most dramatic events in the history of the city (see fig. 39). Savonarola appeared as the apostle of purity, the advocate of liberty. His fiery eloquence soon made him famous, as did his inspired determination to reform the Church. A classical proverb claimed that Jupiter blinded those he wished to be destroyed. For nine long years Lorenzo the Magnificent turned a blind eye on Savonarola's wrathful attempts to undermine the political structure of Florence and destroy her cult of beauty, which had made her the brilliant pilot star of the Renaissance. Savonarola was indeed fortunate in having as adversaries, two of the most tolerant and understanding men of his day, Lorenzo the Magnificent and the Borgia Pope, Alexander VI, who allowed him to attack, insult and threaten them to his heart's content.

Florence was used to living through the occasional revolutionary outburst within her walls. The uprisings and civil wars she had known in the past, however, were aimed only at changing the existing government; Savonarola wanted to make people change their way of life in accordance with their consciences. The reforms he advocated bore into every part of the Florentine way of life, into its morality and even into its aesthetics. It was the monk's firm conviction that Lorenzo the Magnificent was not only a political tyrant, but a real corrupter of souls. The sermons he preached at San Marco attacked, slashed, and blasted the splendid edifice of arts and culture that had sprung up around the banker-prince, which Savonarola branded as the religious instruments of paganism. The reversals of custom, tastes, opinions, and way of life that Savonarola's fanaticism achieved is a psychological freak in Florentine history and even in the entire history of Italian civilization. Florentine society had been only too willing and pleased to be carried away by the excellence of ancient art and to be converted by the humanists to Platonism and the Florentines had rejoiced in the most exquisite forms of perfection and beauty produced by its artists under the inspiration of the ancient world; then suddenly the city underwent a total change of heart. It was literally *converted* and so radically that even those most attracted to paganism, including Michelangelo and Botticelli, joined the ranks of the 'tear-jerkers', the *piagnoni*.

Savonarola was able to use to his advantage the discredit which Lorenzo's son, Pietro lo Sfortunato (1471–1503) cast upon his ancestors. The Medici had also been in power for a very long time and the Florentines, fickle as always, were restless and ready for change. Add to this the fact that the exiled Florentine families, in collusion with the French, saw the advantage of exacerbating internal disorder, and that their intrigues were helped on by the preacher's pro-French and anti-Medici propaganda, and it becomes apparent that the position of Lorenzo's heir and successor was a difficult one. Pietro was nicknamed 'lo Sfortunato', the Unfortunate —inaccurately because most of his mishaps were of his own doing. Bungling would probably have been a better description, for his period of government was marked by a series of '*combinazioni*', political arrangements which might have come off had he been a more skilful politician but which in fact only served to weaken his position further. It was indeed unfortunate for him to be ruling Florence at a time when French armies were swarming over the Alps and into Italy, while Savonarola urged

55. Fountain of Oceanus and the *Vasca dell'Isolotto* (the basin of the islet) designed by Giovanni Bologna in the Bóboli Gardens; the Viottolone avenue is in the background.

them on with tempting promises of victory and glory.

The monk's influence on public opinion had only lightly grazed the surface of Lorenzo's last years, but he did raise serious doubts about the legitimacy of the Medici's all-embracing power. The monk's popularity was of course helped on by his religious fervour but it was more especially his seductive championing of that Florentine favourite, liberty, the familiar ring of which caught and fired the imaginations of the people and of a portion of the ruling class. Although his attempts at religious and moral reforms were a failure in the end—they were condemned by the Pope and the Florentines were glad to be reprieved from their brief spell of enforced puritan virtue—his reforming zeal had very important political consequences. The Medici were forced out of Florence and had it not been for the weakness of the Gonfaloniere Soderini and the existence of the Holy League, they would have been banished for ever. Orators, however, are only effective as long as they continue speaking. After Savonarola was finally silenced and burned at the stake (which he had morally built and fired himself), his attempt to create a dictatorship of God on earth could not last. Up to the end of his domination, however, he was able to take advantage of Pietro the Unfortunate's weakness; indeed the city would probably never have been rid of him had the Pope's condemnation of Savonarola not lost him nearly all his supporters.

In spite of Pietro's weakness, he was an ambitious man. He feared the changeability of democratic governments. It never struck him that he was a citizen 'like anyone else'. From his mother perhaps he had inherited the Orsini's pride and arrogance. He wanted to rise from being a *de facto* sovereign to being a titular ruler, and even sought the rank of duke. He always regarded his fellow citizens with a nervous suspicion. Nor did he hesitate to seek foreign support to bolster his power, not only by hiring foreign mercenaries (which was in any case a Florentine custom) but also by forming a system of alliances with other large states. Although he was aware of the real aims of these powers he fanned their acquisitive ambitions, in the hope of using them for his own ends. Artists and chroniclers sang the praises of his beauty, of his noble face and bearing, the dignity of his ways and his prowess in sports. This façade masked a craven and twisted personality, a cold, violent, and hypocritical nature. He was misguided, over-confident in his own puny cunning and his own opinions, and over-eager to dismiss good advice. He was something of a debauchee and his various personal entanglements were the source of many scandals. His mother had tried to avoid this by marrying him off at an early age to a member of her own family, to Alfonsina Orsini, but Alfonsina did not have Clarissa's strength and intelligence and did not know how to control or keep her husband.

Politically he was a disaster. He committed the folly of breaking up and dispersing the League which had been laboriously contrived by the Italian states to repel possible foreign invaders. The newly unified French monarchy which had begun to reduce the power of the feudal lords and to centralize its power had claims to the Duchy of Milan and the Kingdom of Naples. These claims meant that the French king, Charles VIII, would eventually invade Italy. If this happened, the Emperor was bound to take up arms against him and then the peninsula would be transformed into a European battlefield. The League had aimed to unify the states against a common danger—a distant glimmer of a real *Italian unification* which had been conceived by some hopeful spirits, by Cola di Rienzo in the fourteenth century for instance, and in Pietro's lifetime by Cesare Borgia, Machiavelli, and to some degree by Lorenzo the Magnificent, as well.

Pietro did not rest until he had dissolved this League. He had the silly notion of building up a different one that would better serve his own interests, one which he was vain enough to think he could manipulate. Instead of strengthening his military and diplomatic defences against the French, he made overtures to Charles VIII whom he showered with sycophantic favours at the same time as Savonarola was invoking French thunder upon Italy to punish her impiety. The Dominican wanted to hand the 'sword of God' which he brandished over the Florentines' heads, to the French whom he apocalyptically transformed into the wrathful scourges of divine justice. Charles VIII, encouraged by these allies, who, he expected, would help him consolidate his Italian conquests, invaded Italy in 1494 and won a series of easy victories. His Italian enemies were totally taken aback and paralysed by this attack.

Florence could not decide on what stand it should take in the face of this situation. The Dominican's *piagnoni* were prepared to accept the French as a necessary evil sent them by heaven to punish them; Pietro the Unfortunate was ready to play the French game as long as it helped his cause. The majority of the population however was dead against the idea of foreign interference; the Medieval intrusions of foreigners into the affairs of the city had left long-lasting scars. They became more and more restive and angry as the alien invaders approached. When they reached Sarzana, a town belonging to Florence, the question of whether to fight or surrender became more urgent. Pietro in the throes of one of his typically misguided flights of inspired fantasy decided to throw Tuscany open to the enemy and thus enable the French to advance on Naples more easily, despite the fact that the King of Naples was supposed to be Florence's ally. Pietro imagined that in this way he would win his adversaries' favours and then their support. In order to prove the seriousness of his friendly overtures, Pietro laid all he had at their disposal: supplies, fortifications, and money. He even took envoys from the Signoria with him to demonstrate that the entire Florentine republic acquiesced in this gross humiliation which he light-heartedly forced upon her.

Unfortunately for himself, Pietro misjudged his countrymen. He banked too much on the Medici's traditional prestige and powers of persuasion. The illustrious family's business and political rivals joined forces with the people in feeling outraged that Florence should have yielded to the enemy without a fight. A stormy session of the Council in the Great Hall of the Palazzo della Signoria declared Pietro to be a felon and outlaw, while angry mobs howled in the street below. Pietro's brother, Cardinal Giovanni and the condottiere Orsini tried in vain to appease the crowds but ended by having to run for their lives, the cardinal disguised as a monk. Pietro had barely set foot in his palace when he had to abandon it and gallop for Venice. The mobs followed their time-honoured custom of pillaging their victims' houses, in this case those of the Medici, revelling in the restoration of a privilege given them by the return of the authentic republic, liberty and virtue.

57. Terracotta bust of Niccolò da Uzzano by Donatello, based on an antique bust of Cicero, between 1460 and 1480. (*Height 46 cms.*) *Bargello, Museo Nazionale.*

The flight of the Medici removed the last important obstacle to the 'Dictatorship of God' and to that of his vicar on earth, Savonarola. The city dedicated herself to Christ, who was proclaimed King of Florence. In an orgy of masochistic contrition, the people lit 'pyres of vanity', burning all licentious books and works of art. Children became Fra Girolamo's terrible aids and were allowed to enter homes and destroy whatever they deemed evil: silken wigs, cosmetics, sumptuous or indecent garments. The gleeful outbursts of these young vandals did not however resolve the problem of the city's relationship to the French. It was now up to the Dominican, the master of the city, God's vicar, and the lieutenant of Christ-King to negotiate with them. The problem was greater than he expected. He was appalled by the behaviour of the French troops; did not understand the French leaders. Under the circumstances it seemed best to allow them into the city as they were already masters of a good part of Tuscany. The only way to control them was to prepare a dazzling welcome and so convince them of the good faith and goodwill of both populace and Signoria. This *entente* was, however, short-lived. The French abused and misused Florentine hospitality to such an extent that the same people who had initially welcomed their arrival soon turned upon them. Quarrels broke out between the generals and the Gonfaloniere Capponi who tried to resist their demands, and Charles VIII began to fear a popular uprising. He therefore decided to leave, but not before he had wrested a sizeable contribution towards his war from the city and the Signoria's pledge of allegiance to France.

In the meantime Pietro lo Sfortunato was waiting for an opportunity to join the French and to put himself at Charles VIII's disposal. Their departure from Florence was his chance, and he decided to link his fortunes and his future with those of the invaders. He joined their campaigns in the vain hope of eventually returning to Florence with the help of the enemy's pikes and arquebuses. The rest of Italy, however, formed a new league against the common enemy; Charles VIII's victorious hour was not to last, for he had to leave Naples and head North again. At Fornova in 1495 the French were forced into a great battle, great by the standards of the day, which proved fatal for them. It became clear that they had to pull out of Italy, or they would be wiped out. Pietro, however, was still plotting his return to Florence, which he hoped to recapture by force, and to this end he even hired some condottieri while he egged on his remaining pro-Medici partisans in the city.

There Savonarola's popularity was beginning to wane, for he had lost many of his supporters when Pope Alexander VI came to the end of his patience and excommunicated him. From this the *palleschi*, or Medici faction took heart; at the same time one of those periodic outbreaks of the plague occurred in the city which further weakened Savonarola's position. The Signoria took sides against the Dominican during his trial for heresy at the end of which he was sentenced to die at the stake. On May 23, 1498, the young Machiavelli, who had recently taken a post in the Palazzo Vecchio's offices, watched the event from his window (see plate 27). He saw Savonarola clamber onto the platform with two other monks, while children —perhaps the same children who had eagerly followed the 'prophet' and lit his 'pyres of vanity'—ducked under the ladder and prodded the poor men's legs with sharpened sticks. This ghastly spectacle inspired the future author of the *Prince* to write his disillusioned maxim: 'Unarmed prophets always come to a sorry end.'

Popular unrest, the disruption caused by the French occupation, by the intrigues of the *palleschi*, and by the sad confusion of the *piagnoni*, all called for a powerful man to restore order to the cracking Republic. The 'government by all' had proved its instability, its muddle-headedness and its impotence. After the 'Dictatorship of God' had gone up in smoke along with Savonarola, Florence demanded another dictatorship, but the people required that the dictator be chosen by them. The Florentines thought they had found the very 'powerful man' they needed in Pietro

58. Marble bust of Piero de' Medici (il Gottoso), by Mino da Fiesole, 1453. *Bargello, Museo Nazionale.*

132

Soderini, who was appointed Gonfaloniere.

Soderini was an honest, conscientious and intelligent man. His genuine devotion to the public good was well known. He was a citizen who was widely respected for his upright life, for his impeccable morals and for the modesty of his ambitions. In any case, he seemed to be a contrast to Pietro lo Sfortunato. Machiavelli, ever perspicacious and quick-witted, assessed him rather more accurately when he said of him in a nicely turned epigram that when the Gonfaloniere died he would not go to heaven or hell but to the limbo of babies. Machiavelli, whom Pietro Soderini chose as his adviser—which shows that Soderini was an intelligent man—could not convince him that what was needed was a *policy of strength*. A genius, a born leader, a brilliant, strong and decisive 'prince', all of which Soderini was not, would have been daunted by the many problems which faced him: the intrigues of the factions and parties, the plots of the banished citizens, the most active of whom was Pietro de' Medici, the dissatisfaction of the people, the danger of a new invasion from France under the leadership of Louis XII (1498–1515), the rebellion of vassal cities, the financial difficulties and threats from the hereditary enemies of the city. The Gonfaloniere's government suffered from its precarious position, for it was always on the brink of being dismissed by the councils. It also became unpopular when Soderini tried to pass economic reforms which were so badly needed. He presented a plan for progressive taxation to the Great Council a hundred and six times and it was rejected by them exactly a hundred and six times—much to Machiavelli's amusement.

Pietro, in the meantime, was still preparing his triumphant return to Florence and was seeking military support. He had Cesare Borgia's help for a while but did not succeed in his aim. Louis XII whose support he never ceased to implore, finally decided he was against the restoration of the Medici. Pietro came to an unfortunate end in a shipwreck in 1503 and so never lived to see his native city welcome him home. Upon his disappearance, the financial inheritance, the political aspirations, and the power of the Medici (if one can talk of power at a time when the family was banished and when Florence was less amenable than ever to its return) were passed on to Pietro's two brothers, to Giovanni, who was a Cardinal, and to Giuliano, who was to become Duke of Nemours, and whose sculpted portrait appears in the Medici tombs in San Lorenzo by Michelangelo (see plate 42).

Giuliano who was the new leader of the family, dubbed himself with the nickname by which he was known to his contemporaries and to posterity. He called himself *Popolesco*, to indicate that he was returning to the rank and file, that he merely wanted to be a common-or-garden citizen, a loyal democrat. This token offering to Florentine sensibilities, which were just as touchy, and as vindictive as ever, was to pave the way for a Medici return; this head of the family had declared himself a 'man of the people', a believer in liberal institutions. The Cardinal Giovanni was not regarded as favourably as was his brother; they had not forgotten the part he had played during the commotion which preceded his brother Pietro's expulsion. There was in any case a sizeable opposition to the restoration of the Medici power which paid lip-service to liberal factions but which would probably aim to build up a form of monarchy again. A *de facto* monarchy, if not a titular one, was however what the people probably needed. In spite of its weaknesses the Soderini government continued in power for some years, and was able to survive the attempts of the *palleschi* faction to secure the return of the Medici, as well as the mounting criticism of Soderini from less biased citizens. Cardinal Giovanni de' Medici was not inactive in the meanwhile, however; he had been working for some time for a meeting between the principal foreign powers interested in the future of Italy, and this finally took place in 1511, when King Louis XII of France, the Emperor Maximilian, King Ferdinand of Spain and Pope Julius II met at Mantua to arrange a peace settlement

59. Marble bust of Battista Sforza by Francesco Laurana, mid-1470's. *Bargello, Museo Nazionale.*

for the peninsula. The Cardinal used the opportunity to obtain military backing with which to overcome the city's resistance to the return of his family, by persuading the European sovereigns that Florentine anarchy was the principal obstacle to peace, and that it must be quelled. The result was the formation of a new Holy League, with a condottiere commissioned to put an end to these difficulties.

The Spaniard, Ramon de Cardona, at the head of five thousand men reached the outskirts of Florence on August 20, 1512, much to the dismay of its citizens who were once again threatened with the horrors of a siege and the discomforts of foreign occupation. They were relieved to learn that Cardona would settle for a contribution of one hundred and forty thousand ducats which would be divided amongst the kings; the principal conditions were that the Medici were to be restored and that Pietro Soderini be exiled and thus pay the price of the reconciliation. Soderini was happy to exchange places with the exiled Medici for it saved his life. A few ungrateful councillors had proposed that the Gonfaloniere's head be offered to the enemy and the poor man had to go to great lengths to hold on to it, never walking abroad without a personal bodyguard.

The populace was as ever ready to reverse their opinions overnight. They managed to convert their old hatred into a renewed enthusiasm with an ease and a rapidity that leaves the historian bewildered. The descriptions of the celebrations which welcomed the Cardinal and his brother would lead one to believe that they were overjoyed to receive back the exiled family, which had been regarded as highly dangerous until only a few days before these celebrations. Giuliano was thirty-three, he understood politics and aimed to be an honest and loyal leader. He was determined to keep his democratic promises and to be democratic in every aspect of political life, including his dealings with foreign powers. He shaved off his beard; he dressed in a modest way; he would stop to chat with shopkeepers and tradesmen whenever he walked abroad. He restored order to the democratic institutions and then pretended to keep out of politics and let them evolve freely. He got on with his own business and took up that Medici tradition of patronage which Pietro had interrupted. In spite of this appearance of restraint, however, Giuliano was really little more than an instrument in the ambitious hands of Cardinal Giovanni: in 1513 he became Pope Leo X and from then on directed the Republic's political life according to his own ambitions and interest.

VII   The Medici at the Vatican

Giovanni de' Medici, the future Pope Leo X, was fourteen in 1489, when Pope Innocent VIII awarded him a cardinalate, by way of strengthening relations with the 'uncrowned king of Florence'. Lorenzo the Magnificent had for some time wanted to secure this foothold in the Church government, so that his son could expand and promote the family interests at an ecclesiastical level. Lorenzo's paternal ambitions followed the practice of aristocratic families, in which the eldest son received a title and the domains attached to it, while the younger sons were assigned to honourable and profitable positions as soldiers or in the Church. The temporal power over the Papal States gave St Peter's successors leading rôles to play in the concert of the European states, although their power obviously owed much of its sway to its spiritual weapons, to excommunications and interdictions and to the propaganda circulated abroad by the propagators of the faith, the bishops, priests, and religious orders.

It can be argued, of course, and indeed it became the principal argument of the anti-papal factions, that the authority of the Holy See was contaminated by the materialistic activities involved in governing a state and that the Pope had had to set aside his principal rôle of exemplifying absolute morality because of his involvement in intrigues and compromises which were regulated by the totally relative morality of individuals and groups. The papacy's temporal power was subject to a great deal of criticism during the Middle Ages and still more criticism during the Renaissance. These attacks culminated in the denunciation of the *Donation of Constantine,* the document on which the Pope's temporal power was based, as a crass forgery. Popes had also used and abused their temporal power to wage unjust wars in their own or their families' interest, by which the prosperity and prestige of the Church itself had often been endangered.

A split personality was demanded of the Pope, which often produced that paradox of the Pope who administered his spiritual duties honourably, scrupulously and with dignity, carrying out his spiritual functions correctly and according to the rules of Church dogma and morality, but who then, in the name of his temporal sovereignty, committed flagrant injustices and crimes, or allowed them to be committed under the mantle of ecclesiastical inviolability, such as, for instance, Alexander VI Borgia (1492–1503). Borgia had not been a bad Pope, ecclesiastically speaking, but his power had been badly abused by his son Cesare, who acted as the Gonfaloniere of the Church, Commander-in-Chief of the papal armies, which were called the Regiments of the Keys (after the Keys of St Peter). His position had also been weakened by the activities of his daughter Lucrezia Borgia, whose innumerable marriages were arranged and annulled for purely political reasons, causing such a scandal that she was still talked of centuries later.

It was agreed that Giovanni's election to the cardinalate would not be publicly announced for three years, by which time he would be nearing the legal age of manhood. This would avoid the obvious objections that would be raised by the candidate's youth and by the fact that he was not even a priest. He had received minor orders in 1483, when he was eight and his father had arranged then that he be given some ecclesiastical benefices. This was a first step in the direction of what was to be a remarkably brilliant and prosperous career. His beginnings were modest; his first benefices came from the revenues of a French abbey, the Abbey of Pin, near Poitiers; this was not a bad start for an eight-year-old. He did a little better four years later when he was appointed Abbot of the powerful and magnificent monastery at Monte Cassino.

A little boy could not actually be expected to fulfil these responsibilities. His offices therefore remained honorary and remunerative functions while he continued to study assiduously in the family palace at Via Larga under the tutelage of eminent teachers secured by his father: Gregorio da Spoleto, Ardiani, and the illustrious Hellenist Chalcondylas. This intellectual training was by now an established Medici tradition. It developed Giovanni's literary tastes and interests, while his appreciation and understanding of the visual arts seemed to lag behind; some of his biographers usually criticize him for not having used two of the great geniuses of his time, Michelangelo and Leonardo da Vinci, although he must have known of his cousin Cardinal Giulio de' Medici's plans for San Lorenzo (including a project for his own tomb) which were entrusted to Michelangelo. His favours were, however, given very liberally to Raphael on whom he heaped all manner of kindness.

From the portraits, Giovanni appears as large and heavy; he had a soft face, joined to his shoulders by a short, thick neck. He was on the stout side, but he was also very strong, loved sports, and was particularly fond of hunting and fishing. He had beautiful, white, long, fine-fingered hands. His face displayed little energy or strength of will and character, but was nonetheless sympathetic and very kindly. His protuberant, globular eyes, which unexpectedly stared out at one, have a haggard appearance (see plate 15). His eyesight was less than excellent; his biographers claim alternately that he was long and shortsighted. Some say he could not see very well at all; others claim that his eyesight was so remarkable that he was always the huntsman who saw the game most clearly from the greatest distances. His passion for hunting and his fondness for gaming made these his two favourite pastimes. His morals, however, were at all times beyond reproach, in contrast to the sensual excesses of Alexander VI, who was known as 'the most carnal man alive'. His eating habits were unremittingly sober, although he always offered sumptuous repasts to his guests. He ate small portions of simple fare, either as a way of mortifying his flesh or perhaps to prevent himself from growing too fat. Paolo Giovio, who was his first biographer, and his friend and contemporary, reports that 'he always exercised the greatest restraint, and from his earliest years he took great pains to master his natural instincts and the desires of his senses. His meals were frugal; he partook of no meat on Wednesdays, only of vegetables on Fridays and nothing at all on Saturdays'.

He had a great fondness for exotic animals and established a menagerie in the Vatican which boasted many varieties of animals and rare birds. The star of this collection and his pride and joy was an elephant given him by the King of Portugal. He named the elephant Hanno in memory of the Carthaginian elephants who helped the Punic troops to cross the Alps. When the beast died, the Pope was filled with sorrow and forthwith ordered Raphael to paint his portrait 'life size', and commanded an epitaph from the famous humanist Beroaldo. The gigantic corpse was given an honourable resting place at the foot of one of the towers of the great Vatican wall.

Leo X's chief claim to fame, the virtue which his contemporaries most admired, was his predilection for music. He was a great admirer of the French composer Jacques Consilium (1498–1535), Costanzo Festa (1490–1545) and of the Flemish Arcadelt (c. 1514–c. 1565). Contemporaries tell how he was never seen without his 'choir' about him, and how when he was short of money, he would instead confer ecclesiastical benefices on a singer or instrumentalist whom he liked. This was how

60. Bust of Machiavelli in coloured stucco; sixteenth-century Florentine. *Palazzo Vecchio*.

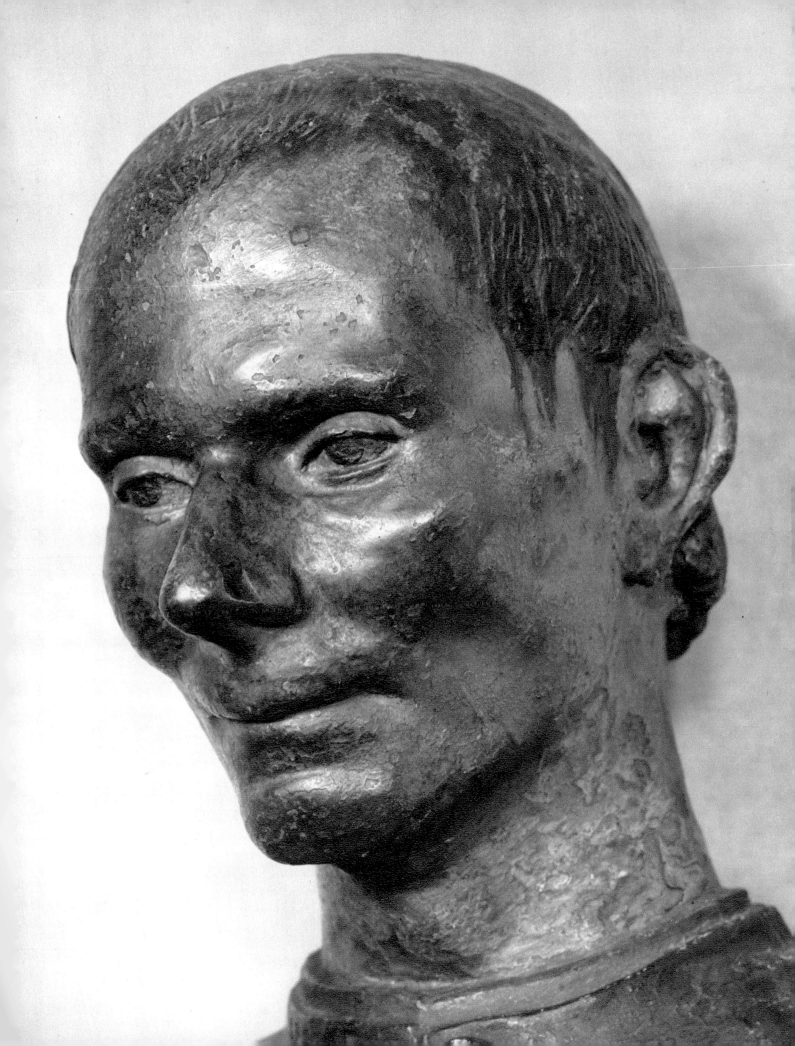

Gabriele Mernio, whose religious inclinations, let alone vocation, had never previously been apparent, came to be Archbishop of Bari. Leo X was also a good Latin scholar with a passion for Cicero and disposed to favour anyone who could speak well in that language.

His relations with Raphael (1483–1520) were of the greatest importance for that artist; he put him in charge of his building operations in Rome, where he was responsible to the Pope for the continuation of the reconstruction of St Peter's, for the construction of the University—the *Sapienza*—and for several new churches. Leo X also undertook the replanning of Rome which the city so badly needed and embellished it and improved its sanitation. In the Vatican itself Leo employed Raphael copiously: first and foremost he continued the commission the painter had received from Julius II to decorate the 'Stanze', official rooms in the Pope's palace, perhaps Raphael's most important work. For Leo he painted the Stanza di Eliodoro (the 'Heliodorus room'), including the portrait of Leo X on horseback as Pope Leo the Great turning away Attila the Hun from Rome (see plate 47). This was followed by the painting of the *loggie*, or balconies, of Leo's apartments in a style reminiscent of ancient Rome which had a profound influence on decorative painting for a long time to come. Raphael also carried out the cartoons for a series of ten tapestries for the lower walls of the Sistine Chapel for Leo, tapestries that were woven in Flanders; Raphael's cartoons were sent to the Brussels factories and seven of them finally entered the collection of Charles I of England, and can be seen in the Victoria and Albert Museum in London (see fig. 42). In their own time Raphael's designs for these tapestries were regarded as being amongst the greatest works of the age.

It was during Leo X's reign also that the Medici first approached Michelangelo to work in the church of San Lorenzo in Florence, which was to house some of his finest sculpture; in 1520 Cardinal Giulio de' Medici (the future Clement VII) commissioned him to work on the design of the *Sagrestia Nuova* (New Sacristy) as a setting of a series of Medici tombs, including those of Lorenzo the Magnificent and Leo X, although in the end Michelangelo only completed those of Giuliano, Duke of Nemours, and Lorenzo, Duke of Urbino, son of Pietro lo Sfortunato (see plate 42 and fig. 43). Earlier he had been asked to design a façade for the Church itself (a model

Fig. 42 Cartoon for the tapestry for the Sistine Chapel, showing the *Healing of the Lame Man*, one of a series made for Leo X by Raphael. (390 × 520 cms.) *London, Victoria and Albert Museum.*

61. Marble bust of the writer and pharmacist Matteo Palmieri by Antonio Rossellino, 1468. *Bargello, Museo Nazionale.*

Fig. 43 Tomb of Lorenzo, Duke of Urbino, in the New Sacristy, San Lorenzo, by Michelangelo.

62. Seated statue of Giovanni delle Bande Nere by Bandinelli, in Piazza San Lorenzo, 1540. The plinth has reliefs depicting his victories.

remains in the Casa Buonarroti) which was never carried out (although his design for the inside wall of the façade was completed); later, in the reign of Clement VII, he also designed and built part of the magnificent staircase for the Library of the Church (see plate 40), founded by Cosimo in 1444, later to become the Biblioteca Laurenziana of the Medici Grand-Dukes. (His designs for the ceiling of the Library and the Library's reading-room itself, were carried out by Vasari in 1571.) Altogether the work done for the Medici Popes by Raphael and Michelangelo was the result of some of the most important commissions that the family had ever given.

The success, if not the birth, of the Reformation in Germany is often attributed to Leo's campaign for the selling of indulgences whose revenues were to finance the completion of the new St Peter's. Previously donations had been collected throughout Europe, but the generosity of the faithful had proved insufficient to meet the building expenses. Indulgences were an old practice. They were a way of purchasing penitence, as a worthy substitute for the usual punishments imposed on sinners. A great

Left:
Fig. 44 Drawing by an unknown 16th-century artist after *Dawn* by Michelangelo. *London, British Museum.*

Right:
Fig. 45 Drawing of Andrea Quaratesi (1512-85) by Michelangelo. The artist may have lived in Quaratesi's house in 1530 when this unusual portrait would have been made. (41.1 × 29.2 cms.) *London, British Museum.*

63. Equestrian statue (bronze) of Grand Duke Cosimo I by Giovanni Bologna in the Piazza della Signoria (1594).

deal has been said about this 'sale' of indulgences, but it was really nothing more than a chance for sinners to expiate their sins by making a payment that corresponded in quantity to the quality and the degree of their wrong. That one could be released from punishment for wrong-doing by paying a sum which would contribute towards the reconstruction of the greatest and most beautiful cathedral in Christendom was regarded by many as sufficiently immoral and indecent to justify direct attack on the clerics that disseminated the indulgences. Through these men in turn it was possible to strike a few indirect blows at the Pope who profited directly from this practice.

The scandal caused by the sale of indulgences should be placed in proper perspective. In order to do this, one must take into account the moral climate of the day and particularly what one might call the *morality of money*. It was, for instance, perfectly acceptable that newly appointed cardinals should commemorate their accession by endowing the pontifical treasury with large sums; hence the claim that they 'bought' their elections and that the highest bidder was the preferred candidate, which is what this practice meant. The remittance of an abbey's revenues to an eight-year-old boy whom he had never seen, and who was never likely to set eyes on the abbey itself, might also appear immoral. Leo X has always been taken to task for his extravagance, but one can also argue that anyone who has ever been in the public eye has at one time or another been called either a spendthrift or a miser. Leo X was always short of money because he distributed it about him so liberally, to humanists, musicians, to the needy, even to jesters. During his audiences or at table he always kept a bag full of money by his side from which he dispensed uncounted handfuls.

Although he was often reduced to selling his own jewelry and to borrowing

money from bankers willing to give him credit, often at the usurious rates of interest
that were current in those times, he never sank to disposing of church property.
He needed the extra money, not to lavish upon table and court in the opulent style
which historians have too often exaggerated, but more to meet the expenses of the
Sapienza, and to cover the costs of his growing Library. He also needed sizeable
sums to steal away university professors, from other universities, to whom he
proffered temptingly high salaries; when these proved insufficient he would sometimes try threats as well. The professors who thus came to the Sapienza were subjected to austere disciplines; the slightest deviations from the prescribed regulations
were punishable by fines to be deducted from their salaries and by reprimands from
the Pope himself. Leo X was of the opinion that lecturing was but a part, and perhaps
the least important part, of university instruction; he required that the professors
should make themselves available to their students outside the classroom and be
ready at all times to answer their questions.

Modern and classical languages were not the only subjects read at the Sapienza.
Natural sciences, botany, astronomy, medicine were also taught. Greek was Leo X's
first love, as it had been for his ancestors. He assembled a circle of ten young members
of aristocratic Greek families whom he placed under the authority of the famous
Hellenist Masurus, so that Greek could be taught in a more modern way than was
usual in universities of the day, which would ensure that the language of Homer
became literally a 'living language' for those who studied it. Leo endowed his
private library and that of the University with all the manuscripts he could lay his
hands on; he even retained scholars to engage in this 'hunt for rare works'. They
scoured the whole of Europe rather like erudite ferrets, going as far afield as the Isle

of Gotland, off the Swedish mainland, covered with old churches whose convent and chapel cupboards yielded some rich finds. The director of the Vatican library under Leo, Cardinal Inghirami, was a well-known humanist, nicknamed Fedra Inghirami because he had written a tragedy about Phaedra which had been modestly successful (see fig. 49).

While the Pope, like all the Medici, devoted considerable time and energy to cultural activities, as much out of a sense of duty as for his own pleasure, this did not prevent him from conducting his affairs with considerable skill, although he was inclined to be a little over-cautious, and indulge in a degree of subtlety which frequently rebounded to his detriment. His tasks were not easy for the Church was in an extremely difficult position. It was during his reign, as we have seen, that the Reformation broke loose in Germany. He took little notice at first and neglected to keep a close watch on the rapid and dangerous turn of events. The result of this was that when he finally had to deal with Luther he was at a loss as to how to control a situation that had already become unmanageable. Giovanni de' Medici's tolerance of Martin Luther's attacks on the Vatican and Catholicism was characteristic of this tolerant, possibly even sceptical humanist. He also held a very Italian view of all heterodoxical movements: 'Everything will sort itself out'. Indeed in Italy, everything did sort itself out. Savonarola's tempest had blown itself out in Florence without too much havoc, except for the rather unimpressive holocaust of the 'pyres of vanity'. All the reforming spirits that had sprung up in the peninsula had died away of their own accord or were easily put down. Joachino del Fiore and Arnoldo da Brescia had had their devotees and had even roused entire provinces, but the 'Joachimism' and the millenarian 'Johannists' which they inspired, only enjoyed short-lived and geographically rather limited successes. Leo X himself was in regular correspondence with the Dutch philosopher Erasmus, whose learning and intellect and lack of sectarian feeling he matched. He ignored the warnings from the Emperor, who was becoming increasingly anxious that the religious insurrection might well become a political one also. Leo X believed in the legitimate association of temporal and spiritual power, as sanctioned in the *Donation of Constantine*, and never really expected the principle or the practice to be seriously questioned. Luther's insults, the publication of the *Treatise on Christian Liberty*, and of the *Ninety-Five Theses* of Wittenberg (1517), the humiliating burning of the Papal Bull calling the Augustinian to return to the fold of the Church (1520), the immense popularity of all the anti-papal propaganda, the debates, the pamphlets, the distribution at fairs of engraved caricatures of the Pope, bishops, priests, and monks, could not make him realize the scale of the oncoming tempest, which would roar through the Church, shatter its structure, and rock its very foundations.

Leo X conducted his relations with other Italian states and with foreign powers in much the same spirit of compromise and with the same desire to achieve his ends peacefully as he did the internal affairs of the church. His methods were relatively, although not entirely, peaceable, for, sharing as he did that Medici urge to get effective solutions, he could be very cruel, as he was in the Petrucci affair, certainly quite as cruel as his father Lorenzo had been to the people of Volterra. When Machiavelli advocated the implementation of immediate and harsh sanctions, whenever the circumstances demanded, he was merely setting down, and thus justifying the standard practice of contemporary Italian politicians. Public opinion, which is always prone to simplify arbitrarily the philosophies of great men, has given Machiavelli the reputation of an advocate of duplicity and violence: he was in fact a believer in the view, which he presented very cleverly, that honesty will always win and that harsh measures should only be taken as a last resort, when no other course is open to ward off even greater evils.

The Petrucci were an old Sienese family, whose fief had been usurped by the

Fig. 48   Silver medal with the head of Michelangelo by Leone Leoni (Milan), 1564. (*Diameter 6.4 cms.*) *London, Victoria and Albert Museum.*

65.   Detail from the frescoes in the Sassetti chapel, *Santa Trinità*, by Domenico Ghirlandaio, showing Giuliano de' Medici (later Duke of Nemours) as a boy, with his tutor, the humanist Poliziano. The frescoes, which were painted for the Sassetti family in 1485, show incidents in the life of St Francis; the scene in which Pope Honorius approves the Franciscan Order contains portraits of Lorenzo the Magnificent, his children and their tutor.

Medici. They had sworn to avenge themselves and to regain their principality. Alfonso Petrucci was a cardinal, and had made several unsuccessful attempts to kill off Leo X, while out hunting. He had even considered stabbing the Pope during one of the sessions of the Consistory, but had dismissed this spectacular plan as too risky; for if he wore a dagger beneath his robes the Pope might well be wearing a coat of mail beneath his. His thoughts then turned to poison, to which the majority of Renaissance intrigues and conspiracies owed their success. He befriended His Holiness's physician, Vercelli, who was wise enough to dismiss this idea on the grounds that it always left tell-tale traces, which quickly led to the author of the crime. Whenever a public figure died, a prince, a condottiere, or a pope, everyone immediately wondered if he had been poisoned. (When Leo X died, in fact, rumour had it that poison was the cause.) The physician conceived a more discreet and foolproof plan. He had been treating Leo X for an anal ulcer for some time. His patient trusted him implicitly. He advised the Pope to submit to an operation that could finally cure him.

The Pope may have been warned because in this kind of plot there were often double-agents; he rejected the surgeon's recommendation, who immediately smelled a rat and took to his heels. Petrucci, fearing that his accomplice may have denounced him, also fled from Rome. A suit was filed against the real assassins. As was the custom, the occasion was taken to eliminate not only the true culprits but also all the possible culprits. Several cardinals were implicated, who were forced to make amends by paying large fines. The main conspirators, Cardinal Petrucci (who had been caught), Cardinal Riario (the same Cardinal Riario who had been involved in the Pazzi plot which had cost Leo X's uncle Giuliano de' Medici his life), and Bandinello de Sauli, were strangled after their death sentences had been read to them by a writer whom one would never have imagined capable of performing such a function, the sweet poet of the *Asolani*, Pietro Bembo. The more inferior-ranking accomplices were hanged, drawn, and quartered.

This severity seemed out of character in a man whose accession to the papal crown had been achieved quite unmelodramatically—rather by skilfully taking advantage of circumstances. Reviewing Leo X's career, one finds few examples of dare-devil intrepidity. He was very much the Cosimo type of circumspect negotiator. He had been a cardinal during Alexander VI's tempestuous papacy (1492–1503) and had managed to survive quite unscathed. Although he had rather unwisely been a rival candidate in the papal election, he never begrudged Alexander his papal crown. Nor did he raise obstacles to the election of his successor Cardinal della Rovere, who became Julius II (1503–1513). He actively supported the new Pope's anti-French policy, because this was a means to regaining control of Florence and to re-establishing his family in their native town and to their position there, which they had lost after the death of Lorenzo the Magnificent. He was appointed papal legate to Perugia, then to Bologna, where he seconded the bellicose policies of the 'warrior Pope', as Julius II came to be known. He was loyal to his superior and refused to be part of a conspiracy of rebel cardinals that plotted against della Rovere and who tried to bring together a council that would depose him. (All the popes of this period, Leo X himself, his predecessors Julius II and Alexander VI, and later Clement VII were haunted by a fear that a council would be called to depose them.)

He was taken prisoner by the French during the siege of Ravenna and was led thus to Louis XII, whose retinue included the rebellious, but free, cardinals who had tried to persuade Louis to support their conspiracy. He made his escape one night disguised as an ordinary soldier, with the help of some trusted friends who had prepared the way, taking advantage of the disorder that prevailed when the retreating French had to ford the Po at Pavia, and crossed safely to freedom himself. After a few adventurous weeks, during which he was again captured and again

Fig. 49 Portrait of Fedra Inghirami by Raphael (1515). *Pitti.*

66. *Tobias and the Angel,* by a follower of Verrocchio, showing Tobias dressed in the height of contemporary Florentine fashion (second half of fourteenth century). *London, National Gallery.*

67, 68, 69, 70. Four lunettes with views of Medici houses—Villa di Castello, Palazzo Pitti with the Belvedere, Villa di Pratolino, Villa di Poggio a Caiano—by van Hutens, a Dutch artist working in Florence towards the end of the sixteenth century. *Museo di Firenze Com'Era.*

150

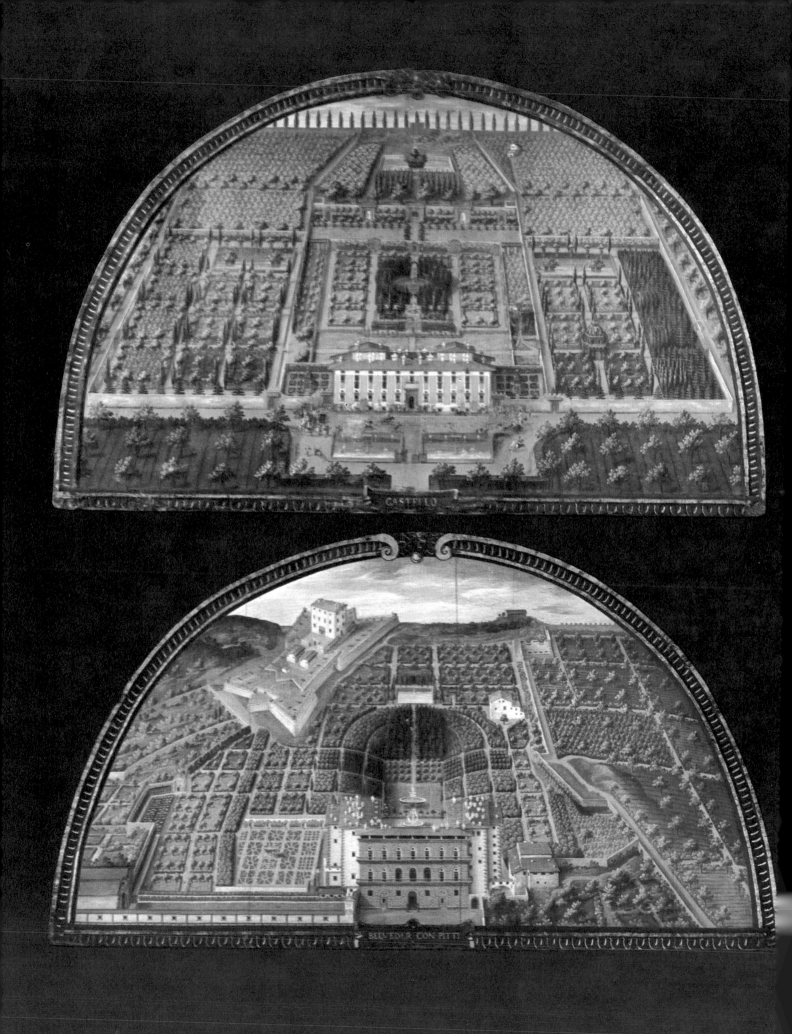

CASTELLO

BELVEDER CON PITTI

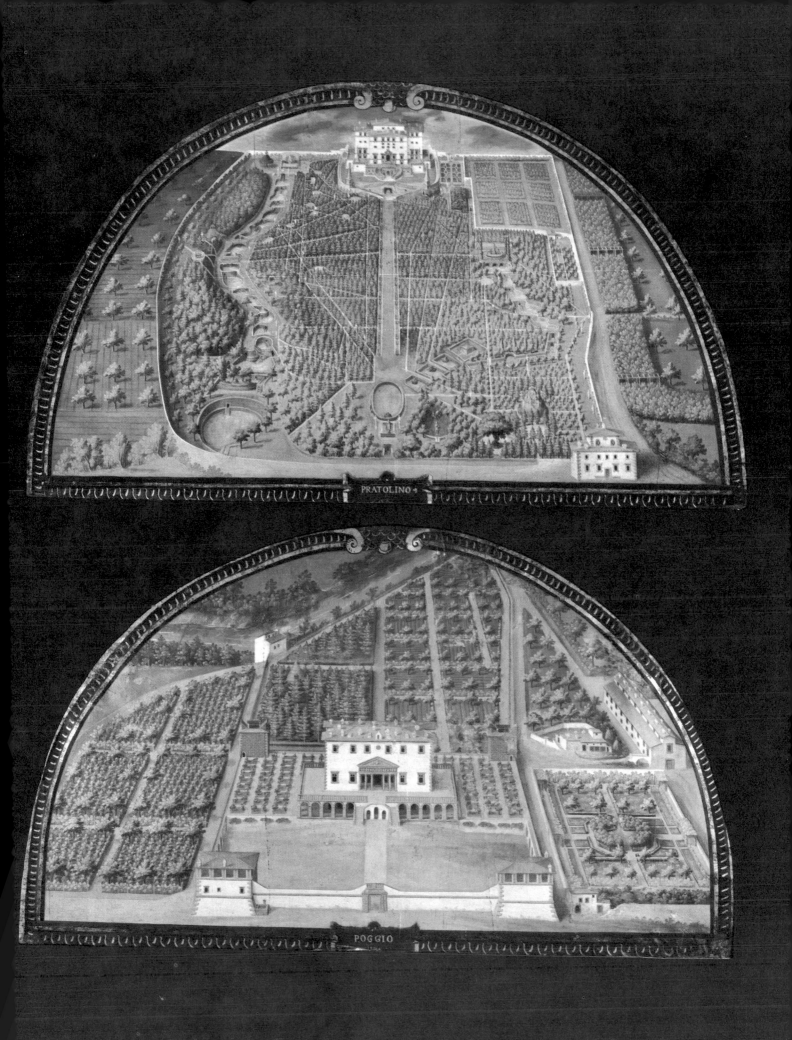

PRATOLINO

POGGIO

escaped, he reached Mantua where he joined some of the opponents of Soderini and the 'popular' government in Florence (who were therefore, by definition, supporters of the Medici). Subsequently, as we have seen, the combined efforts of Pope, Emperor, Venice, and Spain, backed by the terror which German troops provoked in Tuscany, had enabled the Medici allies to re-enter the conquered city on August 31, 1512.

The return of the Medici to Florence, where they had played such a decisive rôle for more than a century, fortified Cardinal Giovanni's position in the College of Cardinals. When Julius II died on February 21, 1513, it was clear that of all the *papabili* (the candidates to be considered for the papacy) the Florentine had the best chance. The conclave lasted seven days, however, before a final decision was reached. Some historians even maintain that Giovanni's abcessed anus which, it was generally thought, would kill him soon, won him the election! Indeed, he only reigned on St Peter's throne for eight years, dying in 1521.

His last years were clouded by a heavy burden of difficult political situations and by his steadily worsening malady. He was forced to undergo an operation in 1516, but he continued to suffer, although he had a robust constitution. It is believed that he contracted malaria at Malliana in 1521, where he was supervising the manoeuvres and the progress of the papal army, which was engaged in expelling the French from Lombardy under the command of Prospero Colonna and Federigo Gonzaga. The Pope's illness soon caused anxiety, although he followed his troops' progress with enormous enthusiasm and was delighted by their conquests of Parma and Milan. He was not, however, to have the pleasure of witnessing their final victory. He deteriorated quickly. Within four days he was so ill that there seemed no hope for him. The priest summoned to administer last unction arrived too late.

Did poison accelerate the decline of this chronically sick man? His cupbearer Malespina was suspected, arrested, questioned, but finally released for lack of any substantial evidence. The corpse decomposed so rapidly that an examination of his viscera would have produced no more convincing evidence. His adversaries' pleasure at being rid of him was expressed in the almost universal outbursts of joy which greeted the news of his death. Florence manifested its glee by declaring a public holiday and putting on a fireworks display; the loyalty formerly shown the illustrious bankers had been dismally eclipsed. This hostility indicates that Leo had unwittingly created much enmity around him, and it was probably the inevitable outcome of his policies. He always tried to avoid endangering himself by taking sides alternatively with and against his various adversaries; this made him no friends and alienated everyone. When his predecessor, the aggressive and warlike Julius II, was asked by Michelangelo how he wished to be portrayed, he replied, 'Put a sword in my hand for I would not know how to hold a book . . .'; Leo X, on the other hand, had always gone into battle reluctantly, except for that one occasion when he actively risked war as a means to regain Florence.

One of the most striking characteristics of Leo X's reign, and also of that of his cousin Clement VII, who became Pope after the short interval of Adrian VI (1521–1523), was an abiding preoccupation with the recovery of Florence, which dominated the Vatican's policies in Italy. The fifteenth-century marriage between the City of the Lily and the Medici family had seemed indissoluble; the city's commercial prosperity and its government's power had been deeply involved in this association. Exiled from the city, which in the end they had ruled almost as kings, the Medici were cruelly humiliated by the replacement of their *palle* with the emblems of the *popolani*. Leo X, who shared his ancestors' pride in the dynasty, never felt that his tiara could compensate for the loss of Florence. He calculated, no doubt, that the immense spiritual and material power he had at his disposal could be manipulated to achieve his main ambition, the domination of Tuscany. This overruling priority

71. Portrait of Grand Duke Cosimo I, by Bronzino, 1545. *Museo Mediceo.*

155

lay at the basis of all his dealings with Milan, Venice, Naples, the King of France, and the Emperors. It coloured and directed his every action, decision, and hesitation, his masterful plans and his errors.

Julius II had loved playing at war. Leo X followed his instinct and disposed his pawns on the European chequerboard by diplomatic methods, convinced that he would achieve his ends more effectively with diplomacy than with force. Tortuous diplomacy is often the instrument of the weak; Giovanni de' Medici's negotiations always betrayed his weakness, his preference for trickery, and his reluctance to commit himself or to risk himself. He used the same methods against the expansion of the German heresy as he did in his negotiations with foreign ambassadors in Rome. His schemes often paid off. At their best, they resulted in the disbanding of the coalitions that formed against him, or through them he managed to sow the seeds of distrust and discord among allies where associations threatened him. His diplomacy, however, always struck his contemporaries as underhand; posterity has not revised this opinion. He was bound to produce this reaction for he possessed neither Alexander VI's unscrupulousness, nor Julius II's taste for violent methods.

Circumstances may have forced him to adopt policies which would previously have been regarded as pusillanimous or cowardly, but it was perhaps already obvious that papal power was on the wane. First it was battered by the assaults of the Reformers, even in Italy; in the College of Cardinals itself a majority of the cardinals had tried to get a decision from one of the Church Councils that the body of the Church as a whole was superior to individual Popes, and that the Popes should not be regarded as omnipotent. The general disenchantment was becoming still more obvious abroad. France resisted the papal authority, her church was essentially Gallican, although she still claimed to be the 'eldest daughter of the Church'; England and the German states were drifting away from the body of Catholicism and not for exclusively religious, dogmatic, or moral reasons, since politics played an important part in these developments. The solidarity and integrity of the Papal States had been on the wane, for the independent principalities in Italy had begun to entrench themselves round the leadership of their main cities, such as Naples, Milan, Venice; this development was especially noticeable after the Empire, Spain, and France began to claim certain portions of Italy, and turned the peninsula into a battleground on which to settle their disputes. Excommunication and interdiction were also no longer the effective instruments that they had been; the states did not capitulate in awed submission when threatened. The growing prevalence of a spirit of debate and of the notion of free will, robbed the Church of its power to assert its infallibility absolutely and so force rebels to capitulate without argument. Alexander VI tried in vain to deal with this progressive decline by advocating a form of political unification, as sought also by his son Cesare Borgia, a unity which would have provided a solid basis for an omnipotent papacy. Julius II had waged war on behalf of papal power like a general. Leo X used all his intelligence, his energy and the prestige that his crown gave him to create discord among the many powers ready to bear down on Italy and to crush him. It was unlikely that the Papal States would be spared in the event of a victorious King of France or a German Emperor deciding to carve up the Italian States to his own advantage.

Leo X reigned at a time in European history when papal authority over kings and peoples had been sharply reduced, and was becoming even weaker. Guicciardini who gave due recognition to Leo X's particular gifts, summed up his career when he said 'he reigned with greater political insight and with more success than was expected'—expected, that is, of a Pope who was devoted to music and literature and totally absorbed by his personal interests. He bequeathed his successor, the Flemish cardinal of Utrecht, who became Adrian VI, a stable enough papacy for him to reign without danger, although he died after only two years. It was left to another

72. Four precious objects from the Medici collection, *Palazzo Pitti, Galleria degli Argenti:*
A. Jasper glass decorated with gold and surmounted by a pearl; French, fifteenth century. (*Height* 18 cms.)
B. Jasper vase in the form of Hydra, surmounted by the figure of Hercules in gold; vase attributed to Michele Mazzafini, and Hercules to Giovanni Bologna, late sixteenth century. (*Height* 34 cms.)
C. Rock crystal box incised with scenes of the life of Christ. Made by Valerio Belli for Clement VII and given to Francis I of France on the occasion of the marriage of Catherine de' Medici to the future Henri II (1533). (*Height* 15 cms. *Length* 26.7 cms.)
D. Vessel of rock crystal in the shape of a mythical bird; Florentine, mid-sixteenth century. (*Height* 33 cms.)

CLEMENS. VII. PONT. MAX. IVLIANI MED. F.

Medici, Giulio, illegitimate son of the handsome Giuliano killed by the Pazzi, who became Clement VII on Adrian's demise in 1523, to live through the darkest hours in the history of the Church and of Italy.

Clement VII could not prevent the Imperial army from sacking Rome in 1527, nor its siege of Florence, both of which were particularly murderous as well as destructive to works of art. He faced political problems which were of the same order and of the same insolubility as those with which Leo X had tried to deal. Like his cousin Giovanni, Giulio found himself caught in the crossfire between the empire of Charles V (reigned 1519–1555), the France of François I (reigned 1515–1547), and the King of England, Henry VIII (reigned 1509–1547), who was trying to manoeuvre the Pope to accept the changes of his marital requirements. He chose to survive this crossfire, as Leo X had before him, by bargaining, evasions, double-dealing. Only the powerful can afford the luxury of straightforward honesty. Fearing that his enemies might overcome their temporary divisions and reunite against him, and fearing that he would be betrayed, he made his own alliances. He did not fail because of any ineptitude on his part, for he was more gifted in the art of intrigue than even Leo X had been, but rather because events were then following an historical course which individual efforts could no longer hope to arrest, let alone reverse.

Giulio de' Medici was forty-five when he became Pope. He is said to have been less artistically inclined than other members of his family, although commissioning the Michelangelo tombs, which he struggled in vain to make the disaffected artist complete. He resembled his father physically (see fig. 51). He was tall and lithe, his features were pleasing and he was fairly amiable. He was more practically minded and tried to encourage the more exacting and utilitarian sciences, mechanics, hydraulics and architecture. Although he was always willing to discuss theological and philosophical subjects, he gave the impression of doing so only as a dialectical exercise. He possessed none of Leo X's easy-going generosity, nor his fat benevolence; he was cold, caustic, calculating, and withdrawn. One suspects that he chose the name Clement VII at his election ironically, for nothing in his nature was remotely akin to clemency. The punitive measures which he used to deal with the Florentine rebels after he regained the city in 1530, make Cesare Borgia's atrocities pale by comparison. He could not have claimed that these horrors were not committed at his behest, nor that he had had no knowledge of them. His adversaries deplored his lack of scruples, his untrustworthiness, and his deceitfulness and his conduct often bore out these charges.

On the other hand, one must stress the gravity of the perils that surrounded him; his only weapon against them was his own intelligence. His greatest fear, as it had been for his predecessors, was that a general council would assemble, for which a large number of churchmen were clamouring; it was bound considerably to weaken his power and that of the papacy in the future. While from without the Church was being attacked furiously by the reformers, from within its time-honoured structure was being called into question by demands for a return to the ancient purity of Christianity. The Church did not have armies great and powerful enough to fight off the European monarchs that invaded Italy; the ecclesiastical hierarchy was not sufficiently secure and trouble-free to quell heretical movements. Clement VII consequently spent his eleven papal years steering as prudently as he could through troubled waters; in spite of the disastrous sack of Rome, and England's and Germany's break with the Church, it can be claimed for him that he did manage to avoid total shipwreck.

An anecdote shows Clement VII in his true light and depicts his cunning methods for extricating himself from difficult situations. A famous soldier, Federigo Gonzaga, Marquis of Mantua, had joined forces with the Emperor, but the Pope wished to lure him over to his side. The Marquis made it known that he would be ready to side with the Pope on condition that he be given a painting of Raphael's that he greatly admired, the portrait of Leo X now in the Palazzo Pitti in Florence (see plate 15). The portrait hung at that time in the old Medici palace. Clement VII accepted the bargain and had the portrait brought to Rome and asked Andrea del Sarto to make a copy of it so that the Medici might keep the effigy of this illustrious member of their family. When the copy was finished, it was identical to the original; it fooled even the sharpest experts, including Giulio Romano, who had been Raphael's pupil. Clement VII decided therefore to keep the original, and send Gonzaga the copy.

It can be argued, of course, that Gonzaga's fidelity to the papal cause was about as genuine as the painting he received, but the story shows that Clement VII was not loath to resort to such stratagems in order to achieve his ends. His principal aims were three: to prevent a general council; to manoeuvre in such a way that the ship of the Church, the 'Navicella', would not be driven onto the rocks; and to keep Florence at all costs under the total, unchallenged hegemony of the Medici.

Three years after his election (1526), rebellion and discontent erupted in Rome itself. The powerful Colonna family, which usually opposed the interests of the Holy See (except when it was occupied by one of its members), joined with the Emperor in an attack on the Vatican. Clement VII had to take refuge in Castel Sant' Angelo reaching it by way of the secret passage built by Alexander VI. This fortress could withstand considerable siege. His enemies were not after his blood, but they demanded that he renounce all claims to Lombardy and dissociate himself from the most recent Holy League, which he had joined. Clement VII recovered his freedom by agreeing to do everything. As soon as he was released, he attacked the Colonna, whose estates he laid waste and whose castle he razed to the ground. Nor did he relinquish François I's cause, which offered continued hope of helping him get rid of the Imperial forces. His loyalty to François I was rewarded by the arrangement of a marriage between his young cousin Caterina de' Medici and the heir to the French throne, the future Henri II. This was a masterly stroke. The family of Florentine bankers had entered the highest aristocracy and were now entitled to

74. *The Death of Procris* by Piero di Cosimo, end of fifteenth century. (65 × 183 cms.) *London, National Gallery.*

75. *Venus and Mars* by Botticelli, mid 1480's. (69 × 173.5 cms.) *London, National Gallery.*

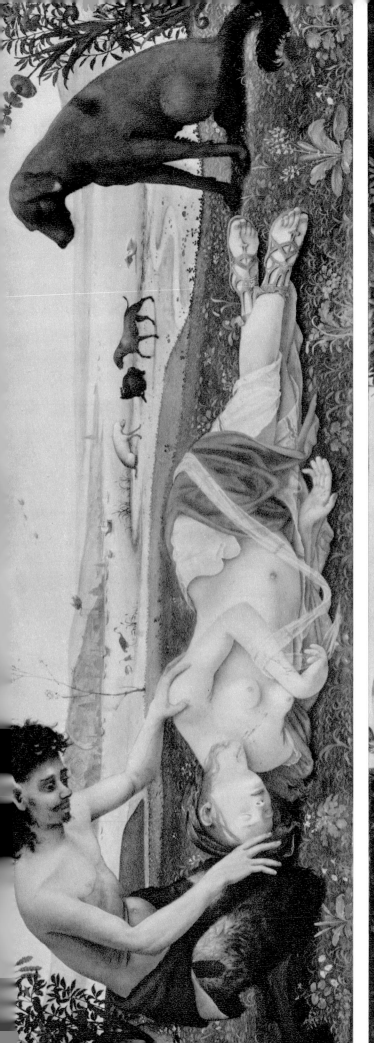

incorporate the lilies of France with the *palle*, one of the golden balls being decorated
with a lily from then on.

The French alliance did not, however, protect Rome from the wrath of Charles V.
His army was largely manned by Lutheran *Landsknechts* (German foot-soldiers)
who, far from merely pillaging Rome, were positively determined to avenge themselves on the 'Great Babylon'. When the German general Frundsberg died, the
Constable of Bourbon took command of the Imperial army and directed its
campaigns. His violence and ferocity overcame any challenge to his march on Rome.
His desire to occupy and devastate the Eternal City became so strong that on May 6,
1527, he insisted on climbing the first ladder laid against the city walls, whereupon
he was struck down by a shot from an arquebus and died. Benvenuto Cellini prided
himself, that it was he who pulled the trigger.

The horrors of the sack of Rome have been told so often that it would be pointless
to describe them again here. Clement VII held out in the Castel Sant' Angelo for
seven months, while the German foot-soldiers heaped destruction on the surrounding
town. The situation became so desperate that the Pope had to ask Cellini, who had
stayed by him, to break up the papal tiara and convert it into gold and jewels to
pay his men. The long incarceration in Castel Sant' Angelo was so depressing that
the captive wondered if the monument that had been built to house the Emperor
Hadrian's tomb would now become his also. He was cut off from any news, other
than the occasional bits of information that reached him when a messenger risked
penetrating the Imperial troops that surrounded him. When he found out from an
audacious, but never identified, messenger that the Papal States like Ferrara and
Urbino were engaged in re-establishing their independence, that Venice was
casting a covetous eye upon Ferrara, and that a revolution had once again expelled
the Medici from Florence, Clement VII made up his mind to escape. Under cover
of darkness, one winter's night, he managed to get out in the guise of a pedlar and
fled to Orvieto.

He could not return to the capital of Christendom until October 1528. He found
Rome burnt and pillaged, her art treasures carried off. The sorry state of Florence,
however, probably enraged him more, true Medici that he was. Once again (in 1527)
the city had fallen into the hands of a 'popular government' and the main representatives of Clement's authority, Alessandro (bastard of the Duke of Urbino) and

Ippolito (bastard of Giuliano, Duke of Nemours), had been chased away. The only way to reconquer the city was to pursue a policy of reconciliation with the Emperor, for Charles V had incontestably established his superior power. Clement therefore made an approach to his former enemy. At the same time he did not, of course, give up his contacts with the French—the royal marriage was still to take place—nor did he forget to make use of Henry VIII's impatient desire to obtain a papal dispensation to divorce Catherine of Aragon, Charles V's aunt.

Although Florentine glory and prosperity had previously been so closely associated with the Medici, the way in which the second Medici Pope made use of the Imperial forces to reconquer the city is a blot on the history of the family. He had barely diverted the Imperial scourge from Rome when he himself re-directed it at the cradle of his dynasty. Florence could easily provide as magnificent booty as Rome, for the mercenaries, when they won a city, generally compensated for the dangers of battle and the boredom of camp life by destroying all they could lay their brutal, thieving hands upon. The Florentine commander Baglioni's treason when he left the Signoria to join the Imperial forces, his successor Francesco Ferrucci's heroic and chivalrous loyalty, Michelangelo's readiness to put aside painting and sculpture in order to devote himself exclusively to reinforcing the city's ramparts and inventing and constructing war machines, are but a few exciting episodes in this tale. The siege of Florence 1529–1530 endowed the city with a new kind of glory, military glory. She withstood the combined armies of the Emperor and Clement VII for ten long months. It was only after the battle of Gavinana, at which Francesco Ferrucci and the Prince of Orange, the commanders of the two rival armies, were both killed, that the city surrendered.

Clement VII promised by the terms agreed upon their surrender to treat the Florentines with clemency and affection, protesting that such had always been his treatment of his people. In fact, he could hardly have been expected to have any affection whatsoever for the rebels who had ignominiously driven his family out of town, raining insults and jeers upon them and declaring this third Medici expulsion to be the lucky final one. As soon as the Medici's private and political attitudes had begun to seem aristocratic, they were unable to avoid displaying the faults of this class or to escape the resentment which the Florentine people felt against it. The ordinary citizens began to dislike them; and their equals resented and envied them. When they advisedly took to employing a personal bodyguard after the Pazzi conspiracy, there were jibes at the 'praetorian guard'. In the same measure that they tried to become the virtual sovereigns of the city, to seek alliances and marriages with Italian princes and the royal houses of Europe, to increase their prestige and their credit abroad, they lost the support and respect of their own people. The banishments were the inevitable outcome, those long periods of Medici absence from Florence, when a 'pure' republican system was restored to the Palazzo della Signoria and Florence sensed that it might very well survive without the Medici.

Cosimo Pater Patriae had known how to handle his people, to live with them and how to please them. The daily confrontation with Cosimo, il Vecchio, 'the old boy', as he was affectionately known, in the street, at market, or in church, who always recognized and greeted everyone amicably, promptly doffing his hat, had continued in the same intimate atmosphere that had been fostered by the founders of the dynasty, by Salvestro, Averardo, and Bicci; they had brought the family out of its obscurity to fame, but they had never ceased to belong to the popular party. Absence had not, however, done the name of the Medici much good in Florence, and the return of the family in 1512, protected by foreign mercenaries, humiliated and offended the citizens who in any case were no longer led by interest and sentiment to support the *palleschi*, the Medici party. In these years also the Medici were at a disadvantage in so far as the Popes tried to govern their ancestral city like a colony

77. *David* by Verrocchio (1476); this work represents a conscious effort to rival the *David* of Donatello, even though it was completed nearly fifty years later. (*Height* 126 cms.) *Bargello, Museo Nazionale.*

from Rome, imposing their will through intermediaries, Lorenzo, Duke of Urbino, or Alessandro de' Medici. In 1527 the Tuscans turned against them again, feeling them to be strangers to the city, even enemies.

The final return of the family was not a joyful occasion. The masses had always been victims of vicious reprisals of one kind or another as is witnessed in the inevitable outcome of every civil uprising in Florence: even the Ciompi disturbance had ended badly for them. Even so the sanctions ordered by Clement VII were perhaps exaggeratedly and gratuitously cruel, especially considering the unpopular use he had already made of the German and Swiss soldiers of Charles V. July 15, 1531, the day Baccio Valori, who had been appointed to carry on the government of the city between the republican Podestà and the papal lieutenancy which Alessandro de' Medici was to assume, yielded his power to Alessandro, was a day of public mourning. Another day of still greater sorrow was May 1, 1532, when the new ruler stood up before the Council assembled in the Palazzo della Signoria and proclaimed that the Republic was officially abolished; the councils and all the democratic institutions were henceforth to be suppressed. Alessandro dealt the fatal blow to the population's pride and dignity by lowering from the belfry at the top of the communal palace, the Vacca, the old bell that for centuries past had always summoned men of all ages to defend their rights and liberty. This gesture added insult to grave injury and to the thousand deaths incurred during the suppression of the republic. Florence never forgave the much-detested Medici this degrading gesture; the divorce between people and master had been decreed. In 1532 also Alessandro was proclaimed Duke of Florence by Charles V and his first act was to construct a fortress whose cannons were not directed outwards in readiness for a possible enemy, but inwards against a turbulent, exasperated mob capable of far greater atrocities. For this situation, Clement VII was largely to blame.

When the news of Clement VII's death reached Florence on September 25, 1534, those who were willing to brave Alessandro's reprisals lit bonfires of joy. The Romans, who held the Pope responsible for their defeat, for the abominations perpetrated during the sack, and for its catastrophic effects, also manifested their joy. In spite of the resentment he caused, Clement VII was a highly intelligent man and a truly talented statesman, but circumstances did not give him an opportunity to let his good qualities shine through. The proletariat's wrath, that had been frustrated and repressed during his lifetime, had a field day with his corpse, which was snatched from its grave several times and returned mutilated and hacked about; one morning he was even found with a sword thrust through his chest. Thus the manhandled mortal remains of this Pope, who pardoned Michelangelo for his support of the republic in order that he could finish the family tombs in the Sagrestia Nuova at San Lorenzo, took a long time to find rest.

78. Panel from the north doors of the *Baptistry,* showing the Annunciation, sculpted in bronze by Lorenzo Ghiberti between 1403 and 1424; Ghiberti was given the commission after a competition in which Brunelleschi and Jacopo della Quercia had also taken part. (39 × 39 cms.)

VIII

A Man of War: Giovanni delle Bande Nere

Giovanni delle Bande Nere (1498–1526) inherited from Caterina Sforza, his mother (1462–1509), her daring, her dashing courage and her proud bearing. She in turn took after her paternal ancestors, the powerful Dukes of Milan, that line of cruel and ambitious condottieri who sprang from peasant stock and who were made famous by Attendolo Sforza, the first of the Sforza condottieri who acquired a kingdom, which they managed successfully to preserve against the claims both of France and the Empire. When Caterina finally consented for political reasons to marry Giovanni de' Medici in 1497, when she was already thirty-five, she had already been married twice, to Girolamo Riario and then to Giacomo Feo. The hazards of a varied life in troubled and dangerous times had taught her to rely almost exclusively on her own courage, her own judgement, and her own capacity to take and carry out quick decisions.

She lived entirely in the world of condottieri. Her first husband was one; her son by Riario, Ottaviano, received a condotta of fifteen thousand ducats from the Pope for his services in protecting the Church. Riario, himself, who was a nephew of Sixtus IV, was also involved in the Pazzi conspiracy, which robbed the handsome Giuliano de' Medici of his life. His reward for this enterprise was his appointment to the captaincy of the papal armies and governorship of the Castel Sant' Angelo. Riario subjected the cities which came under his command to a viciously tyrannical rule, and was universally detested. When Caterina was widowed, she immediately became a target for the deceased captain's enemies. She managed to hold her own and to protect her possessions (which centred on the town of Forlì) only by entering into devious negotiations and even declaring war. Her next husband Giacomo Feo, a cousin of her first husband, was weak-kneed, spineless and without any distinguishing talent but that he had been her lover for some time.

Feo soon began to resent the step-children he inherited from his wife's previous marriage. They in turn were worried about their step-father's ambitions for their property, and even feared for their lives. Feo was assassinated one evening when returning home on the road to Forlì. It was rumoured that Caterina was responsible for his death, because she had wanted to be rid of him as he had become a nuisance; it was even claimed that it was her sons themselves who killed him. She anticipated and parried historians' suspicions when she uttered the famous sentence that has always been quoted to illustrate the customs and ethics of the Italian Renaissance: 'Our family takes care of its own business and if we need to rid ourselves of anyone, we don't need a stranger's hand to kill him.'

Her third marriage bound her to the younger branch of the Medici family, to Giovanni di Piero Francesco de' Medici. She had always been on friendly terms with Florence, where the title of Honorary Daughter of the Republic had been bestowed on her, and her son Ottaviano had been awarded a condotta of fifteen thousand ducats for furnishing the city with some of the formidable Romagna regiments. (Romagna had always produced excellent soldiers.) The child that was to be known as Giovanni of the Black Bands was born in his mother's principality of Forlì, on April 6, 1498. We first hear of him being brought up in a rather strange environment, in a convent, dressed as a little girl and behaving to all outward appearances in perfect accord with his feminine milieu. In fact Caterina Sforza was involved in all sorts of complicated intrigues which inevitably endangered her children. She may have tried to pass her son off as an inoffensive and effeminate boy in the hope of protecting him from some assassin's knife.

When he was eleven, his mother died and he was sent to Florence, where he became a ward of Jacopo Salviati, who was the brother-in-law of Giuliano de' Medici, Duke of Nemours and Giovanni, who became Pope Leo X in 1513. He was raised by his foster parents in a manner which befitted the glorious *signori* of the city. As he only belonged to the cadet branch of the Medici stock (see family tree page 205) he had no claim to the political and financial fortunes of the main line of the Medici dynasty. These Medici took appropriate precautions to ensure that he was excluded from the functions of the family. Their task was made all the easier because the young man manifested no ambition to dominate his fellow citizens and no interest in becoming a banker. His real ambition was to be a soldier. This was his only goal, his burning desire. 'The blood of the Sforza' seemed to prevail; he never showed a single Medici trait. Just as all the cadet members of noble families in the eighteenth century went into the army or the Church, so the bastards and the sons of the minor branches of the great Italian houses were encouraged or forced to become soldiers of fortune. Historians have sometimes suggested that the senior Medici and Leo X in particular made quite certain that Caterina Sforza's child spent his days on the battlefield because they hoped he would meet an untimely death. In fact, Giovanni's actions and what we know of his tastes, feelings and passions, after he had shed his skirts to don male attire, clearly indicate that the young man was eminently suited to wear armour, that famous black armour in which he covered his soldiers, leading his contemporaries and later historians to call them the 'Black Bands', the soldiers in black.

Fig. 54 Medal showing the head of Giovanni delle Bande Nere by the Venetian Danese Cattaneo, mid-16th century. (*Diameter* 5.8 *cms.*) *London, Victoria and Albert Museum.*

In 1515, when Leo X had been Pope for two years, he brought Salviati's ward to Rome; it is not clear whether this was to give him guidance in his career or to keep him under close surveillance. Giovanni had not been in Rome for long, however, before he fell out with the young Roman aristocrats. The election of a Medici to the Holy See, which the leading Roman families regarded as their property, rendered all Florentines unpopular in Rome. The Colonna and Orsini families in particular, in spite of the latter's marriages to Medici, regarded the Medici as intruders and usurpers, and despised them, because they descended from shopkeepers and money lenders. They were thus forced to fight back to defend their power and prestige. Giovanni quickly acquired the reputation of being a bold and impetuous young man, whose quarrels often ended in street fights. When a band of assassins hired by the Orsini ambushed him in a Roman street one night, he is said to have held his own and gave them a thorough beating with the help of a mere ten companions. The Pope congratulated him for his bravery and decided to put his fighting spirit and warrior qualities to good use, where they could flourish to his advantage. The papal army was marching on Urbino under the command of the Pope's cousin Lorenzo de' Medici, governor of Florence and an experienced soldier. Although Giovanni commanded only a hundred men and had to be subordinate to the chief of the army, he was delighted at this chance to realize his life's ambition and gallop over the battlefields at the head of his black-armoured men.

War was not his only passion. He was seventeen and he had left a young lady behind him in Florence. She was Maria Salviati, daughter of his guardian, a charming girl of sixteen. He was in love with her, and before parting they had pledged themselves to one another and sworn to marry. They were both too impatient to put up with a long separation and their hopes were soon fulfilled. Maria Salviati was Giovanni's cousin, for her mother was a Medici and she was a direct descendant of the main Medici branch, her great-great-grandfather being Cosimo Pater

Patriae; Giovanni belonged to the cadet branch that descended from the latter's brother Lorenzo. When the newly weds had been together for only a short while, the young condottiere felt a yearning for adventure; he returned to his regiments dreaming of extravagant deeds, for he was one of those born soldiers who fall into melancholy and boredom as soon as peace is declared. A glorious outlet for his military talents was certainly not hard to find in the Italy of small warring states. Unfortunately Giovanni had too little money to afford to equip a real army. Luck was also against him as peace reigned at this point. So he took to the sea, which bristled with pirates and Barbary buccaneers, and despite his total inexperience, he rigged out three small galleys with which he patrolled the Mediterranean and the Adriatic seas.

The naval interlude was short-lived, however, because Leo X preferred to keep his explosive cousin closer to hand and thought it best that he be employed in the papal states. Rome was at war with Fermo, and the Pope engaged the Black Band, which he reinforced with a hundred cavalrymen and four thousand infantrymen, to fight on his behalf. Military commentators on Giovanni's campaigns have observed that not least among his many innovations was the care with which he looked after his mercenaries' comfort and general welfare, even during a campaign; they also point out the intelligent use he made of infantry. In this respect, Giovanni concurred with Machiavelli, who did not know much about the practical command of troops, but had studied military tactics and the conduct of battles. He realized that the time of chivalrous wars and picturesque knights was definitely finished. The use of artillery, which the old school of condottieri regarded as ignoble (Giovanni was to be victim of this accusation), required new kinds of fortification, as well as new manoeuvres on the battlefield itself. Every Medici was an innovator in his time and circumstances. In the fifteenth century Giovanni di Bicci revolutionized financial systems, later in the sixteenth, the Duke Cosimo I of Tuscany was to rule on the lines of the absolute monarchies of England and France, to turn his duchy into a modern state. Giovanni the soldier (see fig. 54) who had no pretensions and no desires to be anything other than a soldier, revolutionized military strategy. He had as much genius, initiative and intuition for what the changing times required in his particular field as his banking ancestors had had in theirs. His literary style and even his handwriting are original and expressive with a direct and immediate appeal. Cosimo Pater Patriae would have smiled wrily had anyone suggested that a member of his family would become the greatest condottiere of his day, the equal of the most illustrious captains that the Emperor and the King of France found to lead their armies. He would have wanted this soldier-descendant to be the best technician his century and his profession knew. He would have been delighted to hear that public opinion declared him to be 'The Invincible'. Giovanni delle Bande Nere never tasted real defeat. Experts have speculated that if he had been alive when the Constable of Bourbon attacked Rome, the imperial forces would never have triumphed.

The great perceptiveness and circumspection with which he conducted a campaign like a game of chess enabled him to pull off incredible feats of daring which often appeared doomed to failure. In 1521, when Leo X had joined forces with the Emperor against the French King, who was fighting to establish his claims in Italy, he sent Giovanni to French-occupied Milan. Speed was all important; the adversary had to be taken by surprise. A river barred the Black Bands' way; they would lose too much time if they tried to find a ford or boats with which to cross the river. Giovanni threw himself into the water and all his men, cavalry and infantry alike, followed behind him. They clambered ashore on the far side of the Adda before the enemy had noticed them and Milan fell into their hands.

An anecdote from his private life illustrates Giovanni delle Bande Nere's unusual

79. Panel from the *Gate of Paradise* (east doors) of the *Baptistry*, showing *The Creation*, sculpted in bronze by Lorenzo Ghiberti between 1425 and 1452. (79.5 × 79.5 cms.)

qualities, his lightning decisions, his love for gambling with fate while skilfully making sure that all the chances were on his side, his impulsive actions, his pride in defying destiny. Maria Salviati had just given birth to a boy called Cosimo, after the Father of the State, who was to become the founder of the grand-ducal dynasty of Tuscany. Giovanni saw her walking along a gallery carrying her baby in her arms. He ordered her to throw the child to him from the window. The mother hesitated for an instant, then threw the baby to him. He landed safely in Giovanni's arms. Such was the great confidence that Giovanni inspired in everyone. This behaviour was typical of Giovanni: confident in his 'star', sure of his strength and capacities, generous, reliable, daring in the pursuit of realizable goals but with no mind to the impossible. He never saw, or pretended not to notice, the web of intrigues that was constantly woven round his person. He paid no attention to the schemes of the senior branch of Medici to keep him out of Florence, and to put a safe distance between him and their public and financial affairs. This Medici had no interest in making or expanding financial fortunes. If ever he did want money, it was only to see that his soldiers were well paid and well treated and that they had good armaments and fine armour. Indeed their black armour was his only luxury; he never flirted with humanism or financial affairs, electoral intrigues or lavish building projects.

The main branch of the Medici family, which controlled Florence and occupied the papal throne, in fact regarded the young man favourably—provided he kept his distance from the city. When Clement VII became Pope in 1523 after Adrian VI, he followed Leo X's policy towards the soldier-cousin, although the Vatican continued to watch him carefully, if groundlessly, but suspicion of everyone was the Vatican's traditional policy. Maria Salviati, however, was quicker to understand this attitude than her husband. She realized— and warned him in her letters to him— that he was always being sent off into battle in order to keep him away from the political scene. She suffered a good deal during their constant separations; she always felt anxious, always sick with worry that he might be wounded or dead. She would beg him to stay by her and the children for a while.

Giovanni's main preoccupation, however, was to stick by his regiments; he had trained the Black Bands in a particular method of combat, in a certain type of discipline and kind of life, that demanded his constant presence at the camp. The usual situation of the condottiere, as middle-man between the states that hired him and the mercenaries in his employ, exposed him to many dangerous pressures, imposed from both sides. His talents as a leader and his constant surveillance had moulded the Black Bands into a highly efficient instrument of warfare; unfortunately peaceful interludes levied their toll on the best of troops, for they tended to soften up for lack of exercise. The battle against disorder, slackening discipline and sloth began as soon as the adventurer was given respite from his habitual perils. It was as much a matter of moral training as physical fitness. Giovanni's lieutenants were loyal and conscientious, but they could not replace their captain's personal power to inspire zeal and ardour in his men. If he left them or relaxed his control, his formidable system of military discipline would immediately begin to disintegrate. Professional armies, far more than any other, depended entirely upon their loyalty to their commander, whom they followed devotedly and unquestioningly obeyed, and who was the mainspring of their every action, the solid foundation upon which that fragile disciplinary edifice always teetered.

When the states fell out with their condottieri, whether because they were justly dissatisfied with their services, or because they were wrongfully suspicious, or because they wanted to be rid of a man who had ceased to please them or who had begun to frighten them, they invariably struck out at the captain himself, at his very person. This was the only way to be certain of eliminating danger. The condottiere's profession had its own unique psychology and sociology. The relationship

80. Niccolò da Mauruzzi da Tolentino at the Battle of San Romano (1432) between Florence and Siena. One of a series of three paintings of the battle by Paolo Uccello. Niccolò da Tolentino was one of the two principal captains on the Florentine side. (183 × 319.5 cms.) *London, National Gallery.*

81. Detail of the *Cantoria* (choristers' balcony) by Donatello (1433-1440). This marble balcony, like that of Luca della Robbia (see plate 87) was originally made for the Cathedral, but was taken down in the seventeenth century. (*Height of figured area* 98 cms.) *Museo del' Opera di Santa Maria del Fiore.*

between the captain of fortune and his employers was tenuous at the best of times. It was always at the mercy of circumstances, buffeted by rapid reversals of interest and even changes of mood, and weakened by the perennial and inherent mutual distrust they bore each other and the mutual fear of betrayal. There were some exceptions, some virtuous condottieri who were loyal to the causes they championed through thick and thin, who acquitted themselves scrupulously and abided rigorously by their contracts, who were honest because it paid them to be so or because of their personal convictions. Giovanni delle bande Nere was the noblest of this type. He was truly the last of the condottieri, in the real sense of the word, for the idea of national armies caught on quickly. Italy itself took up the practice as a result of Machiavelli's advice to rulers to form civil militias. This was the first step towards the 'armed states' that evolved at the end of the eighteenth century under the influence of the French Revolution.

To understand the status enjoyed by condottieri and their vital rôle in the relationship of the Italian states, we must go back two centuries and see how this institution took root. The condottieri owed their origin to Italian citizens' reluctance to do military service. Machiavelli conceived the civil militias, germ of the national armies, as a means of freeing Florence of its dependence on the wiles, whims, and demands of mercenary soldiers. The man in the street objected to this on the grounds that he did not want to be whisked away from his counter or workshop at a moment's notice and sent charging into battle, but the advantage of Machiavelli's system was that it avoided the heavy expense incurred in maintaining mercenary armies, which could be a severe drain on public resources. The condotta had the advantage over other systems because it did not interrupt public life or interfere with people's normal activities, which were indispensable to the general prosperity of the city. It also cost the city money only when the soldiers were on campaign, while the city actually needed them, and not afterwards. The only problem with this arrangement was that when danger threatened, a city might run the risk of not being able to book the condottieri whose loyalty and courage could be relied upon, either because they were already engaged in the service of other states, or worse still, because the enemy had engaged them first.

War was the condottiere's business and livelihood; peace spelled hard times for all of them. There is a story which tells of a famous soldier of fortune who came out of church one day and gave a poor beggar a gold coin. The beggar was overwhelmed by this act of generosity and thanked his donor saying 'Peace be with you'. The condottiere was horrified. 'Peace! Do you want to ruin me?' he exclaimed grabbing back the money. In Milan Gian Galeazzo Visconti tried to persuade the priests to expunge from the mass the sentence 'Dona nobis pacem'. Aneas Sylvius Piccolomini, who became Pope Pius II, in his book on Sigismondo Malatesta, that perfect example of the soldier-artist-intellectual prince, makes his hero say characteristically, 'Go, be of good courage for as long as I live you shall know no peace.'

Princes vied with each other for various condottieri, competed to retain their services, and rewarded them with money, land and castles. They even became 'tyrants' in the cities whose favour they enjoyed. These condottieri were the ancestors of many of the noblest Italian houses, of the Sforza, Baglioni, Malatesta, della Scala. They were adventurers in every sense of the word, and often hailed from obscure origins, having walked out of some boring, badly paid or menial job and taken up a life of adventure, risk, pleasure, and danger, a life which opened new possibilities of personal power and individual will, and which enabled them to exploit and realize to the fullest extent all their latent capacities. Attendolo Sforza was a peasant from Romagna. One day he saw a squadron of soldiers passing by. They jeered at him because he was there chopping up a tree-trunk while they were setting off for the wars. Without a moment's thought, the woodcutter threw down his axe and joined them.

82. John Hawkwood, known as Giovanni Acuto, fresco in the *Cathedral*, by Paolo Uccello (1436). The fresco was painted as a memorial to the great English condottiere who had led the Florentine forces in 1392 (died 1394).

IOANNES·ACVTVS·EQVES·BRITANNICVS·DVX·AETATIS·S
VAE·CAVTISSIMVS·ET·REI·MILITARIS·PERITISSIMVS·HABITVS·EST

PAVLI·VCCELLI·OPVS·

His descendants were to be the Dukes of Milan, and all the kings were to seek their friendship. Piccinino, the famous strategist, was a butcher's boy; Gattamelata, whom Donatello immortalized in his famous equestrian statue at Padua (see fig. 34) had baked bread in a bakery; Carmagnola, who hailed from a pigsty, was paid the highest possible tribute by Venice, which condemned him to death because it was so terrified of him that his life was regarded as a perpetual threat.

Although these adventurers regarded any means which helped them to escape from their lowly condition and to raise them to princely status as just, honesty was in the end their safest bet. Their first rule was that contracts should always be honoured; when contracts expired, to the nearest hour, the condottiere regained his independence, even if it were in the middle of a campaign or a battle. The Swiss mercenaries hired by France and the Emperor behaved exactly this way. They were loyal and scrupulously correct for the period stipulated in their contracts; these qualities vanished after the deadline. While the contract lasted, the states that employed these 'war contractors' could safely forget about the conduct of a war, except for the occasional spy sent to observe an unreliable captain. The condottieri were paid at monthly or weekly intervals; in return they took full responsibility for manning, arming, equipping, and feeding their armies and for organizing their strategy. They obviously were not expected to fight to the death, or even fiercely, for armies were expensive to man, train, equip, and keep. The soldiers were the condottiere's 'capital'; they had to be sparing with their use of this 'capital' and could not afford to fritter it away. This is why the battles then were so singularly bloodless; on one occasion for instance, when two famous captains fought it out, there was but one single wounded soldier: this poor fellow had wounded himself by accident. The captains always respected their opposite numbers' capital as well. The important point was not to kill, but to take prisoners, whose liberty could then be ransomed for a handsome sum: when a soldier fell from his horse, or sustained an injury, handicapped as he was by all his armour, he became the property of the man who had levelled the blow and could be ransomed at whatever price his captor chose.

The great condottieri were extolled in the chronicles and became legends in their times—Braccio da Montone, Alberico di Barbiano, Boldrino da Panicale—by virtue of their undying loyalty, or their infamous ferocity, or their misfortunes. The one thing they all had in common was their complete lack of moderation. They were all extremists of one kind or another; their good and evil passions were always excessive. Their violent bouts of uncontrolled savagery often mirrored their brutal personalities, but such cruelty was sometimes inspired by a calculated desire to instil terror. Braccio da Montone was thought by his contemporaries to be as handsome as a god, but he was capable of smashing the skulls of nineteen monks on an anvil because their monastery had resisted him.

The relationship between the states and the condottieri was based on mutual service and interest. It thus excluded any sentimental ties. Strength, fortitude, courage, devotion were included in the purchase price paid for men, horses, and armaments. They were only business transactions, and as in business one of the contractors frequently tried to double-deal the other: a condottiere would ask for the largest sum possible in return for as small a service as he could get away with, while the state would try to wriggle out of its part of the deal by defaulting payment whenever it could. The richer and more powerful the condottiere became, the more he frightened his employers. Venice's trumped up case against Carmagnola, who had never faltered in his defence of the Serene Republic's interests, illustrates the fear that the mercenaries inspired in the *bourgeoisie*; his execution was a dastardly and totally inexcusable act. He was beheaded in 1432 in order to avoid paying him for his excellent service.

Another famous story indicates the ambiguous relationship that linked Republics

83. Detail of the head of David with part of the hand holding a sling, by Michelangelo (1501-1503). *Accadèmia delle Belle Arte.*

with condottieri in Renaissance Italy. A tiny state wanted to reward a soldier of fortune for his long and trusty services, but it feared that he might grow too rich, demanding and independent. He had already begun to seem dangerous: what if he hoisted himself to the level of a Baglioni, a Malatesta or a Sforza? A wily senator hit upon a good solution: if he truly represented a threat to the community, he must be assassinated immediately; on the other hand, since he merited recognition for his long and devoted service, over so many years, they would erect a statue in his honour, once he was dead. This weird sort of situation occurred quite frequently at the conclusion of contracts.

In Giovanni delle Bande Nere's case, it was Clement VII who deliberately delayed and finally refused payment for the services of his regiments. It was a nasty trick by which the Pope intended to keep his captain in a subordinate position, to paralyse any dreams of glory and independence he might have had. (Cesare Borgia in the same period, went further: he rid himself of the condottieri Vitelli and Orsini, by having them stabbed in the back, because he feared their treason or defection.) Had Giovanni been more ambitious and less scrupulous, he might well have gained himself a comfortable, independent principality amid the confusion of the Italian states. By 1525, however, there was less chance than in former days for soldiers of fortune to pull this off. Naples, Milan, Venice and the Papal States were on the march, absorbing every possible smaller state; the double danger from France and Emperor was forcing the Italian states to find some arrangement by which to forget parochial differences and offer their common enemies some sort of united front. Even if it was not to be Machiavelli's dream of 'unity', it could have been the beginning.

Leo X ran for protection to the Emperor's arms, but the second Medici Pope, Clement VII, decided to play the French card when in 1525, François I swept down into Italy again, to settle once and for all his contested claims to Milan and the Kingdom of Naples. Northern Italy once more became the private duelling ground for King and Emperor, between two contrary and antagonistic concepts of power. The Papal States could not afford to sit on the fence, for the duel threatened to tumble the whole peninsula into chaos. Clement VII was not so much bothered by the legitimacy of the contestants' claims, as by their respective power. The Italian republics were not pleased at the prospect of Charles V's return in warrior's garb: long-forgotten memories of the Hohenstaufen domination of medieval Italy surfaced and aroused those ancestral hostilities which may have dated from as far back as the time of Alaric and Theodoric, subterranean hostilities which were again to appear in the Risorgimento cry of 'Fuori i Tedeschi' (out with the Germans) of the nineteenth century. Thus Giovanni was happy to rally together his Black Bands to ride off to the siege of Pavia, where he fell from his horse wounded by a shot from a firearm on 24 February.

There may be some symbolical significance in the fact that the last of the great Italian condottieri fell victim to a new weapon which radically altered the conduct of war. Some of the greatest captains, such as the d'Este perfected the use of these new armaments, and some of the greatest artists of this era had even begun to manufacture them: Francesco di Giorgio (1439–1502) undertook the casting of cannons; Leonardo da Vinci invented several ingenious machines, such as a machine gun. Unfortunately we do not know what use Giovanni delle Bande Nere made of the new weapons, if he used artillery to his advantage or kept it in a minor place in his strategy.

The wounded man was taken to Piacenza where he was treated but his leg would not heal properly. When the Medici tombs were reopened in 1857, an examination of Giovanni's bones revealed that his leg bone had been broken and had never fully joined again. The Black Bands, in the absence of their leader, did not acquit them-

84. *Studiolo* of the Grand Duke Francesco I, decorated by various mannerist artists, and with a portrait of Eleonora da Toledo (wife of the Grand Duke Cosimo I), by Bronzino (mid-sixteenth century). *Palazzo Vecchio*.

selves with their customary courage and fighting mettle, and when the French regiments were outflanked by the Imperialists and retreated, the whole of the army fell back and was eventually disbanded.

François I was routed but Giovanni was flat on his back at Piacenza; Charles V stood squarely in Milan and the Pope lost interest in the war. The Pope wrote off the Black Bands as useless and withheld payment of their fees and finally refused to pay. Maria Salviati dipped into her personal fortune to keep the Bands going, to prevent the tightly-knit group of disciplined and loyal soldiers from drifting off to undertake other condotte or to turn to brigandage, an occupation usually staffed by unemployed mercenaries. The assets of the Florentine banks, of which the Salviati Bank was one of the richest, thus began to trickle into the pockets of the mercenaries, but the Black Bands were held together without as much as a penny from the Pope. Giovanni's coffers were not, however, bottomless sources of wealth; the Salviati dowry was dwindling away. Maria, true soldier's wife that she was, shared her husband's concern for his regiments; she left for Rome to entreat with Clement VII.

Fate had given Giovanni of the Black Bands a perfect wife. She was intelligent, cultivated, beautiful and winsome; when the occasion required she could be as bold and tenacious as Caterina Sforza herself. She knew Giovanni had been unfaithful to her, but she understood the demands that a dangerous life made on him and she forgave him; dangerous living was her husband's profession. She intimidated Clement VII to such a degree that he paid into her treasury the overdue six thousand gold florins. She returned to Piacenza and used the money to regroup the mercenaries and to muster arms and equipment so that when her husband regained his strength he would find his army ready to return to battle. The opportunity was not long in coming. Venice, Florence, and the Pope joined forces to stay the progress of the Imperial Army. As soon as the convalescent was able to straddle a horse, Clement VII put him in command of the combined Florentine and papal armies with additional reinforcements of a thousand cavalrymen. The Constable of Bourbon, at the head of the army of Charles V, had superior forces of foot-soldiers, and in November 1526 managed to outflank Giovanni's men, whose insufficient numbers made it impossible for them to hold their own. Giovanni always risked his own person; he rode out at the head of his companies along the banks of the Mincio at Governola. Another bullet shattered the bad leg which he had injured at Pavia. Mantua was the nearest town to the battlefield, and even though the governor Federigo Gonzaga was not on the wounded condottiere's side, he granted him asylum in the ducal castle, a refuge obtained through the skilful and diplomatic negotiations of Giovanni's unlikely friend and companion, Pietro Aretino (1492–1557).

Aretino's character was the complete opposite of Giovanni's. He is best remembered for his *Ragionamenti*, the scurrilous stories of which have established his fame. But he was an important person in his day; he corresponded assiduously with several European courts. His letters are amusing, witty, full of spicy, scandalous gossip. He kept his correspondents up to date on everything happening in Italy. His capacity to twist and exaggerate his reports of events caused incalculable harm to the poor souls who had the misfortune of being counted as his enemies. He boasted that he could make and break an artist's reputation. He was grasping and completely corruptible. He made his fortune by using the terror his writing inspired to obtain gifts of money, jewels, works of art, paintings from his correspondents. His arrogance was such that he even criticized the composition of the *Last Judgement* in the Sistine Chapel: he told Michelangelo that his composition would have been better had he followed Aretino's advice. He asked to be given a present, but it had to be a costly present since he was not someone who accepted mere knick-knacks, a pointed request that was in reality perhaps a veiled threat.

85. Head of a noblewoman; detail of bust by Desiderio da Settignano. *Bargello, Museo Nazionale.*

Fig. 55 Medal with the head of Pietro Aretino by the Venetian Alessandro Vittoria, about 1553. (*Diameter* 7.4 cms.) *London, Victoria and Albert Museum.*

86. Detail of boy with shield from the tomb of the Secretary of State, Carlo Marsuppini (died 1455) by Desiderio da Settignano. *Santa Croce.*

87. Panel from the *Cantoria* (choristers' balcony), showing a group of boys singing, by Luca della Robbia (1431-38). Like the *cantoria* of Donatello (see plate 81) this balcony was originally in the cathedral. (*Height* 328 cms.) *Museo dell'Opera di Santa Maria del Fiore.*

88. *Pietà* by Michelangelo. This unfinished work may have been intended for his own tomb (1548-55), marble. (*Height* 245 cms.) *Cathedral.*

Pietro Aretino was a trickster and a blackmailer with the insolence of a valet. Popes and kings alike waited in fear of him and his ability to spin a web of witty and amusing words round a cluster of fictitious or misinterpreted events. His debauchery was notorious; yet no one dared to criticize him for fear of being stabbed by his venomous pen. He had a veritable harem of concubines, and far from trying to conceal them, he made a point of boasting the joys of this scandalous existence. His portraits show a cocky, vain, self-indulgent, insulting character—a rather sordid man who filed away compromising documents so that he could fish them out and use them in his intrigues. One is surprised to find this *habitué* of corridors and antichambers sitting at Giovanni's sickbed. The surgeon gave Aretino the painful task of informing Giovanni that his broken leg had to be amputated. There were no antiseptics or anaesthetics in those days, and the operation was bound to be as difficult as it was to be painful, for they expected that the patient would resist the operation with all his might, and this was so considerable that ten men were not thought sufficient to hold the sick man down.

Giovanni delle Bande Nere received the news with stoical calm and refused to be strapped down to his bed; he even insisted on helping the surgeon to operate. Throughout the operation he held a candle to light the surgeon's work and his hand never as much as trembled until the instruments had dug deep and long into his festering flesh and shattered bone. When the Medici tombs were opened in 1857, his skeleton was found shrouded in black velvet in a coffin of red wood. The torso was surrounded with the black armour that had distinguished his army; the visor was lowered to conceal his face. Examination of the right leg revealed that his bones had been pulverized by the bullet and the ailing limb had been butchered by the surgeon who sawed brutally through what remained. His gangrenous leg had probably poisoned the rest of his body and killed him.

The captain requested that he be borne on his camp bed and not on the ceremonial litter offered him. He wanted to sleep his last night in his tent, as he had always slept before going into battle. His calm and patience, and silent courage dumbfounded his friends. This twenty-eight-year-old general, who had become Italy's greatest soldier in ten years, this man who was so admired for his military and humane virtues, bore himself on the eve of his death with the quiet dignity of the humanists' beloved Roman heroes. Pietro Aretino's usually wicked pen wrote an unusually moving and tender portrait of his friend: 'He always gave his soldiers more than he kept for himself. He survived the fatigue and trials of war with extreme patience. He never wore any insignia to denote his rank on the battlefield, but his presence among his men was always marked by his fearless carriage. He was first in the saddle and last to dismount. He only honoured men for their personal worth, not for their titles and riches. He always gave more than he offered, but he never tried to dominate a discussion by his great reputation. He was a born leader who had the art of making his men love and fear him. What he hated most was inertia.' The writer gives a final touch to this likeness, when he says, 'Many might have envied him, but none could equal him.'

When the operation was over, Giovanni delle Bande Nere took leave of his family, then turned over to rest on his side. He calmly fell asleep and died, and was buried in the Mantuan church of San Lorenzo. In 1685 his remains were taken back to Florence and placed alongside those of his ancestors in the sacristy of San Lorenzo. So lived and died the only great and noble soldier in the long history of the Medici family.

The Medici, Dukes of Tuscany

IX

The first result of the defeat of Florence by the Imperial army in 1530 was the Medici's return to power. Their supporters also returned from exile and reduced the champions of former liberties to silence. Those who had defended the city against invaders were liquidated or thrown into prison. Valori, Pope Clement VII's legate, had the Gonfaloniere Carducci arrested and beheaded; and as we have seen, his bastard cousin Alessandro (1511–1537) melted down the ancient bronze bell in the belfry of the Palazzo della Signoria which for such ages called the people to the defence of their rights, and recast it into medals commemorating the glory of the great Medici family. There were now no more citizens; there were only subjects whose obedience was ensured by a foreign garrison and whose political opinions were silenced. Charles V and Clement VII decided to make Alessandro governor of the city and ruler of all Florence's Tuscan possessions. Another cousin, Ippolito (the bastard son of Giuliano, Duke of Nemours) whom Titian (and other painters) portrayed in the Hungarian costume he liked to sport (see plate 48) was made cardinal to prevent him competing with his cousin. Competition for power within the new government was in any case limited; the people were meek and terrorized, and there was nothing to fear from any of the other Medici for Alessandro knew how to make himself felt. He even constructed fortifications within the city as a precaution against any possible insurrection. His fear of an uprising led him to move from the badly-fortified Via Larga palace and to set up house in the Palazzo Vecchio. The Signoria itself was dissolved, although the priors continued to meet, theoretically; they were released, however, from their obligation to live in the communal residence and returned to their private life after performing their last political duty of kissing the new sovereign's ring and pledging him their obedience. Charles V accorded Alessandro the title of Duke and promised him the hand of his daughter, the Archduchess Margaret.

The first Medici Duke, helped by the legate Valori and the celebrated historian

Left:
Fig. 56   Medal with the head of Lorenzo de' Medici, Duke of Urbino; Florentine, first half of the 15th century. (*Diameter* 8.3 cms.) *London, Victoria and Albert Museum.*

Right:
Fig. 57   Medal with the head of Alessandro de' Medici, first Duke of Florence; Florentine and made posthumously in 1570. (*Diameter* 9.6 cms.) *London, Victoria and Albert Museum.*

89. A satyr; detail from the *Fountain of Neptune,* in the Piazza della Signoria, by Ammanati (1575).

Guicciardini, whom one is shocked to find ranged by the side of the tyrant, drafted an entirely new constitution for Florence which, to all intents and purposes, replaced old republican institutions. He was perhaps surprised to find that the Florentine notables, who were now, in the new Dukedom, finally to become a real aristocracy backed him to a man. Filippo Strozzi, of the old banking family, declared himself in favour of the monarchy and was seconded by prominent representatives of the greater guilds. They sanctioned reforms that reeked of that 'tyranny' which had been so hated by the Florentines of the fourteenth and fifteenth centuries. Priors were not to be elected or drawn for by lots, but would become ministers selected by the Duke; there would be two councils, one of forty-eight members and the other of two hundred members appointed for life by the Duke, but unable to meet except in his presence. Alessandro's politics were truly egalitarian in so far as everyone from the monarch down enjoyed exactly the same rights or lack of them. A year after receiving his title, Alessandro had the honour of a hereditary dukedom bestowed upon him by the Emperor. Florence had been led by the Medici family since Cosimo Pater Patriae, but now the dynasty, whose influence had originally been legitimized by popular and noble consent, had a new coat of arms and new prerogatives proclaimed their new grandeur.

Alessandro was a corpulent fellow with a low brow, thick lips, heavy jowls, and red hair. Once he was sure that he had no more to fear from his subjects, he abandoned himself to all his natural, vulgar tastes, inclinations and debauchery. He was protected by guards and had confiscated all arms possessed by citizens. He was convinced that Ippolito was too ambitious to be content with a cardinal's hat, and might seek to establish a claim for power in the city. Alessandro therefore had him assassinated on August 10, 1535, and so was rid of the 'noisome wasp', as he called him. Poison took care of this 'wasp', but there was still another Medici, Lorenzo (1515–1548), a member of the Medici branch, which descended (like Giovanni delle Bande Nere) from the brother of Cosimo Pater Patriae (see family tree page 205). Lorenzino, as he was known to his contemporaries, was not dangerous despite his extravagant manners and habits. His cousin Clement VII had brought him up in his circle at Rome and then had to send him away because he had a weakness for beheading antique statues. He was sent to Florence to amuse Alessandro and became his court jester. Lorenzino fulfilled these duties admirably, and by becoming Alessandro's companion in his debauchery, he won the Duke's confidence.

Lorenzino, who was called 'little' Lorenzo not because he was physically small but because he was considered to be such an insignificant character, secretly planned to kill Alessandro. This was certainly not done with the altruistic intention of ridding Florence of her tyrant, although there are those who have called him the 'Florentine Brutus'; Lorenzino was not created of the stuff of which revolutionaries are made. He was no liberator. The murder of the Duke was more likely to have gratified his jealousy, or it may have been an attempt to perform the perfect crime, the 'bellissimo inganno', as Machiavelli called it, an idea which would certainly have appealed to his taste for intrigue and histrionics. As part of his plan, one day he pointed out his sister Laudomia de' Medici, widow of Piero Strozzi, whose beauty was recorded in a portrait painted by Bronzino. He persuaded Alessandro that the seduction of this haughty beauty, who was so irreproachably faithful to her late husband's memory, would be a sure test of his skill as a Don Juan. Alessandro was delighted with the idea, and soon a tryst was arranged by Lorenzino between his sister and his cousin at his own house. An expectant lover does not go to an amorous encounter at a friend's house in coat of mail or with a sword; Lorenzino saw to it that his victim was disarmed before leading him to the appointed room, where it was not the lovely Laudomia that awaited him but an assassin called Scoronconcolo.

Fig. 58   Medal with the head of Lorenzino de' Medici, 1537. (Actual size.) *London, Victoria and Albert Museum.*

90. Detail of *Mercury* from the plinth of Benvenuto Cellini's *Perseus* (completed 1554); in the background a copy of Michelangelo's *David* in front of the Palazzo Vecchio. *Loggia dei Lanzi.*

The murderer planned it so that the encounter would take place during the *Beffana,* Epiphany day, when all Florence was out carousing in the streets. No one saw the Duke enter, as stealth was essential to the preservation of the beautiful Laudomia's reputation, and he did not even take an escort with him.

Once Lorenzino had enticed the Duke into his house, he and his hired assassin murdered him. The crime was so savagely and revoltingly committed that the most cold-blooded professional murderer would be appalled by it; Lorenzino's refined sadism indicates a morbid loathing for his cousin and an irrational jealousy of his importance, which he must have nursed from early childhood. When he had finished with Alessandro, Lorenzino did not rally Florence and proclaim the tyrant's death and the people's freedom. He merely took to his heels. He wandered about Italy for ten restless years, at the end of which he was caught up by the hired assassins of Alessandro's successor, Cosimo.

How did Florence react to this? Alessandro had reduced the citizens to such a state of servility that they felt no inclination to avenge their mutilated tyrant's death, nor did they have the strength to oust the system he had forced on them. The Duke was dead, but the garrisons lived on in the fortresses, which still pointed their cannons at the more turbulent parts of the city. No one lifted a finger. The Duchy had been decreed hereditary and the Emperor chose a successor: the son of the great condottiere, Giovanni delle Bande Nere. Cosimo de' Medici (1519–1574) was a young man of eighteen who had been raised in the country far removed from political life, where his interests had largely revolved around trees and plants. He was the first Medici to adopt that royal custom of placing a number after his name: Cosimo the First is what the general of the German troops in Florence, the condottiere Vitelli, instructed his soldiers to call him. Thus the Council of Forty-Eight and the entire city was obliged to follow suit and use this regal address. Cosimo I (see plate 71) was declared hereditary duke on February 28, 1537. Some thirty years later Pope Pius V elevated him to even greater distinction by creating him Grand Duke. This is the title by which the Medici were known during their two hundred years' reign.

The new monarch's reign stood Tuscany in good stead. He was not an unskilful politician and administrator. He was the head of the largest and most powerful state in sixteenth-century Italy and conducted himself like a king. Cosimo I also sought royal alliances. Because there were no available Emperor's daughters, he married a Spanish princess of great lineage, Eleonora of Toledo, the daughter of the Viceroy of Naples. Her portrait by Bronzino, the Medici court painter, reveals her noble, distinctive beauty and her tender charm (see plate 84). She was seventeen when she married in 1539 and she died tragically in 1562 with two of her sons, Garcia and Giovanni, from a malarial fever she caught during a visit to the swampy Maremma.

Cosimo did not inherit his ancestors' humanistic interests. He was moderately interested in the arts, but it was more out of regard for his family's traditions than out of any real enthusiasm. This may well have not been entirely his fault, because he did not have the good fortune of Cosimo Pater Patriae or Lorenzo the Magnificent who had lived in the time of the greatest Florentine scholars and artists. In the days of Cosimo I, there were some great sculptors; Giovanni Bologna (1524–1608) and Benvenuto Cellini (1500–1571) were employed to celebrate his military and civil successes with massive commemorative statues and bas-reliefs (see plate 63). There were also painters like Vasari (1511–1574) and Bronzino (1503–1572) or older men like Pontormo (1494–1557). But the dazzling age of genius had set over Tuscany. The new ruler had need of docile courtiers more than of fiercely independent and temperamental artists such as Michelangelo (who did not die in fact until 1564), but Cosimo cannot entirely be blamed for not surrounding himself

91. Detail of mannerist fountain in Via Maggio.

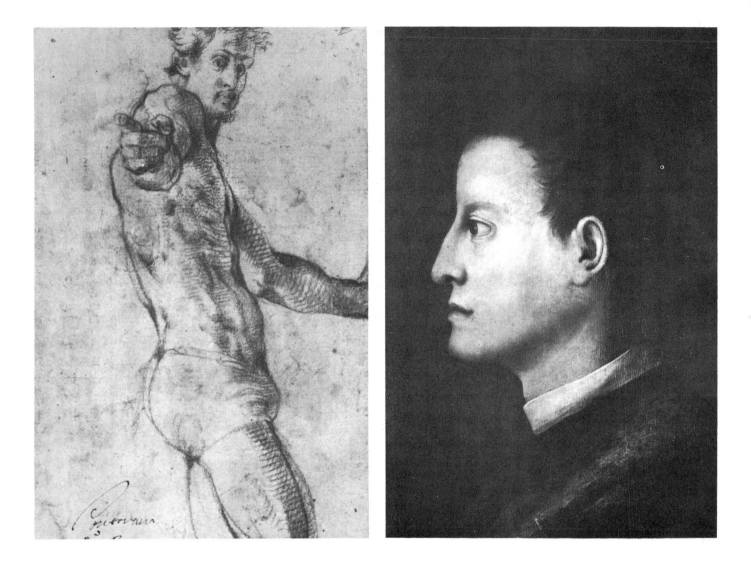

with good artists, for he patronized the best Florence could offer.

He also supported the academies of his time, which, compared to the glories of the group of humanists in the Platonic Academy, encouraged by Cosimo Pater Patriae and Lorenzo the Magnificent, were the very embodiment of stale and decadent pedantry. They were impossibly banal, tasteless and drab, as is often the case with academies; the old virtues which had made their antecedents so lively had been eclipsed; the sublime originality of ideas and the metaphysical energy had disappeared. The inventiveness of these academicians was limited to the selection and award of absurd titles. Cosimo's unenlightened patronage did have one glorious side, however; he put a good deal of energy into the encouragement of Italian music, with the result that music rather eclipsed painting. He also added to the Medici collections, by including many pieces of ancient Etruscan workmanship in which he was interested, and he encouraged research into the Etruscan remains. He was clever enough to know that terror alone would not keep his people loyal, and he devoted some of his energies to amusing his subjects and thus making himself more popular. He added chariot races on the Roman model to the traditional popular entertainments, which were run in front of Santa Maria Novella where the limits of the races are still marked today by posts. Acknowledged botanist and great lover of trees that he was, he sprinkled Florence with gardens; he laid out the beautiful garden on the slopes of Bóboli Hill behind the Pitti Palace, where he took up residence when he left the old and comfortless signorial palace which his wife Eleonora of Toledo found too uncomfortable (see plates 54 and 55). He improved and enlarged the 'herbal nursery' where pharmacological herbs had been grown since the Middle Ages. He encouraged the study of natural sciences at the Tuscan universities, which flourished in the sixteenth century as philosophy, grammar, and classical scholarship had done in the preceding one. In this respect Cosimo I emerges as a truly modern man concerned with anything which might advance the material progress of the state. He developed the ports of Pisa and Livorno, and undertook the digging of a vast network of canals; he built roads and exploited and developed the silver and alum mines; and he introduced new rotating crops to Tuscan soil, some of which were imported from the Orient. He also reformed the administrative and judicial systems, imposing a rigorous judicial structure on Florence, where justice had functioned by custom and tradition since the Middle Ages. This judicial reform won him the reputation of being a man of integrity devoted to upholding the letter of the law.

The reality was rather different. Equestrian statues and bronze bas-reliefs were to immortalize the Grand Duke's military prowess, to celebrate the illustrious soldier. Cosimo did not have the genial, benevolent and lively character of the earlier Medici; portrait painters depict him in armour and lend him the majestic and terrible aspect of the conqueror (see plate 71). His every public action was aimed at evoking fear. He did not have the slightest desire to be his subjects' friend, for he knew what inconsistent friends they would be. He also knew that he owed his power and the maintenance of it to the protection of lances and artillery. He only felt safe when he was circled by the pikes of his Swiss Guards, who camped beneath the splendid Loggia dei Lanzi of Orcagna in the square before the Signoria (see plate 1). He did not inherit his father's warrior virtues and never fought unless he was sure of the weakness of his opponent and thus of overwhelming victory. He wanted to be feared because he feared others. He was nervous of rival states, nervous of dependent cities, nervous of enemies who lurked within his city, nervous of expatriates who conspired against him in foreign courts. He was not to go down in history as an immensely cultivated man of impeccable taste, as a great lover of the arts, as a splendid patron; he is remembered rather as a cruel ruler who founded his power on the repressive measures that wars and revolutions demand. His severe punishment of the men involved in the Strozzi conspiracy and the fierce conduct of his Sienese war illustrate this repressive brutality.

Filippo Strozzi had worked hard for the Medici's return. He had helped Alessandro to rise to power, then he had been disgraced and had to flee from Italy. He found asylum at the French court and François I even gave him a command. Alessandro's sexual excesses, which threatened the virtue of all women, noble or peasant, and then Cosimo's severity, his pride, and arrogance, had altogether alienated a good number of the great families from the Via Larga palace and then from the Palazzo Vecchio. Lorenzino's crime did not inspire the people to rise up and expel its tyrants, but it did re-awaken the old passion for liberty in the breasts of some eager young men. This Liberty, in whose fair name Florence had been subjected to so many covert forms of despotism, once more seemed worth fighting for, now that the heads of state ruled Florence by virtue of foreign armies and not by any merit of their own. Savonarola had been wrong to accuse Lorenzo the Magnificent of tyranny and excite the fanatical mobs against so mild a government, but these accusations could have been justly levelled at the Grand Duke. Strozzi had little trouble in rallying all the most distinguished families round his standard. Piero, Filippo Strozzi's son, got an army together and marched on Florence. Cosimo I's troops encountered them half-way and stopped their advance on July 31, 1537 at Montemurlo in the Apennines. The battle was brief and bloodless, as was the custom, but as many conspirators as possible were caught and made prisoners.

The trial of the rebels was conducted according to the Grand Duke's new judicial code and thus to Cosimo's satisfaction. The tribunal of eight gave a verdict of sixteen death sentences. There were many more guilty parties than this and the Grand Duke had it rumoured abroad that he had put in a plea for mercy. It so happened, however, that all, or nearly all, the insurgents who were not officially hanged died 'accidental', violent, and highly suspicious deaths while still in prison. Those who managed to escape were hunted down by Cosimo's police force and killed in the cities where they had taken refuge; no foreign power was able to save them. The Strozzi, the Albizzi, the Acciaiuoli disappeared from the political scene in accordance with the tyrant's plan for a uniform mediocrity. The supporters of the Medici who had favoured their return in 1512 and 1530 and had helped Alessandro to his ducal powers because they had feared the popular disorders and the anarchy that would have accompanied a popular uprising, now bitterly regretted their own weakness and stupidity. History has preserved a record of the melancholy words of Antonfresco degli Albizzi to Valori, who escorted him to the scaffold where he was to lose his head: 'We have been condemned today by Divine Justice, not for our desire to deliver our country, but for the wrong we did in 1512 when we helped to reduce our land to slavery.'

The brutal suppression of the Strozzi conspiracy throttled all opposition from the aristocrats, whose best men had been removed. The distribution of the police and the billeting of forces at the nerve centres of the city kept the people quiet. This was not all Cosimo I's doing, however, for the Medici's long domination, for all its tolerance (possibly even because of its tolerance), had certainly weakened the lower classes' old fervour for the Liberty which had once inspired the Ciompi. Cosimo

Fig. 61   Bust of Filippo Strozzi by Benedetto da Maiano. *Paris, Musée du Louvre.*

Pater Patriae and Lorenzo the Magnificent had respected their liberty and had increased their general well-being—anything to keep the people calm. In their time the idea of liberty had retained all its attraction as well as a certain literary aura, which appealed to every succeeding generation of young men as they learnt of the glorious feats of classical heroes, of Brutus, or of Harmodius and Aristogeiton. Cosimo's suppression of the young aristocrats, however, dispersed the last serious enemies within the city. He was equally icy, ferocious and methodically destructive when he later waged his war against Siena. The war lasted five long years and his brutality was so successful that by the time the city fell in 1555 the population had dropped from 14,000 to 6,000. The Grand Duke subjected Siena and its surrounding areas to that infamous 'scorched earth' policy which had earned Attila the Hun and the Mongols before him their ghastly fame.

X

The Last of the Dynasty

The last Medici who reigned over Florence from the end of the sixteenth century until Florence ceased to exist as an independent state and became part of the territories of the Empress Maria Teresa of Austria, displayed all the signs that usually accompany a system that is rushing into a decline. First there were the manifestations of *gigantisme*: the desire for conquest, the typical territorial expansionism which always disrupts internal and external harmony and which threw the Florentine republic off balance. Then there was the disappearance of the republic, which had been a democracy despite its oligarchic governments and their attempts at absolutism; this had given way to a monarchic government which had been modelled on other absolute monarchies. The rift between government and people continued to widen with every fresh reign.

Historical forces which were leading rapidly to the formation of the great centralized monarchies, were bound to have a destructive effect on the static little Italian republics which clung obstinately to their conservative and particularist ways, and to their outdated independence which was in any case more theoretical than effective. The desire for autonomy which had so fired the old Communes was to capitulate before this onrush of new conditions. The Florentines would, however, probably not have been nearly so resentful and discontented had the Grand Dukes of Tuscany not been so insistent on their title, which was a flagrant offence to Tuscan egalitarianism, had they not cut themselves off with their royal court, and had they not insulted the people by turning the Belvedere's cannons on them and not on the foreigner without. Until the reign of Ferdinando II, who ruled between 1620 and 1670, all the Medici sovereigns continued to be bankers, as had Giovanni di Bicci, Cosimo Pater Patriae, and Lorenzo the Magnificent. Financial business guaranteed the family's continued wealth. The Grand Dukes felt that in their position it was rather beneath their dignity to remain bankers so they had to supplement their income, for their needs increased in proportion to the rising costs of their court, by resorting to heavier and ever more resented taxes; they were also involved in rather shady transactions which were a far less honourable way of earning their living than that pursued by their predecessors at the sign of the red *palle*.

The disorders and the scandals which emanated from this court, from the Grand Dukes and their entourage, compromised them and served to increase popular discontent and made it the more aggressive and threatening. This in turn only increased the brutality of already excessive punishments and reprisals. Francesco I's suppression of the Pucci conspiracy was not only clumsily executed but ferociously severe. His thirteen years' reign from 1574 to 1587 is distinguished only by disorder. His corruption and negligence of public affairs, his much-hated irresponsibility and his reckless and disastrous fiscal policies, all justified the general antipathy felt towards a family which had abandoned its interest in the general good and which merely exercised its new-found feudal powers. His levies on wheat were particularly hurtful as they struck the needy at the source of their existence and finally succeeded in ruining the agricultural colonies which Lorenzo had set up, and which Cosimo I had developed. Even though the Grand Duke himself was not responsible for all the crimes committed by his entourage, he was blamed for them and for all the refinements of cruelty which usually accompanied such abuses. His brother Pietro, the youngest of Cosimo I's eight children, cruelly neglected his wife Eleonora and spent his time in orgiastic pursuits which vilified him in the eyes of the people, who were kept fully aware of his behaviour. The beautiful and sweet Eleonora who had been cast aside and denied all affection, insulted and dishonoured by her husband, had an affair with a young nobleman, Bernardino Antinori. Bernardino, however, was then involved in a quarrel, in which he finally killed his adversary, whereupon he was imprisoned in his palace. Eleonora, in order to catch a glimpse of the captive, walked up and down beneath his window, which attracted attention. Bernardino was then exiled to Elba, but afterwards brought back to Florence and executed. Three weeks later Pietro ordered his distraught wife to come to the Villa at Caffaggiolo where he simply murdered her.

The death of Cosimo I's daughter Isabella at the hands of her husband Orsini, Prince of Bracciano, was even more frightful. Orsini was the lover of Vittoria Accoramboni, a wild and exciting beauty. He wanted to be rid of his mistress's husband, Peretti, and of his own wife at one and the same time. Vittoria lured her own husband to the Villa Negroni and delivered him over to his assassins. The Princess of Bracciano's death scene was full of the complex horrors which were fashionable in those days. She had joined her husband in his villa at Cerreto Guidi, and when they had finished dinner, he strangled her with a rope let down through a hole that had been made in the ceiling for this purpose, and held by four men from the room above. It was officially announced that she had died in a fit of apoplexy. The crime might have remained a secret had Orsini not then applied to the Pope for leave to marry Vittoria Accoramboni. Gregory XIII opposed the marriage, but Orsini ignored him and went through with a clandestine marriage in the Castle of Bracciano, a fortified structure which could safely withstand an attack launched by papal troops. Gregory XIII died soon afterwards and Cardinal Montalto, the murdered husband's uncle, became Pope Sixtus V. Realizing that he would not escape the Pope's retaliatory measures, Orsini fled to Venice where he died, leaving his fortune to Vittoria Accoramboni, who was then stabbed in Padua by Orsini's next of kin, Ludovico.

The uneasiness and indignation which these atrocities aroused in the Florentines were only aggravated by Francesco I's second marriage. After his first wife Joanna of Austria died in 1578 at the age of thirty, he married the beautiful Venetian Bianca Capello, who had been his mistress and whom he had installed in a nearby palace. The life that this lovely, young, intelligent and charming woman had led since her arrival in Florence was regarded as a public scandal. Popular superstition even claimed she had 'the evil eye', which was the most damning thing an Italian could say or suffer. The superstitions went as far as believing her to be a witch. Every evil that emanated from the ducal palace was soon pinned on her. The source of all these malicious rumours was probably her brother-in-law Ferdinando. Francesco I's reputation was not enhanced by the cost of his wedding, 300,000 florins, or as much as the republic collected in revenues during a whole year; although in fact the money came entirely from his personal coffers, and cost the public treasury nothing. The Venetian woman's very origin damned her from the start, for the city of the Lion of San Marco and the city of the Lily were ever hostile to one another. Altogether the Medici and the rest of Florence hated her so much that when she died they refused to bury her in the family tomb, despite the fact that she was Francesco's lawful wife. Her body was removed from Poggio a Caiano, where she had died on the same day as her husband in October 1587, and was buried secretly in a place which has never since been discovered.

Bianca Capello's story is a very touching one which should have moved her Florentine contemporaries had they not been characterized by a harsh, implacable

Fig. 62   Medal with a portrait of Isabella de' Medici, Princess of Bracciano, by D. Poggini, dated 1560. (Actual size.) *London, Victoria and Albert Museum.*

severity, being rarely moved to compassion and often moved to evil and cruelty. When the young Venetian was seventeen, she had fallen in love with a Florentine employed by one of the Florentine trading companies situated on the Lagoon. The Serene Republic had refused to sanction a marriage between a young noble woman and a foreigner, least of all a Tuscan, who was of an undistinguished family and of dubious morals. They thus married secretly and fled to Florence where they took up residence in 1560. Three years later, in 1563, Francesco I passed by their house on horseback and saw this ravishing beauty at her window and immediately fell in love with her. Bianca had had time enough to realize how vulgar, mediocre, even base her husband really was. Some helpful friends organized a meeting between the Duke and the hapless Venetian and they soon became lovers. In order to keep his mistress close to him, Francesco promoted the husband, who proved quite co-operative, to lucrative offices and gave him a house near his palace to make his access to the lovely Bianca the easier.

Although Francesco I had fallen in love with Bianca Capello, he had to submit to 'reasons of state' and marry a woman in keeping with the rank and interests of a Duke. He thus married the Archduchess Joanna of Austria, sister of the Emperor Maximilian II in December, 1564. He did not love her and she was too aware of the greatness of her family to make much effort to ingratiate herself with her people. She imposed on their court and public life the strict, cold, and elaborate etiquette which were the custom at the Court of Spain. This situation lasted for fourteen years until the Archduchess died in April 1578. Since Bianca's husband was no longer an obstacle to a regular marriage, Francesco and Bianca Capello were wed. Their happiness came to an end at their death nine years later. Poison was naturally suspected, since a double death seemed too much of a coincidence. Francesco's brother and successor Ferdinando I tried to silence the gossipers by proclaiming that both had died of natural causes, the Duke of a cold, and Bianca of a fever which was claiming many deaths at the time.

Attentive observers realized that the Medici's new regal status and their disdain for their family banking profession, which had earned their ancestors' fortunes, implied that they were rejecting all the traditions which had made them prosperous, successful and popular. Cosimo I's successors played at being European monarchs, which was a dangerous game for a small state like Tuscany, and one which could drag them at their own risk and peril into the hazards of European politics. The qualities of Cosimo Pater Patriae and Lorenzo il Magnifico were not discernible in their descendants. The historian, however, must give them their due; their patronage of writers, artists, and scholars, though less striking than that of the Via Larga bankers, did continue to do honour to their house. Their taste was less sure and they were less alive to new artistic developments; indeed, their temperament, intuition and general character were altogether less sympathetic to the arts. Nor was it any longer the Quattrocento, and the great artistic achievements of the Renaissance were no longer possible. Painters, sculptors and architects merely developed the ideas originally evolved in the fifteenth century. The sixteenth century witnessed, however, the effect of scientific discoveries on philosophical thought and on the visual arts. Thus it is not surprising really that the Grand Dukes of Tuscany were much more interested in mechanics, physics, chemistry, and astronomy. Francesco I did set up the Uffizi gallery with studios for young artists, as part of the first attempt to create a public museum, but he himself spent much more time on the chemical experiments he performed in his own laboratory. He spent so much time at his laboratory, in fact, that he soon started receiving his ministers there and discussed the affairs of state without having to interrupt his surveillance of his oven, test-tubes, and flasks.

Aware of how difficult it was to cut rock crystal (which Lorenzo the Magnificent had collected in addition to other vases of *pietra dura* and objects in jasper, onyx, and agate), Francesco I invented a method of melting it. He also studied the porcelain of models imported from China. He invented a process for producing a form of porcelain which enabled local potteries to compete favourably with the imported product. He was also responsible for the establishment of an academy which would devote itself to purifying the language and to separating out the wheat from the tares, the husk from the bran. It was called *la Crusca* (the chaff) and still proudly bears this name today.

His successor Ferdinando I (reigned 1587–1609), was Cosimo I's fourth son. He took no interest in chemistry and little in the other sciences. His great enthusiasm was for classical sculpture. He had been made a cardinal when he was fourteen years old and his hatred for his more fortunate elder brother, who governed Florence, dictated that he should live in Rome during his reign. He had the opportunity to assemble there a considerable collection of Greek statues. It did not matter much that the majority of the statues which he believed to be Greek originals were in reality Roman copies; what really counted was that they were *ancient*. The fashion for antique sculpture was old-established; for instance, when Michelangelo was a young man, he was annoyed by the disdain which his work met with and went so far as to sell one of his statues which no one else would buy, to a collector of antique Roman sculpture. Cardinal Ferdinando built a villa to house his statues, which is still known by the name of Villa Medici by the artists of the French Academy who now inhabit it. It was in this villa that the famous marbles could be seen, marbles which were to give the visual arts a new direction leading ultimately to the development of the Baroque style—under the inspiration of the Hellenistic Baroque, of the Laocoon, the Farnese Hercules, the Belvedere Apollo, and the so-called 'Medici' Venus, and the Niobe. When he acceded to the Grand Duchy of Tuscany, on his brother's death, he took part of his collection with him to Florence, but he left the major pieces at Rome, where they enriched the Vatican Museum.

Ferdinando I modified the Medici's old shield; he replaced the *palle*, the 'besants', which had too many banking associations, with a new emblem, a bee, which, according to the new Florentine master, was supposed to be the symbol of practical activity in the service of the general good and welfare of the community. Ferdinando corrected and repaired the financial and economic errors of his predecessor, suppressed the abuses, and ruled in such a way as to justify his being called the best of the Grand Dukes. His administration restored the comparative order, prosperity and peace which had reigned under Cosimo I, but which had lapsed under the intervening term of his predecessor; it was rarely to be achieved by his successors. All his reforms bore the mark of his concern for the public good. His ancestors had always wanted Florence to have a fleet of merchant vessels which would free her from her dependence on her rivals, on Venice, Genoa, and Pisa, who were fighting for supremacy at sea in the hope of winning a monopoly in Mediterranean trade. Florentine merchants needed their imports to circulate freely over seas as over land. The Mediterranean and Adriatic seas were infested with Turkish galleys, which often raided the coasts and captured ships laden with goods. There were also numerous pirates who attacked and robbed merchant convoys, making sea routes rather hazardous.

There was, in fact, a Florentine fleet which did include a few, but not enough warships. Ferdinando wanted to augment and reinforce the convoys and to build up a powerful home port, Livorno, where ships could harbour and pick up reinforcements and cargo without fear of enemy incursions. Cosimo I had already understood the advantages of this small city, which had previously been of no great importance but which was favourably located. He had laid the foundations for a commercial and military port. Ferdinando resumed this project, which his brother had aban-

Fig. 63 Medal with a portrait of Francesco I de' Medici, second Grand Duke, by Pastorino de Pastorini, dated 1560. (*Diameter 7.2 cms.*) *London, Victoria and Albert Museum.*

doned, and made Livorno the strong naval base which it has continued to be ever since. He not only had to build a new town, but also populate it. A resettlement of Tuscans would have weakened their native towns. The Grand Duke thus hit upon the ingenious, generous and useful idea of attracting those members of other populations whose lives were in difficulty elsewhere and who would there be guaranteed a peaceful existence. Since they would be indebted to the Grand Duke for their asylum, they would be loyal and grateful subjects. Religious tolerance was to be the founding principle of all the institutions of Livorno, despite the fact that Ferdinando I himself was a good Catholic and had, during his cardinalate, founded the great missionary society of the Propagation of the Faith (Propaganda Fide) to go out and teach and convert the non-Christian world. His agents advertised and extended his invitation to the religious persecuted throughout Europe. The response was immediate; a great host of people flocked to Livorno, people whose religious sects had been expelled from or persecuted in their native lands: Protestants came from Flanders and France; Catholics from England and large numbers of Jews from everywhere. The proportion of Jews to the rest of the population of Livorno has always been, and is still now, higher than in any other Italian city.

Ferdinando I's taste for opulence was responsible for the building of an addition to the San Lorenzo sacristies, which house the tombs of the earlier Medici. This huge Baroque monster was intended to house the remains of the Grand Dukes and differed vastly from the Sagrestia Vecchia, where the founders of the dynasty lay, and also from the Sagrestia Nuova (see plates 33, 41 and 42) to which Michelangelo had given the best of his creative genius. The Grand Ducal mausoleum was decorated in the Baroque style, which had started to become fashionable at this turning point between the sixteenth and the seventeenth centuries. This period also saw a good deal of change in music, leading to the birth of a new form, the Opera, although at this juncture it was still at an experimental stage. A large part in the early development and spread of Opera is often and justly attributed to Ferdinando I's support for it. This enthusiasm may well have derived from his love of classical sculpture, which may have led him to regard this entirely new musical form as a sixteenth and seventeenth century interpretation of Greek tragedy. The first performance of the *Daphne* of Jacopo Peri and Jacopo Corsi, one of the earliest operas, took place in one of the galleries of the Uffizi in 1597. There were regular performances of operas at the Uffizi and at the Palazzo Bardi, for the Bardi were as interested in music as were the Medici. This active and lively interest was shown at the same time that Monteverdi was writing his first works at the court of Mantua.

There is no room here to stress and describe the importance which the Italian musical drama, as developed in Florence, Mantua, and Venice, had for the future of European music. One should, however, stress the fact that throughout the long course of Medici patronage from the fifteenth century onwards there was not a single generation that did not devote itself in some way or other to encouraging and subsidizing new forms of artistic endeavour. The tastes of some of the Grand Dukes may appear less refined and less sure than those of the early, modest bankers. Their tastes might even be said to be somewhat eccentric; there was Francesco I's passion for shaping cups, flasks and vases from molten rock crystal and precious metal, then again Ferdinando II's love of mosaics and *pietra dura* and *intarsia* or marquetry (see front of jacket). Ferdinando I's musical tastes were more felicitous. The decorations of his favourite villa, La Petraia, do show that he took pains to employ the best decorators of the time to illustrate in brilliant frescoes the important events which marked the new Medici generation.

Ferdinando I was certainly extravagant. He spent lavishly on his building enterprises, and on his very expensive wedding in 1589, when he married Christine of Lorraine; the magnificent 'receptions' and 'triumphal entries' into the city, and the entertainments he prepared for his princely cousins and royal guests, reflected the new splendour of the Grand Dukes of Tuscany. In spite of this expenditure he left the finances of the state and his own family fortunes in very good repair when he died. Contemporary documents corroborate this appraisal of his financial skill; they put his private wealth at about five million gold florins plus a large quantity of foreign currency which included, for example, 7,000 Spanish *doblas*. The earliest Medici were governed by the economic principle that 'money must be kept circulating', which meant that there were times when their tills were empty because all available funds were tied up in commercial or banking ventures. But Ferdinando I was a devoted money hoarder. He had a reinforced safe, a precursor of the modern bank vault, constructed in his Belvedere fortress (see plates 51 and 68), a strategically located and impregnable stronghold—theoretically impregnable, at least, for there is no fortress that human ingenuity cannot take—which was used to keep the Florentines quiet. The earliest Medici had not found need for such a vault. Buontalenti (1536–1608) the famous engineer, devised an unbreakable door and only the Duke and Buontalenti, who had constructed it, had keys to this safe.

Fig. 64 Portrait of Grand Duke Cosimo II by Sustermans. *Uffizi*.

His eldest son Cosimo, who became Grand Duke Cosimo II (see fig. 64), was only nineteen in 1609 when he had to shoulder a difficult succession. He had married the Archduchess Maria Maddalena, who was the Emperor Ferdinand II's sister, and he restored a youthful, happy, and carefree atmosphere to the Florentine court, which had been lacking since the time of Lorenzo the Magnificent. He inherited his father's tolerance, and also loved architecture and indulged this predilection by enlarging the Grand Ducal palace (still known as the Palazzo Pitti) and by constructing a villa at Poggio Imperiale near Arcetri, where the Medici already had a country seat.

The beginning of the seventeenth century was distinguished by its great scientific advances, particularly in the field of astronomy. The young Duke's intelligence was greatly attracted by this science of the stars. Francesco I had set up his chemical laboratory in his palace and Ferdinando I had put on operas at the Uffizi; so Cosimo II added an observatory to his villa at Poggio Imperiale. There he set up the telescope which Galileo had just invented and which the great scientist had brought with him when he took refuge in Florence.

The first time Galileo Galilei (1564–1642) and the future Grand Duke met was at Padua where Cosimo II was a student for some time and where he may have attended the lectures given by the Professor of Mathematics. When he became ruler of Tuscany, the pupil invited his teacher to relinquish his chair at Padua and to come to Florence. He was immensely considerate of his master and relieved him of all material preoccupations. He set him up at the villa at Arcetri and let him pursue his astronomic researches in peace seeing to it that he was safe from his rivals, his enemies and all those who opposed his 'revolutionary' ideas and wished him harm. The researches Galileo did there led, among other things, to the discovery of Jupiter's moons, which he baptized the 'Medicean Stars' in gratitude of the Grand Duke's support. Unfortunately Cosimo II could not extend his protection for very long, for he died on February 28, 1620 at the tender age of thirty. He left his descendants a testament full of wise counsels, one of which was his exhortation that no Medici should ever dig into the family coffers except in times of public calamity. In such cases it would be right and proper that the riches accumulated by generations of Medici should be tapped to ease the hardships and afflictions of the Florentines, who had helped them realize their glory and prosperity.

His ten-year-old son, Ferdinando II, succeeded him. His wife Maria Maddalena and his mother Christine were to rule as joint regents during the prince's minority. The boy was subjected to a rigorous education; then in 1627, when the young prince was seventeen, he was sent abroad to tour the European capitals which was supposed to widen his cultural horizons and develop his character, and which in fact gave him a rootlessness and indecisiveness which were to spoil his reign. Like his ancestors, he was interested in intellectual pursuits. He organized the regular Conversazioni Filosofiche which were attended by scientists and intellectuals in the Ducal Palace and over which the young prince presided. These salons, however, were a far cry from those informal meetings of the Platonic Academy encouraged by Cosimo Pater Patriae or Lorenzo the Magnificent, which attained such great metaphysical heights in an atmosphere of cheerful simplicity that characterized the Medici entourage. The seventeenth-century court of the Grand Dukes of Florence was very different. Scientific experiments rather than metaphysical questions were discussed by Ferdinando II and his learned court. Francesco I's chemical laboratory and Cosimo II's astronomical observatory had already shown the later Medici's preference for experimental science. Speculative philosophy was rejected, as it was felt that it encumbered the study of natural science, and that it was preferable to concentrate on the observation, analysis, and description of nature as it really was. Ferdinando II founded an academy called *del Cimento*, which was to encourage this type of scientific experiment and to define goals worthy of pursuit.

Ferdinando II was responsible for another innovation, of a more bizarre nature, which met with little success, however—the introduction of the camel into Italy. This animal had found its way into the zoological gardens of princely courts, where exotic creatures and their habits had always excited considerable interest, having often been presented to their owners by oriental sovereigns; giraffes, lions, rhinoceros, alongside the various felines which were bred for hunting. One of the earlier Medici in Benozzo Gozzoli's fresco of the *Adoration of the Magi* in the chapel at the Via Larga Palace (see plate 9) appears on horseback with a cheetah on the saddle behind him. The Grand Duke's attempted innovation was not inspired by scientific curiosity nor by any desire to study the anatomy and habits of the camel, but by the practical idea of adapting for Italian use this domestic species, which was known for its patience and endurance and which he thought might well prove to be a less costly and more useful beast of burden and draft than the horse.

Camel breeding was only one of a list of Ferdinando's projects to reform agriculture, but neither the camel nor his new ideas for treating the soil met with success. The enterprise was a flop; a few camels walked about Tuscany, but they were kept more out of curiosity than out of any hope that they might prove useful. The Grand Duke's efforts were more felicitously employed in the development of a new use for mosaic in *pietra dura,* traditionally produced by one of the larger groups of Florentine artisans. This did not result in great mural mosaics such as those at Byzantium, Salonica, Ravenna, and Venice. They were used instead to form small landscapes and still-lifes in multicolour pieces of marble, in onyx, ivory, agate, and jasper, meticulously assembled (see front of jacket). These artisans became expert in laying and decorating tables in this way and their work was prized and distributed throughout Europe and became a precious source of revenue for Florence. Ferdinando fostered the industrialization of these techniques not only because he knew that the city would profit by it, but also because he liked this sort of workmanship, although it was really more of an oddity than of any intrinsic aesthetic merit. This craft has continued to flourish in Florence to the present day and at the Palazzo Pitti *pietra dura* tables often arouse greater admiration from the tourists than the great masterpieces of the picture gallery.

One wonders why the Grand Dukes of Tuscany did not patronize the arts as extensively as their banker ancestors had in the fifteenth and sixteenth centuries. The answer is that the Medici had changed. When they became sovereigns and joined themselves to the royal houses of France and Austria, the Medici blushed inwardly at their banking profession. Then Ferdinando II removed this shame by shutting up shop and closing down his offices. The later Medici saw themselves as kings and wanted to be ostentatious and to display their wealth and glory to the world. The old 'princes of the spirit' were gone. They were more interested in decking out their ceremonial apartments and offices than in 'art' for its own sake. Thus painting and sculpture were used to decorate and create settings for special occasions and activities. The Grand Ducal Palace, which Ferdinando II extended upwards and outwards, reflects his aesthetic preferences, just as Botticelli, Pollaiuolo or Piero di Cosimo had reflected those of Lorenzo and his grandfather.

The old Medici line was spent, but so was the great era of Tuscan creativity. The advent of the Baroque period with all its torments, movements, pathos, and melodrama, proved alien to Florentine sensibilities and to the traditionally clean, pure Tuscan lines, to their severe forms and their sense of moderate and discreet sobriety. Thus artistic primacy passed on to other more sympathetic cities, to Bologna, Naples, and Rome, and Florence was no longer the artistic capital she had been in the Quattrocento. Like Florence, the Medici themselves had lost the knack and power to stimulate, direct, and foster the development of the arts. The sciences were young and only just beginning to develop and flower and this made them more attractive than the arts, which had become static and had started to fossilize into a lifeless formalism. Tuscan art in the Renaissance had been the art of the city, because in a sense the entire city had participated in it. When it became a courtly pursuit limited to the pleasure of prince and courtier, the Tuscan genius lost contact with its roots, its people, and ceased to be an object of popular delight. This contact was never re-established. The loss was one of the main reasons for the rift which started to yawn from the Renaissance onwards between artist and 'general public'—otherwise known as 'the masses'. The Grand Dukes restricted their favourite painters and sculptors, Bronzino, Vasari, Volterrano, Ammanati, by making them celebrate their reigns as Van de Meulen was forced to develop the iconography of a victorious warrior for Louis XIV.

Many contemporary sovereigns modelled their careers on that of Louis XIV to their detriment, as in the case of Ferdinando II's successor Cosimo III (1642–1723) and in that of Cosimo III's successor Gian Gastone, who was the last of the Grand Dukes. Cosimo III married Marguerite-Louise of Orléans, who was Louis XIV's cousin. His entire reign, which lasted fifty-three long years, while Florence sank into economic and political decay, was devoted to aping the *Roi Soleil,* with whom he had absolutely nothing in common, being arrogant, pretentious, extravagant and not very intelligent. He is the only Medici who never once during his whole reign revealed the slightest inclination or twinge of curiosity for the arts or the sciences, which had so engaged his predecessors.

In 1723, his only surviving son Gian Gastone succeeded him. Gian Gastone was fifty-two years old and an inveterate botanist (see fig. 65). He dug up part of the Bóboli gardens and planted rare species of herbs. He built himself a secluded potting shed where he could while away his days performing his experiments far from the worries of public affairs and other such distractions. His reign could have been a happy one, because he was an intelligent, worthy, and reasonable man. But Tuscany had become a pawn on the European political chessboard, which the Great Powers manipulated at will. The princely marriages which had been entered into with such pride had drawn the Grand Dukes into international politics and intrigue. In October 1735, when Gian Gastone's rule was drawing to a close, for he was to die two years later, these Great Powers agreed in the Treaty of Vienna to treat Florence as so much merchandise for international bartering. The treaty sought to make up for the disappointments of the Polish King Stanislas Leczinsky by awarding him the Duchy of Lorraine. This displaced the ruling duke of that

Fig. 65 Medal with a portrait of Gian Gastone de' Medici, by Pieri, dated 1708. (*Diameter 8.4 cms.*) *London, Victoria and Albert Museum.*

state, François-Etienne, who had in turn to be compensated for this loss; this was especially important as he was the husband of the heiress of the Emperor Charles VI, Archduchess Maria Teresa. He was later himself to become the Emperor and she is to be remembered as a most determined Empress. By the Treaty Tuscany would be given to the dispossessed Duke of Lorraine and to Maria Teresa, which, in view of the fact that Gian Gastone had no obvious male heirs, and that the succession to the Duchy was therefore bound to lead to disputes, was a not uningenious solution. Thus the Medici's estates and possessions were annexed to those of the House of Austria. Gian Gastone was too weak and too ill to offer much resistance, although he did try to utter a few diffident cries of protest, which no one heeded.

Thus the Medici disappeared from the political stage on which they had played for nearly four centuries. The Medici had not, as a rule, excelled themselves as politicians or administrators. They had not greatly influenced the evolution of national movements, but they had left their indelible mark on every creative impulse of their times, on every scientific and artistic movement of their age. The Medici's last magnificent gesture to Florence, which they had ruled for such a very long time, was the priceless treasure that Gian Gastone's sister, the Archduchess Anna Maria Ludovica, bestowed upon their city. She inherited from Gian Gastone the immense fortune of the Medici and the vast collections of works of art that had been assembled from Giovanni di Bicci's day to hers. When she died in 1743, she divided her fortune between her various relatives, friends and servants. Her will also stipulated that all the works of art, all the paintings, sculpture, books, furniture, silverware, stoneware, clothing, medallions, tapestries, and pottery, should become part of the patrimony of the Grand Duchy of Tuscany. The Grand Duchess further stipulated that the Grand Duchy's inheritance would only be valid if this estate, these masterpieces, remained in Florence where they were to be made accessible to anyone and everyone from any and every nation. This insured against any hopes the Austrians may have had of carrying these priceless collections off to Vienna. Thus the Medici legacy ensured that Florence would remain one of the great art centres of the world, to which countless admirers would make pilgrimages from every corner of the earth, there to pay homage and contemplate the diverse manifestations of beauty in the City of the Lily.

Fig. 66 Medal with a portrait of Lorenzo il Magnifico and, on the reverse, the symbol of Florence, by Niccolò Fiorentino, 15th century. *Bargello, Museo Nazionale.*

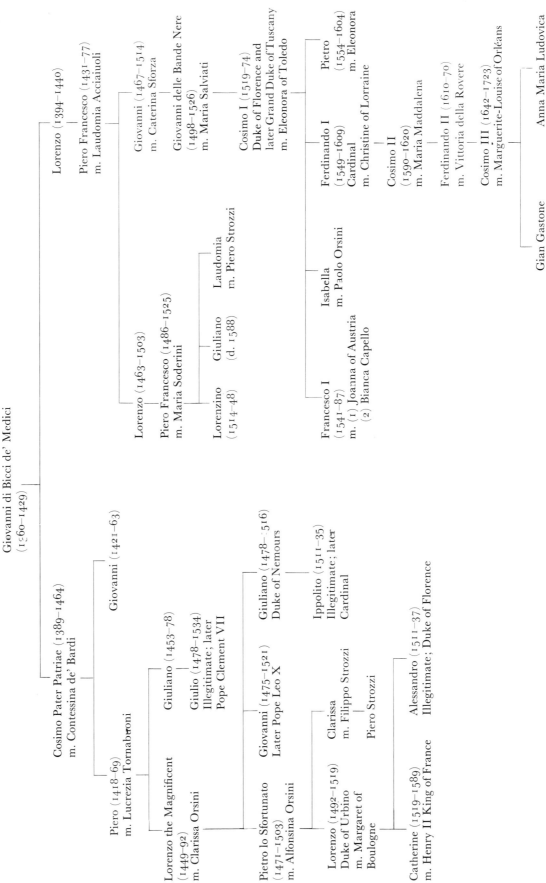

Giovanni di Bicci de' Medici
(1360–1429)

Lorenzo (1394–1440)

Piero Francesco (1431–77)
m. Laudomia Acciaiuoli

Giovanni (1467–1514)
m. Caterina Sforza

Giovanni delle Bande Nere
(1498–1526)
m. Maria Salviati

Cosimo I (1519–74)
Duke of Florence and
later Grand Duke of Tuscany
m. Eleonora of Toledo

Pietro (1554–1604)
m. Eleonora

Ferdinando I (1549–1609)
Cardinal
m. Christine of Lorraine

Cosimo II (1590–1620)
m. Maria Maddalena

Ferdinando II (1610–70)
m. Vittoria della Rovere

Cosimo III (1642–1723)
m. Marguerite-Louise of Orléans

Anna Maria Ludovica
(1667–1743)

Gian Gastone
(1671–1737)

Cosimo Pater Patriae (1389–1464)
m. Contessina de' Bardi

Giovanni (1421–63)

Lorenzo (1463–1503)

Piero Francesco (1486–1525)
m. Maria Soderini

Laudomia
m. Piero Strozzi

Giuliano
(d. 1588)

Lorenzino
(1514–48)

Isabella
m. Paolo Orsini

Francesco I
(1541–87)
m. (1) Joanna of Austria
(2) Bianca Capello

Piero (1418–69)
m. Lucrezia Tornabuoni

Lorenzo the Magnificent
(1449–92)
m. Clarissa Orsini

Giuliano (1453–78)

Giulio (1478–1534)
Illegitimate; later
Pope Clement VII

Giuliano (1478–1516)
Duke of Nemours

Giovanni (1475–1521)
Later Pope Leo X

Ippolito (1511–35)
Illegitimate; later
Cardinal

Pietro lo Sfortunato
(1471–1503)
m. Alfonsina Orsini

Clarissa
m. Filippo Strozzi

Piero Strozzi

Lorenzo (1492–1519)
Duke of Urbino
m. Margaret of
Boulogne

Alessandro (1511–37)
Illegitimate; Duke of Florence

Catherine (1519–1589)
m. Henry II King of France

Bibliography

Accascina, M. *L'oreficeria italiana,*
Firenze, 1933

Ady, Cecilia M. *Lorenzo dei Medici and
Renaissance Italy,* London, 1955

Alazard, J. *L'art italien de l'ère baroque au XIX
siècle,* Paris, 1960

Albertini, R. von *Das florentinische
Staatsbewusstsein im Übergang von der Republik
zum Prinzipat,* Berne, 1955

Allodoli, E. *I Medici,* Firenze, 1929

Andrieux, M. *Les Médicis,* Paris, 1958

Antal, F. *Florentine Painting and its Social
Background,* London, 1947

Armstrong, E. *Lorenzo de' Medici and Florence
in the Fifteenth Century,* London, 1896

Aubenas, Roger, and Ricard, Robert *L'Eglise
et la Renaissance,* Paris, 1951

Barbagallo, C. *L'Età della Rinascenza e della
Riforma,* Storia Universale Vol. 4 pt. 1,
Torino, 1936

Barfucci, E. *Lorenzo de' Medici e la società
artistica del suo tempo,* Firenze, 1945

Baron, A. *The Crisis of the Italian Renaissance,*
Princeton, 1955

Benedeni, B. *Il carteggio della Signoria di Firenze
e dei Medici coi Gonzaga,* Roma, 1962

Benoist, Charles *Le Machiavélisme avant
Machiavel et Le Machiavélisme après Machiavel,*
3 vols. Paris, 1907–1934

Berence, F. *La Renaissance Italienne,* Paris, 1951

Berence, F. *Laurent le Magnifique ou la quête de
la perfection,* Paris, 1949

Berenson, B. *The Florentine Painters of the
Renaissance,* London, 1896

Biagi, G. *The Private Life of the Renaissance
Florentines,* London, 1896

Bignami, L. *Nel crepuscolo delle signorie
Lombarde; Gian Giacomo de' Medici 1495-1555,*
Milano, 1925

Bizzarri, E. *Il Magnifico Lorenzo,* Verona, 1950

Block, W. *Die Condottieri,* Berlin, 1913

Blunt, A. *Artistic Theory in Italy 1450–1600,*
Oxford, 1940

Bocchi, F. *Le Bellezze della Città di Fiorenza,* ed.
Cinelli, Firenze, 1677

Brion, M. *Laurent le Magnifique,* Paris, 1937

Brion, M. *Le Pape et le Prince. Les Borgia,*
Paris, 1953

Brion, M. *Machiavel,* Paris, 1948

Brion, M. *Savonarola,* Paris, 1948

Brucker, G. A. *Florentine Politics and Society
1343–1378,* Princeton, 1962

Buck, A. *Der Platonismus in den Dichtungen
Lorenzo de' Medicis,* Berlin, 1936

Burckhardt, J. *The Civilization of the Renaissance
in Italy,* London, 1878

Burdach, K. *Vom Mittelalter zur Reformation,*
Halle, 1893

Buter, B. *Lorenzo di Medici als italienische,*
Leipzig, 1879

Caggese, Romolo *Firenze dalla decadenza di
Roma al Risorgimento d'Italia,* Firenze, 1913

Camerani, S. *Saggio di bibliografia medicea,*
Firenze, 1940

Canestrini, G. *Documenti per la Storia della
Milizia italiana,* Firenze

Canestrini, G. *La Scienza et l'arte di stato
descarta dagli atti ufficiali della Republica
Fiorentina e dei Medici,* Firenze, 1862

Capasso, A. *Tre saggi sulla poesia italiana del
Rinascimento Boiardo, Lorenzo, Ariosto,*
Genova, 1939

Cappelli, A. *Lettere di Lorenzo de' Medici.*
Modena, 1863

Carbonara, C. *Umanesimo e Rinascimento,*
Torino, 1944

Cassirer, E. *Individuum und kosmos in den
Philosophie der Renaissance,* Leipzig-Berlin, 1927

Cassirer, E. (with P. O. Kristaller and V. J. H. Randall) *The Renaissance Philosophy of Man*, Chicago, 1948

Ceccherelli, A. *I libri di mercatura della Banca Medici*, Firenze, 1913

Cecchi, Emilio *Lorenzo il Magnifico*, Roma, 1949

Chabod, Frederico *Machiavelli and The Renaissance*, London, 1958

Chastel, A. *Art et Humanisme à Florence au temps de Laurent le Magnifique*, Paris, 1961

Chedovsky, K. von *Der Hof von Ferrara*, München, 1921

Chiapelli, G. *Formazione storica del commune citadino*, Firenze, 1927

Ciasca, R. *L'arte dei Medici e speziali nella storia et nel commercio fiorentino dal secolo XII al XV*, Firenze, 1927

Cipolla, C. *Money, Prices and Civilization in the Mediterranean World, Fifth to Seventeenth century*, Princeton, 1956

De Roover, R. *The Rise and Decline of the Medici Bank*, Cambridge, Mass., 1963

Di Napoli, G. *L'immortalità dell' anima nel Rinascimento*, Torino, 1963

Di Pino, *La poesia di Lorenzo dei Medici*, Firenze, 1952

Dorini, Umberto *I Medici e i loro tempi*, Firenze, 1947

Ewart, Joseph *Cosimo de' Medici*, London, 1899

Fabbri, Mario *Alessandro Scarlatti e il Principe Fernando de Medici*, Firenze, 1961

Fabriczy, C. von *Italian Medals*, London, 1904

Fabroni, A. *Laurentii Medicis Magnifici Vita*, Pisa, 1784

Ferguson, W. K. *The Renaissance in Historical Thought*, Boston, 1948

Ferrara, Mario *Prediche e scritti di Savonarola*, 1930

Ferrari, M. *La Congiura dei Pazzi*, Roma, 1945

Les fêtes de la Renaissance, Paris, 1956

Filarete, A. A. *Filarete's Essays on Architecture, the Art of Drawing, and on Building by the Medicis*, edited by W. von Oettingen, Vienna, 1890

Fiori, F. G. *Lorenzo il Magnifico*, Firenze, 1937

Gandillac, M. de *La sagesse de Plotin*, Paris, 1952

Garin, Eugenio *Italian Humanism: Philosophy and Civic Life in the Renaissance*, Oxford, 1965

Geiger, Ludwig *Renaissance und Humanismus in Italien und Deutschland*, Berlin, 1892

Gengaro, M. L. *Umanesimo e Rinascimento*, Torino, 1948

Gentile, Giovanni *Il Pensiero italiano del Rinascimento*, Firenze, 1940

Gingins, M. de *Dépèches des ambassadeurs milanais sur les campagnes de Charles-le-Hardi Duc de Bourgogne de 1474 à 1477*, Paris, 1858

Giovannoni, G. *Sàggi sulla architettura del Rinascimento*, Milano, 1931

Gnoli, D. *La Roma di Leone X*, Milano, 1938

Gromore, G. *L'architecture de la Renaissance en Italie*, Paris, 1922

Gutkind, K. *Cosimo de' Medici, Pater Patriae 1389–1464*, Oxford, 1938

Hay, D. *The Italian Renaissance in its historical background*, Cambridge, 1950

Haydn, H. C. *The Counter-Renaissance*, New York, 1950

Holzhausen, W. *Studien über den Schatz das Lorenzo il Magnifico*, Firenze, 1929

Horsbrough, E. L. S. *Lorenzo the Magnificent and Florence in the Golden Age*, London, 1908

Jacolo, E. F. ed. *Italian Renaissance Studies. A tribute to the late Cecilia Mary Ady*, London, 1960

Krakowski, Edward *Plotin et le Paganisme religieux*, Paris, 1933

Kristeller, Paul Oskar *Studies in Renaissance Thought and Letters*, Roma, 1956

Labande, E. R. *L'Italie de la Renaissance Duecento—Trecento—Quattrocento*, Paris, 1954

Lavedan, P. *Histoire de l'Urbanisme, Renaissance et Temps Modernes*, Paris, 1941

Lestocquoy, J. *Les villes de Flandre et d'Italie sous le gouvernement des patriciens*, Paris, 1952

Lipari, A. *The Dolce Stil Novo according to Lorenzo di Medici; Study of his poetic Principio etc.* New Haven, 1936

Lungo, Isidoro del *Florentia uomini e cose del Quattrocento*, Firenze, 1897

Luz, P. de *Histoire des Papes*, Paris, 1960

Machiavelli, N. *Opere complete di N.M. con aggiunte e correzione tratte dai manoscritti originali*, Firenze, 1843

Mahon, Denis *Studies in Seicento Art and Theory*, London, 1947

Margotto, G. *Un mercante fiorentino e la sua famiglia nel secolo XV*, Firenze, 1881

Martelli, Mario *Studi Laurenziani*, Firenze, 1965

Martin, A. von *Soziologie der Renaissance*, Stuttgart, 1932

Martini, G. S. *La bottega di un cartolaio fiorentino nella seconda metà del Quattrocento*, Firenze, 1956

Maulde de la Clavière, R. de *La Diplomatie au temps de Machiavel*, Paris, 1892

Meltzing, O. *Das Bankhaus der Medici und ihre Vorläufer*, Milano, 1937

Misciatelli, P. *Personnaggi del Quattrocento italiano*, Roma, 1914

Monnier, P. *Le Quattrocento*, Paris, 1901

Montani, G. *Gli organismi finaziarii della Repubblica di Firenze*, Rimini, 1886

Moreni, D. *Lettere di Lorenzo il Magnifico*, Firenze, 1830

Morlay, Collison *Les Borgia*, Paris, 1934

Müntz, E. *Les arts à la cour des Papes pendant le XV & XVI siècle*, Paris, 1879

Müntz, E. *Les collections d'Antiques formées par les Medicis au XVIe siècle*, Paris, 1888

Nagler, A. M. *Theatre Festivals of the Medici 1539–1637*, New Haven, 1964

Nitti, F. *Leone X e la sua politica secondo documenti e carteggi inediti*, Firenze, 1892

Nordström, J. *Moyen Age et Renaissance*, Uppsala, 1929

Notizie Letterarie ed istoriche intorno agli uomini illustri dell' Accadèmia fiorentina, ed. Rilli, Firenze, 1700

Operti, P. *Il Condottiere, Vita di Bartolomeo Colleoni*, Torino, 1957

Orsi, Pietro *Signorie e Principati (1300–1350)*, Milano, 1900

Palmarocchi, R. *Lorenzo de' Medici*, Torino, 1941

Palmarocchi, R. *La politica italiana di Lorenzo de' Medici. Firenze nella guerra contro Innocenzo VIII*, Firenze, 1933

Panella, Antonio *Storia di Firenze*, Firenze, 1949

Passerini, G. L. *Curiosità storico-artistiche fiorentine*, Firenze, 1866

Pepe, G. *La politica dei Borgia*, Napoli, 1945

Perrens, F. T. *Histoire de Florence*, Paris, 1877–1888

Pierraccini, G. *La stirpe dei Medici di Caffaggiolo*, Firenze, 1924

Portigliotto, Giuseppe *I Condottieri*, Milano, 1935

Randolph, G. *Florentine Merchants in the Age of the Medici*, Cambridge, Mass., 1932

Renard, George *Histoire du travail à Florence*, Paris, 1913–1914

Renaudet, A. *Machiavel*, Paris, 1956

Reumont, Alfred von *Lorenzo de' Medici il magnifico*, Leipzig, 1874–1883

Rho, E. *Lorenzo de' Medici*, Torino, 1932

Ricci, P. G. and Rubinstein, N. *Censimento delle lettere di Lorenzo di Piero de' Medici*, Firenze, 1964

Ridolfi, Roberto *Studi savonaroliani*, Firenze, 1935

Robb, N. A. *Neoplatonism of the Italian Renaissance*, London, 1935

Robion, Emilio *Gli ultimi dei Medici e la successione al granducato di Toscana*, Firenze, 1905

Rodocanachi, E. *La première Renaissance. Rome au Temps de Jules II et de Léon X*, Paris, 1912

Roover, R. de *The Medici Bank, its Organization, Management, Operations and Decline*, New York, 1948

Roscoe, W. *Life and Pontificate of Leo the Tenth*, Liverpool, 1805

Roscoe, W. *Life of Lorenzo de' Medici, called the Magnificent*, Liverpool, 1795

Rossi, L. *Il Quattrocento*, Milano, 1949

Rubinstein, N. *The beginnings of political thought in Florence*, London, 1942

Rubinstein, N. *The Government of Florence under the Medici 1434 to 1494*, Oxford, 1966

Saitta, G. *Il Pensiero italiano nel Umanesimo e nel Rinascimento*, Bologna, 1949–1951

Sapori, Armando *Studi di storia economica medioevale*, Firenze, 1940

Schiaparelli, A. *La casa fiorentina e i suoi arredi nei secoli XIV e XV*, Firenze, 1908

Schillmann, Fritz *Florenz und die Kultur Toskanas*, Wien, 1938

Segni, Bernardo *Storie fiorentine dall'anno 1527 al 1555*, Firenze, 1857

Semerau, Alfred *Die Condottieri*, Iena, 1909

Semprini, G. *I Platonici italiani*, Milano, 1926

Shevill, F. *History of Florence*, New York

Sismondi, Simonde de *A History of the Italian Republics*, 1832

Sorbelli, E. A. *La scomunica di Lorenzo de Medici in un raro incunabulo romano*, Bologna, 1937

Symonds, John Addington *Renaissance in Italy*, London, 1900

Tenhove, Nicolas *Memoirs of the House of Medici from its origins to the death of Francesco....etc.*, Bath, 1797

Testi umanistici sull'ermetisme, ed. C. Vasoli, Roma, 1955

Thomas, Gabriel *Les Révolutions politiques de Florence*, Paris, 1887

Tinti, M. *Il Nobilio fiorentino*, Milano, 1929

Toffanin, Giuseppe *Il secolo senza Roma*, Bologna, 1943

Toffanin, G. *Il Cinquecento*, Milano, 1929

Torre, Arnaldo della *Storia dell'Accadèmia Platonica*, Firenze, 1902

Troger, H. *Beiträge zur Kunstgeschichte von Italien*, Basel, 1898

Truc, G. *Florence et les Medicis*, Paris, 1936

Truc, G. *Leon X et son siècle*, Paris, 1941

Ullmann, B. L. *The Origin and Development of Humanistic Script*, 1960

Vagaggini, Sandra *La miniatura fiorentina*, Milano, 1952

Valeri, Antonio *L'italia nell'età dei principati, dal 1343 al 1516*, Milano, 1949

Valori, L. *Laurentii Medicis Vita*, Firenze, 1740

Varillas, Antoine *(Anecdota...) Or, the secret history of the House of Medici*, made English by F. Spence, London, 1686

Vasoli, C. (*see* Testi)

Venturi, Adolfo *A Short History of Italian Art*, London, 1926

Violini, C. *Lorenzo il magnifico. La vita, la politica, l'arte, gli amori*, Milano, 1937

Voigt, George *Die Wiederlebung des klassischen Altertums*, Berlin, 1959

Wackernagel, Martin *Das Lebensraum des Künstlers in der Florentinische Renaissance. Aufgaben und Auftraggäber Werkstatt und Kunstmarkit*, Leipzig, 1938

Warburg, A. *Gesammelte Schriften*, Leipzig, 1932

Weisback, Werner *Trionfi*, Berlin, 1919

Welliver, W. *L'impero fiorentino*, Firenze, 1957

Wind, Edgar *Pagan Mysteries in the Renaissance*, London, 1958

Winspeare, F. *Isabella Orsini e la corte medicea del suo tempo*, Firenze, 1961

Wittkower, Rudolph *Architectural Principles in the Age of Humanism*, London, 1949

Young, G. F. *The Medici*, London, 1910

Zeller, J. *Italie et Renaissance*, Paris, 1863

List of illustrations in the text

Acknowledgements

The Publishers would like to express their gratitude to the museums, libraries and organizations which supplied photographs of paintings, statues and objects in their collections.

The following photographs were taken by Wim Swaan: jacket front, plates 1, 2, 3, 4, 5, 6, 7, 8, 16, 17, 18, 19, 20, 21, 22, 23, 31, 32, 38, 39, 40, 41, 42, 49, 50, 51, 52, 53, 54, 55, 56, 57, 58, 59, 60, 61, 62, 63, 72d, 73, 75, 76, 77, 78, 79, 81, 83, 84, 85, 86, 87, 88, 89, 90, 91, jacket back; figures 3, 5, 6, 10, 11, 12, 19, 29, 39, 43. Other illustrations are acknowledged to the following sources: Scala, Florence: plates 9, 10, 11, 12, 13, 14, 15, 24, 26, 27, 28, 30, 43, 44, 45, 46, 47, 48, 65, 67, 68, 69, 70, 71. Cleveland Museum of Art: plate 25. Guido Sansoni, Florence: plate 29. Reproduced by courtesy of the Trustees of the British Museum, London: plates 33, 34, 35, 36, 37, 64; figures 1, 16, 17, 27, 28, 40, 41, 44, 45, 46, 47, 52, 59. Reproduced by courtesy of the Trustees of the National Gallery, London: plates 66, 74, 75, 80, front and back endpapers; figures 15, 30. Fratelli Alinari, Florence: plate 82; figure 66. Gabinetto Fotografico delle Gallerie, Florence: figures 2, 21, 22, 25, 32, 49, 64. Musées Nationaux, Paris: figures 4, 8, 13, 61. The Mansell Collection, London: figures 7, 9, 14, 20, 23, 24, 31, 34, 60. Biblioteca Medicea Laurenziana, Florence: figures 18, 36, 37. John R. Freeman, London: figure 26. Uffizi Gallery, Florence: figures 33, 35, 51. Reproduced by courtesy of the Victoria and Albert Museum, London: figures 38, 42, 48, 54, 55, 56, 57, 58, 62, 63, 65. National Gallery of Art, Washington: figure 50. Windsor Castle, Royal Collection, by gracious permission of Her Majesty the Queen: plate 36; figure 53. Plates 72, a, b, c, were taken from *Il Tesoro dei Medici* published by Silvana Editoriale d'Arte, Milan.

The Publishers would also like to acknowledge their appreciation for the help and courtesy shown to Mr Swaan of the following: Guido Morozzi, il Soprintendente, e Marco Chiarini ai Monumenti delle Provincie di Firenze, Arezzo e Pistoia; il Ragionere, Opera di Santa Maria del Fiore di Firenze; Sindaco di Firenze, Palazzo Vecchio; i soprintendenti delle Amministrazioni delle Fabbriche delle Chiese di Santa Maria Novella, Santa Trinità, Santa Croce, San Miniato al Monte, Convento di San Marco, San Lorenzo, Santo Spirito.

Index